The Oldest House in London

THE
OLDEST HOUSE
IN
LONDON

FIONA RULE

For my sister, Lindsay Rule.

First published 2017

The History Press
The Mill, Brimscombe Port
Stroud, Gloucestershire, GL5 2QG
www.thehistorypress.co.uk

British Library Cataloguing in Publication Data.
A catalogue record for this book is available from the British Library.

ISBN 978 0 7509 6837 9

Typesetting and origination by The History Press
Printed and bound in Great Britain by TJ International Ltd

CONTENTS

FOREWORD

Searching for London's Oldest House

Finding the oldest house in London was not an easy task. Over the centuries the city's buildings have adapted and evolved to meet the demands of an ever-changing metropolis. Consequently, some structures that were originally built as houses are now commercial premises while ancient workshops and warehouses have been converted into sought-after private homes. The inexorable growth of the metropolis over the centuries has also meant that houses that once stood in an Essex, Surrey or Middlesex village now possess a London postcode.

Early on in my research, I developed simple but strict criteria for identifying the oldest house in London: it had to have been built as a private residence within the precincts of the city and it still had to be someone's home today. My self-imposed rules eliminated several strong candidates. For example, the elaborate building now known as Prince Henry's Room at 17 Fleet Street and the Staple Inn on High

7

Holborn were built in 1610 and 1585 respectively, but both were originally inns, not private houses. The Old Curiosity Shop on Portsmouth Street WC2 predates both of the above and the upper rooms of this extraordinary sixteenth-century property were undoubtedly domestic for much of its long history. However, today, as its name suggests, the building is a shop, selling an interesting range of rather expensive shoes. Likewise, 74 and 75 Long Lane EC1 were built as houses back in the late 1590s but ceased to be private homes many moons ago. Further out of central London, stranded on the grimy northern approach to the Blackwall Tunnel, Bromley Hall's elegant Georgian façade conceals a much earlier house that was built in the 1490s by Holy Trinity Priory. However, its location was not part of London until the late 1800s.

Ultimately there was only building that met my criteria. Built as a domestic residence in 1614, it originally formed part of the City Ward of Farringdon Without. Today it is still used as a private home and its story, along with that of its inhabitants, is told in this book.

Acknowledgements

I would like to thank the staff of London's archive centres and Matthew Bell, the current owner of London's oldest house, whose help has been invaluable. I would also like to thank my husband Robert, the rest of my family, and my friends, particularly Sharon Tyler, for their interest and support. As always, the wisdom and guidance of my agent, Sheila Ableman, has been invaluable and I am very grateful to The History Press for their belief in me and my books. Finally, I would like to thank Jean Rule for her enthusiasm and encouragement over the years. Sleep well.

INTRODUCTION

This is the story of a house. Today it is the oldest private home in the City of London, but its outward appearance gives few clues to its fascinating and ancient heritage. In fact, most people are unaware of its existence. It hides in plain sight at 41–42 Cloth Fair – a narrow street sandwiched between the glass and iron splendour of Smithfield Market and the high walls of Bart's Hospital. Cloth Fair's Smithfield entrance yields an unpromising view, but anyone who cares to venture a little further down the street will be rewarded. Victorian brick quickly gives way to ancient stonework as the magnificent Church of St Bartholomew the Great looms into view. Slip through the gate in the railings and you find yourself in a shady churchyard where the bustle and noise of the nearby market dulls to a distant murmur. Here, a straggly collection of trees and shrubs frame a strangely timeless view of 41–42 Cloth Fair – its fine gabled projections and glinting leadlight windows tantalisingly hinting at a history that stretches back into a time long forgotten.

Over the centuries, 41–42 Cloth Fair has weathered many storms as, all around it, history unfolded. Its inhabitants witnessed events that moulded Britain into the country that it is today. They saw plague, fire and war. They struggled through financial crises, religious strife and commercial revolutions. They are our ancestors, and through their own personal stories we can learn how world-famous events affected ordinary people like us. Names of former residents such as Henry Downing, Elizabeth Witham and Paul Paget do not loom large in the history books but they nonetheless have incredible stories to tell: the first was an eyewitness to the English Civil War and the Great Plague of 1665; the second was a key figure in the foundation of the Methodist movement; and the third was responsible for saving some of London's most iconic buildings after the ravages of the Second World War. It is hoped that their stories, along with many others, will go some way to prove that every property in Britain has its own, unique history – you just have to look for it. Even twenty-first-century houses stand on land as old as time itself that holds myriad secrets waiting to be uncovered.

Today, public interest in Britain's architectural heritage is at an all-time high but, nevertheless, not a month goes by without a much-loved building being sacrificed in the name of progress. As *The Oldest House in London* shows, it is not only mansions and palaces that have extraordinary histories. Homes built for ordinary people can be equally fascinating. It is up to us to preserve the buildings we love by exploring their past and, most importantly, divulging their secrets to others.

I

LAND GRAB

On a cool May morning in 1538, as the sun rose over the rooftops of London, Brother John Forest was dragged from his bed, dressed in a coarse woollen shift and thrust down the steps of the Franciscan friary in which he had been under house arrest. A horse stood waiting in the street, a rough wooden hurdle trailing behind its haunches. Forest was thrown to the ground, strapped to this wheel-less carriage and with a sharp crack of a whip, the horse took off through the streets of London.

Being dragged through the dung-ridden, filthy thoroughfares was just the start of John Forest's ordeal. When the grim spectacle reached the outer precincts of St Bartholomew's Priory, the horse was forced to slow in order to make its way through a large and rowdy crowd that had congregated outside the priory gate. Once at the centre of the mob, the full horror of the scene unfolded before John Forest's terrified eyes. A high scaffold had been erected on which sat the city's noble elite, watching in keen expectation. A few feet in front of this grandstand, gallows rose ominously above the crowd. Forest was untied from the hurdle and strong chains were wrapped around his waist and arms and then slung over the top of the gallows. A sharp tug on the end of the chains elevated him several feet off the ground and, as he dangled helplessly in mid-air, Hugh Latimer, the Bishop of Worcester, pushed his way through the throng, Bible in hand. For almost an hour, the bishop beseeched Forest to renounce the Pope and accept King Henry VIII as the Supreme Head of the English Church. Despite knowing his dreadful fate was just minutes away, Forest refused to listen and retreated into mute prayer while, beneath him, a bonfire of hay bales and kindling was assembled.

When the Bishop of Worcester had finished his long diatribe, the crowd fell silent, knowing that this was John Forest's last chance to save himself from the horrors to come. But no words passed his lips as torches were thrust into the bales. As the flames rose Forest grabbed a ladder propped against the gallows and to this he clung in excruciating pain as the conflagration slowly consumed him.

The dreadful execution of John Forest took place just as Henry VIII's opprobrious Dissolution of the Monasteries was about to swing into full effect. By the time it was over, hundreds of England's religious houses had been swept away, their valuable land and property seized by the king and his inner circle. The Dissolution was effectively the biggest land grab since the Norman Conquest. It transformed the landscape of England and, had it not happened, 41–42 Cloth Fair may never have been built.

The events that paved the way for the creation of 41–42 Cloth Fair began way back in the 1120s when an extraordinary man named Rahere founded the Priory and Hospital of St Bartholomew at Smithfield. Rahere's life was split into two distinct chapters. His early years were spent at the court of Henry I, where he used his considerable charm and keen intellect to become a close confidante of the king. However, as he approached middle age, he began to tire of the shallow frivolity of palace life and rejected its earthly pleasures to become a canon at St Paul's Cathedral.

Shortly after entering the Church, Rahere embarked on a pilgrimage to Rome, where he fell gravely ill. As he lay in a semi-delirious state, he vowed that if he survived, he would devote the rest of his life to caring for the sick and poor, for whom he would found a hospital. Miraculously, his prayers were answered. The fever subsided and he returned to London, where he immediately set about keeping his vow. Taking full advantage of his affluent and influential contacts at the royal court, Rahere persuaded the king to grant him a large tract of Crown land just outside the city wall at Smithfield, inauspiciously adjoining a public execution site. He then embarked on the monumental task of building a hospital and priory to accommodate the monks and nuns who would act as staff. The complex was completed in 1123 and dedicated to Saint Bartholomew.

Although St Bartholomew's Hospital is now one of Britain's oldest medical institutions, its early years were fraught with financial difficulties. The majority of patients came from the most deprived sphere of London society and they had no means of paying for their care. Consequently, the hospital relied solely on charity and just ten years after its foundation the coffers were running dry. Faced with imminent closure, Rahere appealed to the king for help and to his intense relief was granted a lifeline that would ultimately result in the development of the street now known as Cloth Fair. In 1133, a royal charter was drawn up for an annual fundraising event in the grounds of the priory on the feast day of St Bartholomew (24 August).

At first Bartholomew Fair admitted any type of trader, but as the years passed it became especially popular with dealers in silks and wool, which earned it the sobriquet 'Cloth Fair'. Over the next 200 years the Cloth Fair became an important event on Britain's commercial calendar. Every August the land on which 41–42 Cloth Fair would eventually be built was given over to densely packed wooden stalls on which eager traders displayed a dazzling range of fabrics designed to catch the eye of discerning tailors and drapers.

However, by the 1300s the fair was becoming a victim of its own success. Keen to make as much money as possible out of the event, the priory began to rent pitches to any trader prepared to pay the fee. Consequently, stallholders selling fine cloth had to contend with the rowdy distractions of beer vendors and street entertainers performing to crowds of excitable onlookers, many of whom had no connection to the cloth trade. In addition, numerous traders of questionable reputation began to frequent the fair, selling inferior goods and using very short yardsticks and dubious scales.

Inevitably, the sheer volume of people at the Cloth Fair – and the amount of cash that was changing hands – also attracted London's criminal element, who silently darted among the throng relieving unwitting visitors of their valuables whenever they got the opportunity. By 1363, pickpockets and conmen had become so troublesome that a group of influential cloth merchants threatened to boycott the fair unless matters improved. In response, the Corporation of London dispatched constables to keep the thieves at bay and weights and measures men to check that goods were being sold honestly. The Drapers' and Merchant Taylors' Companies also sent officials to test the quality of the merchandise and any miscreants were swiftly dealt with by the Pie Powder Court – a corruption of the French '*pieds poudrés*', referring to the dusty feet of itinerant traders – which met daily at St Bartholomew's Priory.

Despite problems with law and order, the Cloth Fair successfully funded the good work of St Bartholomew's Hospital for 400 years. In the meantime, the priory grew in both size and wealth. By 1500, the complex occupied a roughly triangular island site separated from its hospital by a narrow thoroughfare known as Duck Lane (now Little Britain).

Like many other religious houses, St Bartholomew's Priory was a self-contained community. At the southern tip of the site lay Bartholomew Close – a sunny green with a deep well at its centre – bordered on two sides by large, timber-framed houses occupied by merchants whose rental payments swelled the priory's coffers. Beyond the close were the imposing redbrick domestic quarters of the priory, including a spacious dormitory for the monks, an infirmary with adjacent chapel, a long refectory and a kitchen complete with its own garden stocked with fruit trees, herbs and vegetables.

Further north were two open squares – one containing a burial ground, the other a quiet garden leading to the prior's house. This was the largest dwelling in the complex and it was connected via a galleried walkway to the centrepiece of the estate – the Church of St Bartholomew the Great. By 1500, the church's twelfth-century nucleus had been extended to form a truly magnificent cruciform edifice. At its head, a stone chapel dedicated to the Blessed Virgin overlooked a small green and the parish burial ground. Beyond, the lofty choir and presbytery contained the altar and Rahere's brightly painted tomb, while an enormous nave stretched westwards to the church's grand entrance at West Smithfield.

Next to the Smithfield gateway lay the entrance to the fairground and the priory's laundry – a small, L-shaped building bordering a large, square expanse of grass on which the washing was pegged out to dry. Known as 'Launders Green', this open space would later become the site of 41–42 Cloth Fair.

There is little doubt that the Priory of St Bartholomew the Great was one of the medieval city's most impressive enclaves and the annual fair was renowned throughout the land. However, as the sixteenth century unfolded, events occurred that would leave the historic site in ruins.

By the time Henry VIII came to the throne in 1509, England's religious houses were in disarray. The Church was the second largest landowner in England (after the Crown) and its monasteries, abbeys and priories possessed priceless artefacts. However, over the centuries some religious houses had been corrupted by their vast wealth and instead of using it to benefit the community, they devoted huge sums to the earthly pleasures of wine, women and song. Clearly reorganisation was desperately needed and the king was the one person with the power to bring it into effect. Unfortunately, it transpired that his agents were just as corrupt as those they sought to reform.

The initial aim of Henry VIII's Reformation was purely to restore order and piety to the most self-indulgent religious houses. In 1519, the king instructed his Lord Chancellor, Cardinal Wolsey, to launch an inquiry into the most notorious establishments. Twenty-nine were found to be utterly corrupt and so Wolsey shut them down, employing Thomas Cromwell (then a young and ambitious attorney) to handle the disposal of their assets. Part of the proceeds were used to found Cardinal College (now Christ Church) in Oxford and a second college in Wolsey's home town of Ipswich. The remainder went into the royal purse and, in doing so, sowed seeds of avarice in the minds of the king and his advisors.

In the meantime, Cardinal Wolsey's attempts at stamping out corruption in the English Church opened the floodgates of public resentment. Tenants across the country complained of the astronomical rents charged by their ecclesiastical landlords and general opinion held that at least some of the monasteries' enormous wealth should be diverted to poor relief and education. In 1528 Simon Fish published an influential tract entitled *A Supplication for Beggars*, in which he claimed that England's corrupt religious houses were run by 'ravenous wolves' responsible for 'debauching 100,000 women'. Although his argument was crude, it represented the popular view.

As religious dissatisfaction grew, Henry VIII began to take a keen interest in the growing Protestant movement in Europe and when the Pope failed to nullify his marriage to Catherine of Aragon, he contentiously severed ties with Rome, declaring himself the Supreme Head of the Church of England. The events that followed would almost totally destroy England's ancient monastic system.

In 1534, Henry launched another inquiry into England's religious houses, this time led by Thomas Cromwell, who was instructed to assess the wealth of each establishment and investigate allegations of malpractice. Sensing an opportunity to assert the king's religious authority and swell the royal coffers in one fell swoop, Cromwell assembled a team of commissioners and instructed them to make the most of any misdeeds they uncovered.

Their reports, which were published as the *Valor Ecclesiasticus* in 1535, did not disappoint. According to the commissioners, England's monasteries were veritable dens of iniquity. William Thirsk, head of Fountains Abbey in Yorkshire, was accused of stealing church treasures, wasting his estate's resources and using donations to hire prostitutes. The canons of Leicester Abbey were said to be indulging in sodomy and the abbot of West Langdon was branded 'the drunkenest knave living'. Nuns were not above reproach either; two of the supposedly celibate sisters at Lampley Convent were found to have nine children between them.

Although corruption was widespread, Thomas Cromwell initially concentrated his efforts on small houses that could offer little resistance. Thus, the resulting Suppression of Religious Houses Act (1535) stated, 'The manifest sin, vicious carnal and abominable living is daily used and committed amongst the little and small abbeys, priories and other religious houses of monks, canons and nuns where the congregation of such religious persons is under the number of 12 persons.' However, as the huge extent of monastic riches became clear, Cromwell's campaign snowballed. Within months, every religious house in England was affected by the events now known as the Dissolution of the Monasteries.

The Dissolution began in earnest in March 1536 and progressed with frightening speed and efficiency. Fearing that valuable possessions would be spirited away before they could be seized, the king's bailiffs quickly descended on abbeys, priories and nunneries across the land and took away anything of value, from precious altarpieces to the lead on the roof. In the meantime, all income from monastic estates was diverted to the Crown. In order to oversee this unprecedented rape of England's religious houses, Thomas Cromwell established the Court of Augmentations and appointed as its head one Richard Rich – the man who was destined to own the land on which 41–42 Cloth Fair would be built.

Richard Rich was ambitious and greedy in equal measure. Born in the London parish of St Lawrence Jewry in around 1496, he initially trained as a lawyer and used his cunning, keen intellect to work his way up the legal ladder, eventually becoming Solicitor General in October 1533. In this post, he viciously persecuted any members of the Church who refused to accept Henry VIII as Supreme Head and looked on with indifference as John Forest horrifically burned to death outside St Bartholomew's Priory in 1538.

Richard Rich's vindictive streak was only exceeded by his syco-phancy towards the king. After being made Speaker in Parliament, his opening speech compared Henry VIII to the sun, which 'expels all nox-ious vapours and brings forth the seeds, plants and fruits necessary for the support of human life'. His biographer, A.F. Pollard, described him as 'the most powerful and the most obnoxious of the king's ministers'. Nevertheless, his working partnership with Thomas Cromwell proved devastatingly effective during the Dissolution of the Monasteries. By the time the purge was over, Richard Rich had acquired a fortune from the spoils, including the estate of St Bartholomew the Great.

The acquisition of St Bartholomew's required a long and devious negotiation with distinctly shady undercurrents. The priory could not be closed on the grounds of being corrupt as the adjacent hospital was proof that any profits were being put to good use. Instead, Thomas Cromwell and Richard Rich were forced to play a long game that required some clever tactics.

Their chance came when the priory's head, William Bolton, became gravely ill. With no time to lose, Cromwell made contact with Robert Fuller, the abbot of Waltham Holy Cross, who also happened be a commissioner on the *Valor Ecclesiasticus*. Fuller had already proved he was open to bribery by handing over some of Waltham Abbey's land to the king in return for personal reward and so the two men entered into a verbal agreement to systematically dispose of St Bartholomew's estates in a similar manner as soon as they had the chance.

Prior Bolton died soon after their meeting and just days later Fuller wrote to Cromwell asking him to settle 'this matter for the house of St Bartholomew', reiterating that his palm would be greased in return. 'Such matters shall be largely recompensed on my part, not only in reward for your labours, but also for such yearly remem-brance as you shall have no cause to be sorry for.' Thus, Robert

Fuller became the new prior of St Bartholomew the Great on the understanding that the priory would be relinquished whenever it pleased the king.

Although he was little more than Thomas Cromwell's puppet, Robert Fuller was at least benevolent to his underlings. During his time as prior of St Bartholomew's he took pains to ensure that his canons would receive pensions once the priory ceased to exist. He also looked after the priory's employees. For example, over at Launders Green, Fuller made a point of recording that resident laundryman John Chesewyk and his wife Alyce had signed an agreement to launder all the priory's linen and take responsibility for any lost or stolen items. In return, they received wages of £10 a year and a rent-free house in the priory close along with a gallon of ale and a 'caste' of bread every Friday. This agreement would prove invaluable when the Chesewyks came to claim compensation after the priory's inevitable closure.

St Bartholomew's finally ceased to exist as a priory on 25 October 1539 and Richard Rich's Court of Augmentations immediately set about stripping the buildings of their valuables. Auditor John Scudamore was instructed to 'make sale of bells and superfluous houses and have the lead melted into plokes and sows, weighed and marked with the king's marks'. Five of the bells were sold to the neighbouring Church of St Sepulchre but five others remained in situ, probably because local residents argued that they would be put to parish use in the future.

The priory's plate, jewels, vestments and cash were taken to Sir John Williams, Master of the King's Jewels, who happened to live in Bartholomew Close. Some of this treasure was subsequently sold to the Royal Mint at the Tower of London. Meanwhile, the redundant parts of the priory complex were dismantled. The nave was, in the words of Henry VIII, 'utterly taken away', and its site was converted into the parish burial ground. The chapel was also removed and thus the once great Priory of St Bartholomew was reduced to a parish church, with services conducted in the twelfth-century choir.

As had been agreed with Thomas Cromwell, the canons and staff of the priory received compensation for losing their livelihoods. The day after the official closure, the Court of Augmentations granted the canons handsome pensions: Robert Glasier, the sub prior, received £15 a year; the senior canons (William Barlowe and John Smyth) got an annual allowance of £10 13s 4d apiece; and the junior canons received sums ranging from £5 to almost £7 a year. The Chesewyks at Launders Green also received an 'annuity', the value of which was not specified.

Unsurprisingly, the duplicitous Prior Robert Fuller benefited most from the Court of Augmentations' bequests. He was granted the priory's share of the profits from the annual fair along with all the real estate in the complex, with the exception of the prior's house, which Richard Rich had earmarked for himself. However, Fuller did not enjoy his share of the spoils for long. Just a few months later, he died suddenly from causes unknown.

Although there is no evidence that Richard Rich had any involvement in Robert Fuller's death, he certainly took advantage of it. Many of the houses in Bartholomew Close were quickly let to his cohorts at the Court of Augmentations and, by 1544, Rich was ready to buy the whole complex. In preparation for this, he instructed a surveyor to produce an inventory that was used to calculate ridiculously low values for the property. For instance, valued at just £6 was the old prior's house, along with the priory's halls, chambers, chapel, kitchen, buttery, gallery, dormitory, cloister, refectory and numerous outbuildings.

Although the valuation of Launders Green, other buildings in the complex and the annual proceeds of the fair were more sensible, Rich was able to acquire the entire site for just over £117.

The closure of St Bartholomew's Priory left the adjacent hospital facing ruin, as it now had no form of income. This problem was shared with all of London's hospitals that had traditionally been attached to now defunct religious establishments. As their future hung in the balance, the people of London expressed grave concern that if the hospitals closed the patients would be forced out into the streets, spreading disease and death in their wake. This very real threat was finally addressed in 1546 when Henry VIII granted St Bartholomew's, along with St Thomas's, Bridewell and Bethlem Hospitals, to the Corporation of London on the understanding that the city would pay for their maintenance.

Although St Bartholomew's Hospital survived the Dissolution of the Monasteries, the bustling trade fair that once funded its work did not. By the time Elizabeth I acceded to the throne in 1558, improvements in England's roads and modes of transport meant that London's cloth merchants found wider markets for their goods.

As a result, the old Cloth Fair completely lost its original purpose and degenerated into a lawless and drunken carnival that stretched over a fortnight. The look of the ancient fairground also began to change during Elizabeth's reign. In 1567, Richard Rich died and the land passed first to his son and then to his grandson, Robert. Eager to earn more from the site than just the proceeds of the annual August festivities, Robert Rich began issuing building leases on the land in 1583. Development of the fairground began and, by 1598, John Stow noted in his *Survey of London*:

Now ... in place of booths within [St Bartholomew's] churchyard – only let out in the Fair time, and closed up all the year after – be many large

houses built, and the north wall towards Long Lane taken down, a number
of tenements are erected for such as will give great rents.

The Rich family profited from the spoils of St Bartholomew's Priory
for three generations but ultimately Richard Rich's carefully forged
links with royalty proved to be a poisoned chalice. By the 1630s, public
mistrust which once had been directed at England's religious houses
now turned towards the Crown and the Rich family's loyalty to the
king was severely tested. However, shortly before the situation spiralled
into turmoil and violence, 41–42 Cloth Fair was built.

2

THE EAGLE & CHILD

The Oldest House in London is Built

Richard Rich's carefully tended relationship with the Tudor dynasty was successfully maintained by his grandson, Robert. However, Elizabeth I's death heralded a new era. In 1603, James I (who had reigned as King of Scotland since 1567) acceded to the English throne. Keen to curry favour with the new monarch, Robert Rich lost no time in introducing him to his 13-year-old son, Henry, who made an instant and lasting impression on the middle-aged monarch. By all accounts, young Henry's 'features and pleasant aspect equalled the most beautiful of women' and were combined with a personality described by the chronicler Clarendon as 'a lovely and winning presence, to which he added the charm of genteel conversation'. James I soon became infatuated, showering him with gifts, usually of the monetary variety – the historian James Granger claimed that the king 'wantonly lavished £3,000 upon him at one time'.

The precise nature of Henry Rich's relationship with James I is unproven, but there is evidence that he may have cynically exploited the ageing monarch's infatuation. In 1847 the American journalist Eliakim Littell declared, 'From the dawn of his youth, true to his ancestral characteristics, Henry Rich was a selfish politician', adding that his handsome countenance concealed a dark heart. 'In private life he was violent and haughty; nay more, he was a man of utmost selfishness, unmitigated by any of those loftier qualities which sometimes, coupled with a fiery, overbearing disposition … will not permit us quite to hate.' Walter Scott's *Secret History of the Court of James I* went further, stating, 'Rich, losing that opportunity his curious face and complexion afforded him, by turning aside and spitting after the king had slabered his mouth.'

Whatever the truth of his association with the king, Henry Rich prospered at the royal court and in 1612 his social status was elevated further when he announced his engagement to Isabel, the daughter and heir of Sir Walter Cope – an immensely wealthy landowner who presided over his vast estates from an enormous mansion known as Cope Castle, the grounds of which stretched across the modern west London enclave of Kensington.

Delighted to be forging links with the influential Cope family, Henry's father Robert rewarded him with the valuable deeds to the St Bartholomew estate. Determined to squeeze as much profit as possible from his wedding gift, Henry resolved to develop its last available plot of land – Launders Green.

Although it promised to be a lucrative speculation, Henry Rich's plan for Launders Green received a lukewarm reception from both the locals and the City's Court of Aldermen, who had long since felt that the precinct of St Bartholomew's was becoming dangerously overcrowded. Aware that his new development had its detractors, Rich offered some reassurance by promising to issue strict, thirty-one-year leases forbidding multiple tenancy. This had the required effect and the project was given the green light by the authorities.

Once the fear of overcrowding had been allayed, Henry Rich set about designing a neat square of eleven tall townhouses on Launders Green. As was common practice at the time, each property served as a live/work unit. Subterranean storage cellars led up to an open-fronted room at street level that could be used by the inhabitants as either a workshop or a retail premises. Keen to maximise his return on these shops, Henry Rich stipulated that they had to be vacated each year at fair time so he could let them (for hefty rents) to traders. In order to minimise the inevitable disruption this would cause for the inhabitants, he incorporated staircases in Launders Green's inner courtyard that gave direct access to the living quarters without going through the shops. The first storey of these airy chambers comprised, in modern estate-agent parlance, 'reception rooms' in which the inhabitants relaxed, ate and entertained guests. On the floor above, similarly proportioned rooms provided sleeping quarters while further bedrooms and servants' accommodation were found in the steeply pitched garrets.

Building work on Launders Green began in 1613. Unusually for the time, wattle and daub walls were eschewed in favour of bricks, which were almost certainly crafted locally. Ever since Dutch brickmakers had opened a field near reconstruction work at London Bridge in 1404, the practice of creating brickfields close to development sites had become common and rather neatly resulted in buildings being created from the earth on which they stood.

By the time Launders Green was developed, brickmakers were capable of producing bricks in different shades, which could be used to create attractive geometric patterns on frontages. However, although this style was popular in Europe, the brickwork on English houses was often left plain and embellished with intricate plasterwork designs instead. The Worshipful Company of Plaisterers (plasterers) was granted its first charter by Henry VII in 1501 and, over the following century, elaborate plaster mouldings became a popular form of house decoration, both inside and out. Examples still survive today across Britain – Canonbury House (once part of St Bartholomew's Priory's extensive portfolio) has ornate sixteenth-century plasterwork, as does the Charterhouse in nearby Charterhouse Square.

Over at Launders Green, it seems unlikely that Henry Rich would have gone to the expense of decorating his rental properties with expensive plaster designs. However, tantalising illustrations published in the *Gentleman's Magazine* in 1800 reveal that some of Cloth Fair's oldest buildings did indeed possess them. The jettied upper floors of a butcher's shop are shown sporting four gargoyles, and a townhouse – possibly one of the Launders Green houses – is embellished with three huge plaster casts of flowers and animals, measuring around 6ft in height.

While their walls and foundations were built of brick, the floors of the Launders Green houses were almost certainly made from broad and sturdy oak boards. This durable wood was also used to panel interiors of the period and many examples survive today, their light honey brown surfaces blackened by centuries of smoke. Elsewhere in the houses, elm was probably used for doors and window shutters while fences around the construction site would have been made from wicker hurdles of woven hazel, alder and willow.

Transport logistics meant that wood used in house building often came from local estates, so Henry Rich's land at Kensington may well have yielded the timber for his properties at Launders Green. However, if no local supply was available, a large yard at St Benet Woodwharf in the City stocked Estrich (or Eastland) boards from the Baltic. The standard 8ft 6in length of these timbers dictated ceiling heights on timber-frame buildings and subsequently became the standard height for rooms in domestic houses of the period, even those built of brick or stone.

Protecting the Launders Green houses from the elements were steeply pitched, tiled roofs and wooden pentices, which acted as awnings over the shop front and were a useful place to hang banners advertising the goods inside. However, as traders competed to make their banner the most visible pentices grew to dangerous proportions and jutted so far into the street that unobservant horse riders were regularly knocked off their mounts. Thus, by the time Launders Green was developed, the City authorities had decreed that all pentices had to be raised at least 9ft from street level.

The principal features inside the Launders Green properties were undoubtedly the fireplaces. In the early 1600s fires were used for heat, light and culinary activities and, even on a hot summer's day, at least one hearth would be lit in any given home. The paramount importance of fires led to the curious tradition of placing a shoe inside the chimney stack, either on a ledge or in a purpose-built cavity behind the hearth. The sheer number of shoes discovered in seventeenth-century chimneys make it extremely likely that some were hidden inside the Launders Green houses, but today we can only guess at why they were put there. It may be that builders left them as a sort of personal signature or they may have been installed by the occupants as a fertility talisman – the ancient nursery rhyme, 'There was an old woman who lived in a shoe' tells the story of a home overrun with children, shoes and boots were tied to the back of honeymoon vehicles, and Lancashire women who wanted to conceive often wore the shoes of someone who had recently given birth. However, whether these traditions have any connection to the mysterious shoes in chimneys is a moot point.

Obscure superstitions notwithstanding, the Launders Green houses were completed in the winter of 1614 and Nos 41–42 Cloth Fair – today the only surviving section of the square – became part of London's cityscape. Now that the last piece of available land at St Bartholomew the Great had been developed, Henry Rich was eager to discover how much his estate was worth. With this in mind, he employed surveyor Gilbert Thacker to visit the site and compile a list of every building, its value and the name of the leaseholder. Amazingly, Thacker's survey survives and today it provides a fascinating and unique snapshot of Cloth Fair at the beginning of the 1600s. It also reveals that, from the outset, today's 41–42 was let as one house containing 'two cellars, two shops, four chambers and two garrets opening both front and west'. Its first tenant was a man named William Chapman.

Details of ordinary people who lived in England during the early 1600s are frustratingly scant. However, William Chapman had sufficient personal wealth to leave a very detailed will from which glimpses of the man can be snatched. By the time he purchased 41–42 Cloth Fair, he was probably in his late forties or early fifties, a partner in a successful business with a gentleman named John Martin and married to Joan. There is no evidence that he had any children but members of his extended family, including his 'kinswoman' Frances Fullwood and nephew Robert Chapman, lived nearby.

It transpired that William Chapman had innovative plans for his new house. After acquiring a thirty-one-year lease from Henry Rich on 14 December 1614, he set about converting the ground floor and cellars into an alehouse to serve the busy local area.

Seventeenth-century alehouses offered victuals, warmth and a convivial escape from the trials of everyday life. The beverages on offer were similar to those available in modern pubs, with the notable exception of wine, which since 1553 had been restricted to specially

licensed taverns. As their name suggests, alehouses traditionally specialised in ales, many of which were home brewed. However, by the
time William Chapman opened his establishment on Cloth Fair, ale
sales were rapidly being overtaken by beer, which was easier to produce and could be stored longer without deteriorating. Three strengths
were available, the most potent being 'double beer', which sold for
around 20s a barrel and was marketed using thrillingly ominous brand
names such as 'Dagger' and 'Pharaoh'. 'Middle beer' was a cheaper,
more diluted brew that could be purchased for around 8s a barrel and
'small beer' was so weak that it could be consumed by children – the
term survives today, describing something of little consequence.

In addition to ale and beer, early seventeenth-century alehouses
often served 'aqua vitae', a devilishly strong spirit distilled from ale
dregs that was either made in-house or purchased from a local distillery.
The drink was so potent that it was said that just one pint of the stuff
could send ten men into a stupor. Consequently, aqua vitae proved
immensely popular and over the course of the 1600s it was gradually
refined into the beverage we now know as gin.

Although they served a similar purpose to the modern pub, the
drinking rooms of alehouses were sparsely furnished and decorated.
As they possessed no bar, drinks were dispensed direct from the barrel
into a vast array of vessels including pewter tankards, wassail bowls
and wooden cups known as noggins. The cheaper ales and beers were
served in earthenware pots or leather-handled wooden cans lined with
pitch, known as black jacks. Most of the drinking vessels held either
a pint or a quart (2 pints) but larger versions – some holding up to
2 gallons – were available for communal drinking.

Another crucial feature of the seventeenth-century alehouse was
the hearth, which was especially valued by poorer customers who
could not afford to heat their own homes. Set around it were simple

trestle tables, benches, stools and perhaps a chair or two. A few upmarket alehouses also provided reading matter in the form of a Bible on a lectern, but in an age when literacy was low this was by no means essential. Walls were usually left plain, although some alehouses decorated them with murals, often depicting biblical stories such as Daniel in the lion's den.

Officially alehouses were supposed to have just one entrance and exit. However, numerous contemporary court hearings record instances of customers creeping out of back doors to escape creditors, angry spouses or the local constable. Outside the front door, alehouse keepers were required to hang a lantern and a sign that could be understood by any passer-by, regardless of whether they could read. Originally these signs were known as 'ale stakes' and comprised a removable pole that was placed into a slot whenever the ale was ready to serve. If a house sold wine, a 'bush', or bundle of twigs, was hung on the end. However, as alehouses grew in number and home brewing was superseded by wholesalers, alehouse keepers sought to distinguish their business from competitors by creating bespoke signage. For his house at 41–42 Cloth Fair, William Chapman chose a particularly cryptic name – the Eagle & Child.

The meaning of the Eagle & Child was probably derived from an ancient legend concerning Alfred the Great. During a hunting trip, the king was distracted by a baby's cries and, on further investigation, his men discovered a boy dressed in purple and wearing gold bracelets (the mark of Saxon nobility) in an eagle's nest. Alfred named the child Nestingium and took him into the royal household. During the 1300s, the legend was appropriated by a nobleman named Sir Thomas Lathom, probably to legitimise a son born out of wedlock. According to this later story, the infant was found in an eagle's nest in Lathom Park and adopted by Sir Thomas as his heir. Eventually a descendant of the child married into the Stanley family and, to this day, the eagle and child appears on the Stanley coat of arms. That said, there is no evidence that William Chapman had any connection to the Stanley family and the legend was not well known when he opened his alehouse on Cloth Fair.

In 1710, 'British Apollo' was so bemused by obscure alehouse names that he wrote the following verse:

I'm amaz'd at the signs
As I pass through the town,
To see the odd mixture –
A magpye and crown,
The whale and the crow,
The razor and hen.
The leg and seven stars,
The axe and the bottle,
The tun and the lute,
The eagle and child,
The shovel and boot.

Whatever the reason behind his choice of name, William Chapman's Eagle & Child alehouse was a gamble. During the early 1600s, victualling was a notoriously volatile business and an estimated two out of every three alehouses went bust within five years of opening. Their failure was due to the dual threat of stiff competition and the authorities' endless quest to combat public drunkenness.

The latter was a particular problem in the parish of St Bartholomew the Great during fair time. By 1600, the event had degenerated into a fourteen-day carnival of debauchery, the neat rows of cloth stalls replaced with puppet booths, freak shows and pop-up brothels bearing the poetic sign of a soiled dove. In 1613, Ben Jonson described the scene in his play, *Bartholomew Fair*: 'The place is Smithfield, or the field of smiths, the grove of hobby-horses and trinkets. The wares are the wares of devils and the whole Fair is the shop of Satan.' Nevertheless, any attempts to curb drinking proved unsuccessful and, by 1641, Richard Harper noted, 'Cloth Fair is now in great request; well fare the Ale houses therein.'

Given the precarious nature of alehouse keeping, William Chapman wisely opened the Eagle & Child as a sideline rather than his main business. His wife Joan may have run the house at first, but when she died, management passed to a widowed servant named Bridget Warner. William Chapman's will reveals that he treated Bridget with generosity and respect, but this was not always the case in alehouses of the period. Female servants in some establishments were enthusiastically encouraged or even pressured into offering 'personal services' to the male clientele. A seventeenth-century report from Anglesey shamelessly stated, 'Most of our alehouses have a punk [prostitute] besides, for if the good hostess be not so well shaped as she may serve the turn in her own person, she must have a maid to fill pots.'

Although Bridget Warner was not expected to offer sex to customers, she almost certainly had to contend with a criminal element. In around 1612, Robert Harris complained, 'Too many [alehouses] are nurseries of all riot, excess and idleness', and court records from the period are littered with reports of alehouses being used as a criminal resort. A particularly atrocious London establishment even ran an academy for cutpurses and alehouses in Bermuda (a rookery in St Clement Danes) swarmed with 'persons accused of murder and other outrageous offences'.

It is clear that running an alehouse was not for the fainthearted and consequently women like Bridget Warner were typically feisty characters. One of her contemporaries – Mother Bunch – was said to have a laugh so loud that it could be heard from Aldgate to Westminster, and the broadside ballad 'Kind Believing Hostess' recorded another formidable landlady:

> To speak poor man he dares not
> My hostess for him cares not
> She'll drink and quaff
> And merrily laugh
> And she his anger fears not.

Despite the challenges of alehouse keeping, Bridget Warner excelled in her duties and the Eagle & Child may even have provided the 'cool tankard' traditionally imbibed by the Lord Mayor at the opening of the annual Cloth Fair. In fact, the business performed so well that William Chapman eventually took on another alehouse further along the street named the Holly Bush, which was run by victualler Ambrose Bourchier.

William Chapman lived in his spacious private rooms above the Eagle & Child until his death on 18 October 1623. In accordance with his will, he was buried in St Bartholomew's Churchyard and the bulk of his estate passed to his nephew, Robert, who lived close by in the parish of St Sepulchre. However, William Chapman also remembered his faithful servant in his will, stipulating that Robert:

> will within one month of my decease make unto Bridget Warner, widow, a good and sufficient lease in law of the … Eagle & Child now in the possession of me … with the benefits as now are thereto belonging and enjoyed by me for and during the term of ten years … for the yearly rent of 20 shillings … I also give Bridget Warner all the beer as shall be in the

cellars belonging to the said tenement at the time of my decease, [she] paying unto Robert Chapman for every barrel … the sum of eight shillings.

With her future secure, Bridget Warner married James Tench at St Bartholomew's Church just seven weeks after her employer's death. However, her time as proprietor of the Eagle & Child was short-lived. She died in 1625 and was buried at St Mary Somerset in the City of London. The alehouse subsequently passed into the hands of Robert Chapman, but by this stage storm clouds were beginning to gather over England that would result in bitter conflict between the inhabitants of Cloth Fair and disaster for landlord Henry Rich and his family.

3

THE PROUD, BLOODY CITY OF LONDON

Cloth Fair in the Civil War

As night drew in on 4 January 1642, the patrons of the Eagle & Child became locked in furious debate when news arrived that their king, Charles I, had broken centuries-old protocol and stormed the House of Commons. The reason for the king's rage was the refusal of five Puritan MPs to answer accusations of treason. However, when Charles demanded to know their whereabouts, the Speaker of the House, William Lenthall, curtly informed the stunned monarch, 'I have neither eyes to see nor tongue to speak in this place but as this House is pleased to direct me.' With Lenthall's insolent words ringing in his ears, the humiliated king left the chamber empty-handed amid a chorus of catcalls from infuriated MPs.

News of the king's ignominy was received with particular interest by the Eagle & Child's freeholder, Henry Rich, who had fallen from grace at the royal court. The early years of Charles' reign had brought him great rewards, including an influential office as Groom of the Stole and the titles Baron Kensington and Earl of Holland. However, as the years passed his egocentricities got the better of him and his influence waned. By the end of the 1630s, King Charles suspected that Henry Rich was not the devoted courtier he claimed to be. Over the next decade, he was to be proved absolutely right.

While Henry Rich mulled over the implications of the king's humiliation in the House of Commons, the opinion of his tenants at Cloth Fair became fiercely divided. Some felt Charles had wantonly abused his royal privilege; others believed he had been chosen by God and so should do as he saw fit. However, no one foresaw that it was a pivotal event in a bitter saga that would lead to civil war.

The first seeds of trouble had been sown back in 1625 when, on the advice of none other than Henry Rich, Charles had wed Henrietta Maria, the devoutly Catholic daughter of Henry IV of France. Knowing the marriage would be opposed by Puritan MPs, who were already pressing for Protestant reform in the Church of England, Charles deliberately delayed the opening of Parliament until the ceremony had taken place. This high-handed decision was seen by many as an attempt to undermine the government and to manoeuvre the English Church towards Catholicism. Charles' appointment of William Laud as Archbishop of Canterbury in 1633 caused even more outrage when the primate began to introduce changes to church services that had distinctly Catholic undertones. When a group of Puritan ministers criticised his actions, the archbishop's response was swift and brutal – the men had their ears severed and their faces branded as a warning to others.

Charles I's reforms were not only restricted to religion. Traditionally, funding of the royal purse had been agreed by MPs but when they failed to support the king's tax policy of 1629, he controversially shut down Parliament and declared Personal Rule, which lasted for eleven long years. During this period, Charles dramatically increased his income by imposing a series of brutal levies that had a devastating effect on Robert Chapman and his neighbours at Cloth Fair. New customs duties reduced merchants' profits, and the sale of monopolies and patents put some of the street's small traders out of business. In addition, every household was compelled to pay 'ship money' to protect England from invasion (previously this tax had only been enforced in coastal towns). It is hardly necessary to state that Charles' new taxes were universally unpopular. However, any opposition was quickly subdued in the Star Chamber – the monarch's personal court.

Eventually it was his religious reforms, not taxes, that ended Charles' term of Personal Rule. In 1637, he and Archbishop Laud attempted to enforce religious reform on the Church of Scotland, but the feisty Scots rebelled. Incensed at their audacity, Charles dispatched around 20,000 soldiers to the north. Among them was a cavalry led by Henry Rich, who encountered Scottish rebels at the border town of Kelso. What followed epitomised his vainglorious character. When the Scots cleverly deployed along the brow of a hill to make their force look far larger than it was, Rich fell for the trick and instead of attempting an attack he ordered his men to retreat and hastened back to London where he urged the king to begin peace talks.

In the event, the entire campaign against the Scottish rebels was a disaster, but Charles was determined to continue the fight. However, his war chest was virtually empty and, unable to raise more funds independently, he was forced to recall Parliament. At this point, the House of Commons had a golden opportunity to woo the public firmly and permanently to their side, but the chance was wasted. After refusing to raise money to pay off the Scots, a group of Puritan MPs accused the king's chief minister, Lord Strafford, of treason. Still smarting from the king's rejection of his advice, Henry Rich traitorously manufactured 'proof' of the peer's guilt and thus ensured that Strafford's appointment with the executioner was kept. Soon afterwards, a group of MPs published 'The Grand Remonstrance', a document that set out their grievances against the king.

As Charles half-heartedly considered their request for constitutional reform, his subjects began to split into two factions: the Royalists and the Parliamentarians. England was about to slide into a bitter and brutal civil war, and over at Cloth Fair, Henry Rich, the patrons of the Eagle & Child and their friends, foes and neighbours would all be drawn into the conflict. Many were forced to fight on the battlefields; others heroically defended their city. A few – including Henry Rich – sought only to protect themselves.

The start of the English Civil War was not marked by a declaration on either side. Instead it was sparked by a sudden escalation of tensions in the early months of 1642. Despite his humiliation in the House of Commons on 4 January, King Charles refused to give up his pursuit of the five MPs wanted for treason. The very next day, he burst into a meeting of the Common Council, demanding to know their whereabouts. When the councillors refused to answer, a rumour began to circulate that the king's men were poised to seize the city that very night and hold it to ransom until the men were found.

As dusk fell, gunshots and the clash of swords were heard and a group of panicked citizens descended on the house of the Lord Mayor, pleading with him to call out the local militia. When he refused, they decided to take matters into their own hands and, from Cloth Fair in the west to the Tower in the east, there was 'great bouncing at every man's door to be up in their arms presently and to stand on their guard … so the gates were shut and the cullisses let down and the chains put across the corners of our streets'.

The residents of Cloth Fair and its surrounds spent an agonising night waiting for the imminent arrival of the king's soldiers. For some, the terror was too great – rumours abounded of pregnant women miscarrying and the wife of Alderman Thomas Adams was said to have died of fright. However, the Royalist army never materialised and the next morning it transpired that the fighting that had been heard was nothing more than an accidentally discharged carbine, combined with the sound of a mock duel being enacted by drunken courtiers in Covent Garden.

Although the citizens did not know it, seizing the city could not have been further from King Charles' mind. Realising that his dogged pursuit of the five MPs had outraged many of his subjects, and fearful of an uprising, he fled London on 10 January 1642 and headed northwards. This inevitably cast him as a coward in the minds of many of his subjects and, more importantly, it handed control of London over to Parliament.

Realising that his property and money were now at the mercy of the Parliamentarians, Henry Rich conveniently forgot his allegiance to the king and refused to heed the monarch's call to arms at York on 23 March. Three weeks later he received word from the king's minister, Lord Falkland, that he was to surrender his office as Groom of the Stole immediately. By all accounts, the order had been instigated by Queen Henrietta Maria, who was so infuriated by his ingratitude that she declared she would 'never live in the court if he kept his place'.

After the king's departure from London, Parliament staged a triumphal parade of the city's trained bands, which were destined to play a crucial role in the war. In the absence of a formal army, the county bands were England's only permanent militia. In London, membership was compulsory for all male property owners and their sons, which of course included the proprietor of the Eagle & Child, Robert Chapman.

The London Trained Bands comprised around 6,000 men, arranged in twenty companies and armed with muskets and pikes. There was no cavalry and in the decades preceding the war the trained bands' main function had been ceremonial. Nevertheless, the men were expected to meet once a month for drill or field exercises. Unsurprisingly, attendance was low in bad weather and wealthier members like Robert Chapman would employ servants to carry their equipment on long marches, which left them ill-prepared for real battle.

In addition to attending drills, the trained bands' soldiers were expected to buy their own weapons and equipment. 'Directions for Musters', in 1638, stated:

Pikemen must be armed with a pike 17 feet long, head and all; the diameter of the staff to be one inch three quarters, the head [armour] to be well steeled, eight inches long, broad, strong and sword-pointed; the cheeks two foot long, well riveted; the butt end bound with a ring of iron, a gorget [throat armour], back, breast, tassets [upper leg protection] and head piece, a good sword of three foot long, cutting and stiff pointed with girdle and hangers ... The musketeer must be armed with a good musket, the barrel four foot long, ... a rest, bandolier [ammunition belt], head-piece, a good sword, girdle and hangers.

There was no official uniform, although some members favoured 'trained band buff' – a simple leather coat with cloth sleeves. In addition, the musketeers often eschewed the prescribed metal helmets in favour of broad-brimmed hats or peaked 'Montero' caps.

Although they were taught to use weapons, few men in London's trained bands had seen any action and the outbreak of the Civil War must have filled many of them with dread. In an attempt to allay fears, the Corporation of London hastily conscripted 2,000 more men and reorganised the militia into six regiments, each comprising inhabitants of a specific city ward and named after the colour of its banner: Red, White, Yellow, Orange, Blue and Green. Three additional regiments (Tower Hamlets, Southwark and Westminster Liberty) were added in 1643.

The residents of Cloth Fair formed part of the Orange Regiment, which drew its members from the ward of Farringdon Without. For much of the war, the regiment's colonel was John Towse, a grocer and city alderman who had served as Sheriff of London in 1641. Although Colonel Towse proved an able commander, some of his peers had hitherto only played at being soldiers and the thought of actual combat terrified them. This led to an embarrassing incident on 10 May 1642 when Thomas Atkins, colonel of the Red Regiment, became so jittery during a parade at Finsbury Fields that a sudden discharge of muskets caused him to experience a violent 'yearning in his bowels'. Although the incident caused a great deal of hilarity, it demonstrates the intense anxiety felt by ordinary civilians forced to become soldiers.

While London's trained bands were whipped into shape, Parliament laid plans to ensure that the Corporation of London – the city's governing body – was in their pocket. Elections on the eve of the war had already ensured that the Common Council and aldermen supported Parliament and in August 1642 the Royalist Lord Mayor, Sir Richard Gurney, was deprived of office and replaced by a Puritan merchant named Isaac Pennington. With London now fully under Parliamentarian control, the trained bands were ordered to join the Earl of Essex – head of the Parliamentarian forces – who was poised to march on the Royalists at Nottingham.

At this point, it is important to note that not all Londoners supported Parliament's cause. As an example, at the Eagle & Child there were three major reasons why Robert Chapman might have opposed it. Firstly, in the years preceding the war, business at the alehouse had been brisk and the war threatened to destroy this burgeoning trade. Secondly, Robert Chapman may well have welcomed Archbishop Laud's reforms to services at St Bartholomew the Great. Since it had become a parish church in the 1540s, Rahere's majestic sanctuary had been reduced to a cold, uncomfortable place of solemn and dull worship. Laud's reintroduction of music and ceremonial pomp had been wholeheartedly welcomed by many congregants who feared it would be lost again if the strongly Puritan Parliament was victorious. Finally, like every other member of the trained bands, Robert Chapman would have feared not only for his own safety, but also for that of his kinsmen. The men of the Orange Regiment were primarily tradesmen not soldiers, were poorly trained and had no experience of warfare.

In addition to the concerns above, many of Robert Chapman's contemporaries were shocked at the rough treatment meted out to people perceived to be Royalist sympathisers. A notable victim of this prejudice was Thomas Westfield, the rector of St Bartholomew the Great. Although his reputation for delivering melancholy sermons had earned him the unflattering nickname 'Mournful Jeremy', the Reverend Westfield was a thoughtful and sensitive man – when asked to preach before the king, he fainted with fright – and during his forty-year tenure at St Bartholomew's he became well known and widely liked. This made his subsequent treatment by the Parliamentarians even more shocking.

During the early stages of the war, Reverend Westfield was openly bullied by Parliament's sympathisers and ignored by Henry Rich –

the man who was supposed to be his supporter and patron. Indeed, Westfield's contemporary, David Lloyd, wrote:

> Nothing was thought too much for him by [Rich] before the troubles and nothing too little since. To disturb his devotion they removed and burnt the rails he had set about the Lord's Table ... those who were glad formerly to converse with him in their houses would not have communion with him in church.

Thomas Westfield lamented this appalling state of affairs in a sermon preached at St Paul's Cathedral on 14 November 1641. He sadly told the congregation:

> The time was ... that people did esteem us as the Ministers of Jesus Christ, that they knew and did acknowledge us worthy, and accordingly had us in exceeding great love ... [Now] God hath bidden them to curse us and revile us and traduce us and load us with all these contumelies and reproaches.

By May 1643, Thomas Westfield's position at St Bartholomew the Great had become untenable. Preparing to sequester his property, a Parliamentary committee reported, 'His tenants refuse to pay him his rents', and recommended that he and his family be given safe conduct to Bristol, where they had been offered shelter by the bishop. Reverend Westfield left soon afterwards. His sadness was recorded in St Bartholomew's Church register where a Latin inscription simply read, 'In prosperous times friends number without end. When fortune wanes who then will be your friend?'

Thomas Westfield never returned to his London ministry. He died in Bristol on 25 June 1644, a broken man, and David Lloyd later admitted,

'He was glad to go from London to Bristol to avoid the tumults, but he was gladder to be translated from Bristol to Heaven, quite heartbroken with the rebellion'.

Eight months before Thomas Westfield's banishment, his congregation learned that the men of the Orange Regiment were to join a sortie against the king led by the Earl of Essex. To add to their misery and foreboding, they were expected to fund the campaign, and each household was assessed to see how much cash could be extracted from them. Those who refused to pay up were thrown into gaol and this dubious method of fundraising continued throughout the war.

Some residents were exempted from paying because of previous sacrifices to the Parliamentarian cause. For example, Lady Digby, who lived in Bartholomew Close, was excused owing to the recent death of her husband in battle. Others did their best to avoid the levy by hiding their wealth. The home of St Bartholomew resident Mr Fox was raided after informants claimed he had 'plate and treasure walled up in the house', and Edward Wortley was accused of hiding jewellery belonging to the wife of Sir Henry Griffith. In this tense and suspicious atmosphere, the patrons of the Eagle & Child dared not air their views in the alehouse lest their comments be overheard by enemies. However, there was one matter on which everyone was united: the defence of the city.

The first months of the war passed by with no blood being spilt and the prospect of the king returning to London seemed remote. However, on 23 October, the Earl of Essex's troops finally engaged with the Royalist army at Edge Hill, Warwickshire. However, the king's men were just as poorly prepared as the Parliamentarians and a ferocious battle ensued during which neither side was able to gain a decisive advantage. An anonymous eyewitness described the scene in all its horror:

[Royalist] Arms were the great deficiency, and the men stood up in the same garments in which they had left their native field; and with scythes, pitchforks, and even sickles in their hands, they cheerfully took the field, and literally like reapers descended to the harvest of death.

There were similarly horrific fates for the Parliamentarian troops and after the inconclusive battle was over, horribly maimed and traumatised soldiers limped back to London accompanied by hundreds of frightened refugees from sacked towns.

Through them, the people of London learned to their horror that the Earl of Essex had withdrawn to Warwick Castle, leaving the route into the metropolis unguarded. Fears grew that the Royalists were poised to lay siege to the city and, determined that they would not suffer that unconscionable fate, they sprang into action. On 7 November 1642, Giovanni Giustiniani, the Venetian Ambassador, described the preparations for the defence of London: 'All the troops are currently kept at arms. There is no street, however little frequented, that is not barricaded … and every post is guarded.'

The preparations were timely. On Saturday, 12 November, Royalist troops under the command of the king's nephew, Prince Rupert of the Rhine, attacked Brentford, which was being guarded by Denzil Holles – one of the five MPs wanted by the king. The inexperience of the Parliamentarians combined with a woeful lack of artillery meant that Prince Rupert's men quickly gained the upper hand. John Gwyn, a Royalist soldier, wrote:

We beat them from one [end of] Brainford [*sic*] to the other, and from thence to the open field, with a resolute and expeditious fighting, that after firing suddenly to advance up to push of pikes and butt end of muskets, which proved so fatal to Holles [and] his butchers and dyers that day, that abundance of them were killed and taken prisoners, besides those drowned in their attempts to escape by leaping into the river.

Once they had overpowered their adversaries, the Royalist troops sacked the little town before pressing towards London. By this stage, news of the disastrous battle had reached the Earl of Essex who hurriedly mustered the London Trained Bands, including the Orange Regiment, at Chelsea.

The militiamen of Cloth Fair seemed set to get their first taste of battle and they were emboldened when they were joined by hundreds of their civilian neighbours, determined to protect their city, whatever the cost. By the time the Parliamentarians were ready to take on their adversaries, their numbers had swelled to around 24,000 men.

One of the few detractors in their ranks was Henry Rich, who did his level best to dissuade the Earl of Essex from engaging the Royalists. However, Essex ignored his pleas and ordered his men to march west. They soon caught sight of the enemy at Turnham Green and took up a strategic position where their impressive size could intimidate the better armed but significantly smaller Royalist force. As they loomed into view, King Charles (who was present on the battlefield) saw that many of Parliament's men were civilians. Realising that slaying hundreds of unarmed labourers would not pave the way for a triumphal return to London, he hastily ordered his generals not to press the matter and, after a brief burst of cannon fire, the Royalist army withdrew.

The people of London had managed to stop the Royalist advance, but they knew that the king still had their city in his sights. Bad weather prevented any further attacks during the winter of 1642–43, but when peace talks failed in January it became clear that it was only a matter of time before the Royalist army unleashed a new onslaught on London.

In response, the inhabitants resolved to turn their city into a fortress. Plans for this formidable scheme were laid in early March 1643 when Parliament decreed that 'the Lord Mayor and Citizens of the City of London ... shall have power to trench and stop all ... highways ... leading into the City, as well within as without the Liberties'. The money to build the fortification was raised through taxes. Families living in property valued at £5 or less paid 6*d*, while those in more valuable dwellings were taxed at a rate of 2*d* in the pound. Anyone reluctant to cough up was warned that they would 'answer the contrary at their peril'.

By April 1643, a plan of the fortification – known as the London Line of Communication – had been finalised. The defences were designed to form an impenetrable ring around the metropolis, from the Tower in the east to Constitution Hill in the west, at a distance of about 2 miles from the centre of the city. Dotted along its perimeter were a series of wooden forts, complete with artillery, connected by broad earthwork ramparts on which lookouts could patrol.

Construction of the fortification was overseen by London's trained bands. The Orange Regiment worked on the section nearest to the ward of Farringdon Without, which comprised Waterfield Fort, at the northern end of St John Street (near modern Islington Library), and Mount Mill Fort, which was built around an ancient mill that stood by the side of today's Goswell Road (a narrow cul-de-sac named Mount Mills now commemorates the site).

Amazingly, London's fortress was completed in little more than five months and, although the trained bands formed the core of the workforce, this stupendous feat could not have been achieved without the help of ordinary citizens. By the time the works were at their peak in the spring of 1643, 20,000 Londoners, including numerous inhabitants of Cloth Fair, were working on the defences. Mr May witnessed the construction and wrote:

> It was the custom every day to go out by the thousands to dig; all professions, trades and occupations taking their turns; and not only inferior tradesmen, but gentlemen, and ladies themselves, for the encouragement of others, carrying spades, mattocks [pickaxes], and other instruments of digging; so that it became a pleasant sight in London to see them go out in such an order and number with drums beating before them.

Scottish minister William Lithgow was also in the city during the early months of 1643 and admired the way both rich and poor came together defend their homes and livelihoods:

> All sorts of Londoners here were wondrous commendable in marching to the fields and outworks; as merchants, silk men … shopkeepers, etc., with great alacrity, carrying on their shoulders iron mattocks and wooden shovels, with roaring drums, flying colours and girded swords, most companies also being interlarded with ladies, women and girls, two and two carrying baskets for to advance the labour.

By summer 1643, the London Line of Communication was complete and the forbidding fortress sent a clear message to the king that he would not reclaim the city without facing considerable resistance. Indeed, as Royalist John Berkenhead later lamented, '[If posterity asks] who would have pulled the crown from the king's head, taken the government off the hinges, dissolved the monarchy, inslaved the laws, and ruined their country, – say t'was the proud, unthankefull, schismaticall, rebellious, bloody city of London.'

That said, the remarkable creation of fortress London was driven more from the citizens' fear for their livelihoods than passionate allegiance to the Parliamentarian cause. Refugees from Brentford and the Midlands' battle towns had told of how they lost everything in the wake of Royalist occupation, and the prosperous merchants and tradesmen from streets like Cloth Fair were determined not to suffer the same fate.

It also did not mean that London was devoid of Royalists. While construction of the fortification was still under way, the Cheapside Cross (an ancient memorial to Queen Eleanor) became a place of pilgrimage for the king's supporters, some of whom even dared to remove their hats and genuflect as they passed. This prompted the City's Common Council to order its demolition, on the basis that the cross was a place of 'spiritual fornication', and contractor Robert Harley was dispatched to take it down. He was met by such vehement opposition that the local militia had to be summoned to quell a potential riot. The diarist John Evelyn, who was in London on business, witnessed the sorry scene and wrote, 'I returned [to Hertfordshire] with no little regret, for the confusion that threatened us. Resolving to possess myself in some quiet, if it might be, in a time of so great jealousy.'

The atmosphere of paranoia that infected London during the Civil War manifested itself again later in May when politician and poet Edmund Waller and his associates were arrested for plotting a Royalist uprising. Earlier in the month, Waller, his brother-in-law Nathaniel Tomkins and their friend, Richard Challoner, had met in Tomkins' home to discuss destabilising Parliament by persuading supporters of the king to withhold their taxes. Unfortunately, their conversation was overheard by a servant, the men were arrested and soon alehouses like the Eagle & Child hummed with gossip that a rebellion was imminent.

On 8 June, a London news-sheet reported, 'Master Waller and about 20 more of the chief plotters' planned to seize 'the Tower, the Magazines, and the new erected Forts about the City', capture the Lord Mayor and his councillors and 'to have massacred all the honest and well-affected people in and about London'. In fear for his life, Edmund Waller agreed to give evidence for the prosecution at the ensuing trial and, after receiving £10,000 for his betrayal, he was released and banished from England. His friend and brother-in-law were sentenced to death for treason and executed on 5 July.

By the time Nathaniel Tomkins and Richard Challoner faced the executioner's axe, many Londoners, including some inhabitants of Cloth Fair, were growing frustrated at the prolonged conflict. Although the men of the Orange Regiment had been spared fierce battle, their conscription into the Parliamentarian army had forced many to leave their businesses in the control of staff or, in some cases, temporarily shut them down. They had been promised compensation for the inevitable financial disadvantages, but as the war raged on this became increasingly scarce. In addition, battles in the Midlands were severely affecting trade with other counties and spot-checks at the new fortification made travel in and out of London tiresome. Although it was scheduled to go ahead as usual in August, the annual Bartholomew Fair – during which the Eagle & Child gleaned a large proportion of its annual profit – was looking unlikely to happen.

On a more personal level, pleasant diversions from the horrors of the war were in short supply. Following fears of Royalist propaganda being spread, Parliament shut down all of London's theatres and the suppression of the Church of England meant that even weddings became joyless civil affairs conducted by city aldermen. By the summer of 1643, there is doubt that Robert Chapman, his relatives and neighbours had much enthusiasm for continuing the war.

As divisions began to open up within the ranks of the Parliamentarian army, its general, the Earl of Essex, pressed for renewed peace talks, claiming that his poorly trained and ill-equipped troops were simply not capable of overpowering the king's forces. Over in Cloth Fair, the men of the Orange Regiment began to question the earl's commitment to the cause and the mood prompted the Common Council to petition for all the London Trained Bands to be placed under the control of a committee.

Sensing rebellion in the air, Parliament tried to subdue both sides by providing the Earl of Essex with 4,500 more men and handing control of the London Trained Bands to Sir William Waller, a general who was well respected in the metropolis. Nevertheless, many people still believed that the militia was too reliant on the command of noblemen. In September 1643, the colonel of an East Anglian regiment – one Oliver Cromwell – wrote, 'I had rather have a plain russet-coated captain that knows what he fights for, and loves what he knows, than that which you call a gentleman and is nothing else.'

In the meantime, Henry Rich had given up hope of a peaceful resolution and joined the royal court at Oxford, confidently expecting to be welcomed back into the fold and restored to his office as Groom of the Stole. To his surprise (if no one else's) only two members of the Privy Council were in favour of admitting him back into the royal court and King Charles himself bitterly complained that he had made no attempt to apologise for his misconduct. Henry Rich spent two months trying to curry favour with the court, but when his old office was awarded to the Marquis of Hertford he admitted defeat and returned to London. However, by this stage, Parliament were fully aware of his selfish nature and only allowed him to return to his seat in the House of Lords after the Earl of Essex intervened. The Commons remained suspicious of Rich's intentions and consequently pressured the Upper House to pass an ordinance preventing peers who had deserted Parliament from voting on legislation without the agreement of both houses.

The enmity of the House of Commons was studiously ignored by Henry Rich and in December 1645 he audaciously petitioned for compensation to the tune of almost £40,000 for financial losses caused by the war. Unsurprisingly, the petition was rejected by the Commons, but he remained upbeat and instead turned his attention to drawing up an independent peace treaty in a vain attempt to resolve the conflict in his favour. The treaty was ignored by both sides, and as the conflict dragged on, the mood within the ranks of London's trained bands became increasingly mutinous. In July 1644, Sir William Waller wrote to Parliament complaining that his troops were growing rebellious and warned, 'An army compounded of these men will never go through with your service, and till you have an army merely your own that you may command, it is in a manner impossible to do anything of importance.'

The attitude of the London soldiers was shared by Parliamentarian troops across the kingdom and, by early January 1645, the situation had reached breaking point. In a desperate bid to reunite the army, the Earl of Essex was relieved of command and the New Model Army was established with Sir Thomas Fairfax as its captain general. Fairfax quickly commissioned his ally Oliver Cromwell as Lieutenant General of Horse and effectively his second in command. This set Cromwell on a path that would ultimately lead to greatness.

The New Model Army officially comprised 22,000 soldiers split into eleven cavalry regiments, twelve of infantry and one regiment of dragoons. New regulations were set out in a 'Soldiers' Catechism' and the standard daily pay was 8*d* for infantry and 2*s* for cavalry. The soldiers were also provided with sufficient food and clothing – two things that had previously been woefully lacking. For the men of the Orange Regiment who chose to join its ranks, the New Model Army presented unprecedented opportunities for advancement. Believing firmly in the abilities of all men, Oliver Cromwell ensured that soldiers would be promoted for their proficiency rather than their social status. Consequently, wealthy but ineffective officers who had bought their way into the army became surplus to requirements and were discharged. This reformed Parliamentarian force proved so effective that it eventually helped to effect a temporary cessation of hostilities in 1646. However, the Civil War was far from over.

In the meantime, London remained a violent and paranoid city. On 10 January 1645, Archbishop Laud – the architect of the religious reform that had so infuriated the Puritan MPs – was executed on Tower Hill, and soon afterwards the celebration of all religious festivals was outlawed. This move was not well received by the citizens of London and caused Royalist satirist John Taylor to lament, 'Thus are the merry lords of misrule suppressed by the mad lords of bad rule at Westminster.'

The banning of religious celebrations, especially Christmas, caused some unexpected problems for Parliament. The young apprentices who toiled in the workshops of Cloth Fair and beyond were understandably furious at having their holidays cancelled and businesses that tried to open on Christmas Day soon closed their doors again when an angry mob appeared outside.

Nevertheless, Parliament's curtailment of Church censorship inadvertently gave rise to an explosion in printing. When Jan Comenius, an intellectual from Bohemia, visited London during the 1640s he was amazed to see the number of new bookshops in the city. This printing revolution is encapsulated in the activities of George Thomason, a London bookseller, who collected a copy of every book and pamphlet he came across. In 1640, he bought twenty-four books; in 1642 the number had risen to 2,134. The era also heralded the first regular newspapers, which reported on the war and spread propaganda. By 1644, the residents of Cloth Fair were able to choose from a dozen 'news books' every week, not all of which supported Parliament. The most widely read Royalist publication was the *Mercurius Aulicus*, which was printed in London and Oxford throughout the conflict.

The wealth of books and pamphlets available on London's streets inevitably encouraged intellectual debate among the city's inhabitants, particularly on the subject of religion, and soon a Nonconformist movement gained momentum, although it faced strong opposition from the authorities. In September 1645, Henry Burton (one of the ministers who had had his ears removed by Archbishop Laud) was locked out of St Mary's Aldermanbury for delivering independent lectures, and his associate John Goodwin was removed from St Stephen's Coleman Street for preaching controversial theories. Despite this, the Nonconformists' popularity grew and by 1646 the sheer number of new 'sects' prompted Puritan clergyman Thomas Edwards to publish *Gangraena*, which he declared to be 'a catalogue and discovery of many of the errors, heresies, blasphemies and pernicious practices of the Sectaries of this time'.

Most importantly, the printing revolution gave Londoners a voice. Sick and tired of the seemingly unresolvable divisions between king and Parliament, Richard Overton voiced the popular view in July 1646 when he published *The Remonstrance of Many Thousand Citizens*. This explosive pamphlet opened by reminding MPs that 'the cause of our choosing you to be Parliament was to deliver us from all kind of bondage and to preserve the commonwealth in peace and happiness ... But ye are to remember, this was only of us but a power of trust, which is ever revocable.' It then swiftly cut to the chase, urging Parliament to abolish the monarchy without further delay:

> You maintain the king can do no wrong and apply all his oppressions to 'evil counsellors' ... as if you were resolved to make us believe he were a God ... We do expect [that you] declare King Charles an enemy, and to publish your resolution never to have any more, but to acquit us of so great a charge and trouble forever, and to convert the great revenue of the crown to the public treasure.

Londoners showed their support for *The Remonstrance* by withholding their taxes – between June and September 1646 only a quarter of all monies due was collected and, in February 1647, the inhabitants of Cloth Fair were involved in fierce riots when a trader at Smithfield Market refused to pay duty on his livestock. As he began to remove the beasts he was stopped by guards, but the crowd leapt to his defence and later that day a mob led by butcher William Taylor burned down the market's excise office. A hastily printed pamphlet declared, 'Parliament never met with their match ... until they began to vex the Butchers of London'.

The riots outside Cloth Fair inspired the local apprentices to agitate again over the loss of their holidays. After a renewed campaign to enforce the closure of shops and businesses during religious festivals – by force if necessary – the apprentices raised a petition to be given alternative days off and, to their astonishment, Parliament acquiesced, awarding them a holiday on the second Tuesday of every month.

Although insurrection in London was a major worry for Parliament, their main concern was the future of the English monarchy. By the summer of 1646 the Royalist army was at the point of capitulation and King Charles made it clear that he was willing to discuss his future role.

Nevertheless, severe discontent on both sides still simmered. Parliament was loath to allow Charles to return to London for fear it would spark an uprising and, while an agreement between king and Parliament remained elusive, resentment began to grow within the ranks of the previously exemplary New Model Army.

The soldiers' discontent was due to several factors. Firstly, Londoners' refusal to pay tax meant that they had not received all the pay they had been promised. Secondly, Parliament refused to give them indemnity for so-called 'war crimes' such as stealing Royalist horses for their cavalry. Thirdly, Parliament's refusal to even discuss the king's future role made the soldiers wonder what they had been fighting for in the first place.

In an attempt to settle their grievances, an Army Council was formed and a list of the men's concerns was formally handed to Parliament, along with their proposals for constitutional reform. Meanwhile, many London-based soldiers joined forces with a radical group known as the Levellers and published the *Agreement of the People*, which pressed for political reform, including the right for every man to have a vote. Realising that the New Model Army was capable of occupying London to achieve their aims, the beleaguered Common Council warned the Orange Regiment that it might soon have to mobilise again, this time against men who had once been their compatriots.

In the event, the New Model Army did indeed occupy London, but they did so with the support of its citizens. This forced Oliver Cromwell to finally instigate talks at a series of hearings known as the Putney Debates, which began in October 1647.

While the Putney Debates slowly rolled on, Parliament's persistent reluctance to make any decisions concerning the constitution created a power vacuum. Vying for supremacy were the Royalists, who wanted to return to the old constitution, independents from the New

Model Army, and Presbyterian MPs, who were pressing for political and religious reform. The ensuing struggle between these groups led to a period of renewed conflict and London descended into chaos as pro-Royalist riots broke out in March and April 1648.

Seizing the opportunity to redeem himself with the king, Henry Rich once again offered his services to the Royalists and succeeded in obtaining a commission as a general from the Prince of Wales. On 4 July he left London for Kingston in Surrey where he hoped to recruit an army and attack Parliamentarian soldiers at Colchester. However, only around 600 men joined his ranks and he was defeated by Parliamentarian forces before they had even left the county. The residue of his army marched northwards but were overwhelmed at St Neots, and Henry Rich was sent in chains to Warwick Castle. However, before Parliament could decide his fate, events overtook them.

In December 1648, Colonel Thomas Pride and his supporters succeeded in expelling over 100 Presbyterian MPs from the House. The remaining members formed what became known as the Rump Parliament and finally instigated legal proceedings against King Charles, indicting him with high treason. Tired of war, but fearful of the future, the incarcerated Henry Rich and his tenants at Cloth Fair waited in grim anticipation of what would happen next.

Charles I returned to London as a prisoner in early 1649 after seven long and violent years of absence. His trial began on 20 January at Westminster Hall and a week later he was found guilty as charged and sentenced to death. England's monarch was executed on 29 January outside his former banqueting house on Whitehall in front of a large crowd of ghoulish spectators. Standing in their midst was Philip Henry, who later summed up the prevailing mood when he wrote, 'The blow I saw given and can truly say with a sad heart; at the instant thereof, I remember well, there was such a groan by the thousands there present, as I never heard before and desire I may never hear again.'

The death of Charles I signified the end of the English monarchy, for the time being. However, although his was the most significant execution in 1649, it was not the last. On 10 February, Henry Rich appeared at the High Court charged with treason. Shrewd to the last, he argued that he had only agreed to surrender at St Neots after being assured that his life would be spared. However, both judge and jury were wise to his stories and he was sentenced to death. Subsequent interventions by several high-ranking Parliamentarians ensured that the sentence was debated in the House of Lords but, in the event, they narrowly voted against a reprieve.

Henry Rich was beheaded at Whitehall on 9 March 1649. On ascending the scaffold, he protested his innocence to the last, declaring, 'God be praised, although my blood comes to be shed here, there was scarcely a drop of blood shed in that action I was engaged in.' With that, the executioner's axe fell on one of the most cunningly self-serving characters of the Civil War.

4

THE SIGN OF
THE RED CROSS

Death Visits Cloth Fair

After Henry Rich's execution, his widow Isabella successfully petitioned to have his sequestered lands returned and soon afterwards Robert Chapman's lease on the Eagle & Child expired. The property was subsequently let to Robert Downing, a long-term resident of St Bartholomew's parish, and his wife Elizabeth.

The Downings had lived in the area since the early 1620s and in the years leading up to the Civil War they had six children, but only two survived into adulthood – Henry (born in 1627) and Deborah (born in 1639). Although his profession is unknown, Robert Downing was clearly a successful man – the Eagle & Child was one of three properties he held in and around Cloth Fair, his personal residence being a house in neighbouring Long Lane. Downing had prospered during the war years and those that followed, even though during this period the character of England changed significantly. After the execution of Charles I, the country was declared a Commonwealth, presided over by the House of Commons and a new Council of State, which replaced the king's Privy Council and the House of Lords. In December 1653, Oliver Cromwell became the head of state when he was appointed Lord Protector and, under his leadership, Parliament strived to restrict what they regarded as the excesses of Charles I's reign. Festivities at Christmas and Easter continued to be suppressed and any public meetings, be they in church, theatre or pleasure ground, were strictly regulated.

Quite what the inhabitants of Cloth Fair thought of the Commonwealth regime can only be guessed, as any clues that may have been found in the records of St Bartholomew the Great have been lost. However, Parliament's administrative reforms directly benefited the Eagle & Child's new owner, Robert Downing. In a bid to create accurate population statistics it was decreed that England's parishes should keep a secular record of every birth, marriage and burial that occurred within their bounds, entered into a parish register by a trusted resident elected by the local rate payers. On 22 September 1653, Robert Downing was chosen as the registrar for St Bartholomew the Great and, a week later, he presented himself at the offices of Alderman Robert Tichborne clutching a certificate confirming his election. In return, he was handed a sturdy, leather-bound book in which he would record the relevant events.

His subsequent entries in the ledger were inscribed in a fine, strong script that gave no indication of illness or old age. Nevertheless, after serving as registrar for just nine months, Robert Downing suddenly died.

Downing's last will and testament gave detailed instructions on how he wished to be laid to rest and to whom his worldly goods should be distributed. In accordance with his wishes, he was buried in St Bartholomew's Churchyard and, rather intriguingly, he specifically requested that the ceremony should be conducted using the Book of Common Prayer, which had been banned by Parliament back in 1645 — a fact he was surely aware of in his capacity as parish registrar. Perhaps to compensate for the clandestine use of the prayer book, he stipulated that the minister presiding over his funeral should receive payment of 3s. After the service, the mourners were invited over to the Eagle & Child where they were treated to 'Rosemarie White or Claret Wine, two gallons of port and Naples biscuits', before being presented with a pair of gloves to wear in memory of the departed, as was customary at the time.

After the funeral, Robert Downing's estate was divided between his family. His wife Elizabeth inherited the house on Long Lane and most of its contents, while his 15-year-old daughter Deborah received a bed, some silverware and £50, which was placed in trust until she either married or reached the age of 21. The rest of his estate passed to his son Henry, including the Eagle & Child, another house on Cloth Fair and personal possessions such as a 'great trunk', a seal ring and a number of books. Henry Downing also inherited his father's role as parish registrar.

After his father's will had been proved, Henry Downing moved into the spacious chambers above the Eagle & Child, leaving the alehouse in the capable hands of his servant, John Tocock, while he pursued his career as a master tailor. This was a potentially engrossing trade but unfortunately during the 1650s, fashion afforded little opportunity for creativity or self-expression. Londoners were reluctant to wear elaborate apparel for fear of being branded Royalist sympathisers and instead their clothes were invariably made from plain, drab fabrics. Men wore short, unstructured jackets and wide breeches that hung loose to the knee over thick, black stockings. Women's clothing was no more inspiring and usually comprised a high-necked, sleeved bodice and gathered skirt, covered by a plain shawl and apron. Lace collars and cuffs were sometimes worn by the more daring members of both sexes, but generally the starched linen varieties were considered the safer option.

Although his creativity was stifled, Henry Downing's early years at 41–42 Cloth Fair nevertheless seemed promising. On 18 September 1657 he married Rebecca Pratt, a young woman from the nearby parish of Trinity the Less, in a simple, civil ceremony presided over by Sir John Bollastone, a local Justice of the Peace. In his capacity as registrar, Henry recorded the union in his own hand, and the following year he registered the marriage of his sister Deborah to John Hobbs, one of the parish churchwardens, and that of his widowed mother Elizabeth, who wed William Dowks. Tragically, a month after Elizabeth and William's wedding, Henry's wife Rebecca suddenly died, possibly during childbirth. However, on 19 January 1659 he married again, this time to Judith Atkins of Holborn.

By the time of Henry Downing's second marriage, Oliver Cromwell had been succeeded as Lord Protector by his son Richard and the populace were beginning to tire of Parliament's regime. The Protectorate was subsequently abolished, the Commonwealth disintegrated and, on 25 May 1660, Charles II returned to England from exile. He was crowned king at Westminster Abbey on 23 April 1661.

The restoration of the monarchy released the population from the conservatism that had dominated the post-war period we now know as the Interregnum. Previously banned plays opened at theatres across the country, religious festivals were enthusiastically celebrated and a feeling of optimism prevailed.

The ebullience of the new era was reflected in fashion. Daniel Defoe noted in his dramatised *Journal of the Plague Year* (1722), 'The court brought with it a great flux of pride and new fashions; all people were gay and luxurious.' This inevitably prompted Henry Downing to replace his dowdy stock at his tailor's shop with brightly coloured (and more profitable) silks and brocades that were snapped up by clients who were keen to rid themselves of their old Puritan attire.

The restoration of the monarchy also brought a significant increase to the population of London. Royalist families who had fled the capital during the war returned and soldiers from the disbanded armies set up in trade. This sudden influx of people had a positive effect on the city's economy and the mood of oppression lifted, but there was a darker side to life in Restoration London.

In the months following Charles II's triumphant return to the capital, his father's foes, whether living or dead, were relentlessly persecuted. Oliver Cromwell's body was exhumed, subjected to a posthumous execution and allegedly hung in chains at Tyburn, where it was decapitated. The head was then rumoured to be displayed on a pole outside Westminster Hall until 1685. The truth of this story is debatable as another rumour suggests that, in the months leading up to the Restoration, Cromwell's remains were moved to a secret location to protect them from the inevitable wrath of Royalists.

Nevertheless, Charles II's desire to avenge his father's death was indisputably real, and during the first years of his reign the parish of St Bartholomew the Great developed a reputation as a citadel for his opponents. The poet John Milton, a fierce critic of the monarchy and erstwhile Latin Secretary to the Council of State, hid in a house next to the churchyard at Cloth Fair for several weeks to evade the king's men. He was eventually arrested and, although ultimately released without charge, was subjected to the humiliation of seeing his political writings symbolically burnt outside Newgate Gaol.

Soon after Milton's arrest, intelligence was received at the royal court that the parish of St Bartholomew had also become a resort of religious Nonconformists. In response, the king ordered the Lord Mayor to conduct a detailed search of all its houses to rout the dissenters, but by the time the mayor's men arrived on the scene, most of the 300-strong congregation had disappeared. Nevertheless, ten men and thirty women were arrested and imprisoned.

Cloth Fair and its surrounds remained a Nonconformist stronghold throughout the early years of Charles II's reign, but before the king could progress any further with its suppression, the district was overwhelmed by an outbreak of the most feared disease in England – the plague. In September 1664, Dutch sailors arriving at the Port of London described a plague epidemic that was devastating the cities of Amsterdam and Rotterdam. Word quickly reached the Lord Mayor, who called a series of meetings to discuss ways of stopping the disease spreading to London, but no measures were implemented and the capital was left vulnerable.

Spread by *Yersinia pestis*, a bacterium carried by fleas living on the bodies of rodents, the plague manifests itself in three forms. The septicaemic strain infects the blood, the pneumonic type assaults the respiratory tract and the bubonic plague attacks the lymphatic system. Any one of these strains is potentially fatal and it is thought that the outbreak that ravaged London in 1665 was a devastating combination of two, or perhaps even all three.

Plague was by no means unknown on the streets of the capital. Epidemics broke out every twenty or thirty years and thus physicians were quick to recognise symptoms, particularly those of the bubonic strain, which caused agonisingly tender boils known as buboes to swell on the neck, armpits and groin of the victim. However, although the plague was relatively easy to diagnose, physicians were baffled as to how it spread. It was generally suspected that the disease was carried on board ships because the first cases of an epidemic often appeared in areas close to international ports. Some scientists went so far as to assert that it was specifically contained in bales of cotton from Egypt; others blamed cargoes from Italy and Cyprus. There was even a school of thought that plague was spread by a hostile foreign power in an early attempt at chemical warfare.

While the scientists posited their theories, the ordinary people on the street thought it most likely that plague was spread either by animals or the very air they breathed. For instance, when the disease swept through the Buckinghamshire village of Ellesborough in 1665, the inhabitants placed blame squarely on a stray dog that had been seen wandering the lanes shortly before the outbreak began. In London, it was widely thought that the plague was carried by odours and this gave rise to quack physicians who claimed they could detect it in aromas as diverse as spring flowers (epidemics usually manifested in April or May) and rotting carcasses. The most fanciful even claimed to see the plague lurking in cloud formations, while amateur scientist William Boghurst published a table of signs foreshadowing outbreaks of the disease. Some of the portents were plainly ridiculous, such as 'Comets, gleams of fire or fiery impressions in the air'. Others inadvertently strayed close to the truth, in particular, 'an increase in vermin'.

The first signs of the plague epidemic of 1665 had appeared in London just before Christmas the previous year, when Dr Nathaniel Hodges attended a young man suffering from a high fever. Suspecting blood poisoning, Hodges gave him an antidote, but two days later he was summoned to the house again and recorded in his diary that 'two risings about the bigness of a nutmeg broke out, one on each thigh; upon examination of which I soon discovered the malignity, both from their black hue and the circle around them, and pronounced it to be the plague'.

Luckily Dr Hodges' patient recovered, but in January London's weekly bills of mortality began to grow. Usually this cold, hard month claimed the lives of around 250–300 people but, by the week ending 24 January 1665, the number stood at 474. The writer Daniel Defoe later recalled, 'This last bill was really frightful, being a higher number than had been known to have been buried in one week since the preceding visitation in 1656.'

The first manifestations of plague centred on the densely packed parish of St Giles-in-the-Fields, some distance away from Cloth Fair. Consequently, Londoners gave the district a wide berth and only ventured there if absolutely necessary. This unofficial containment initially appeared to work and over February and March the bills of mortality decreased, but the plague never completely left the streets of London. As the winter frosts gave way to spring, the disease was reported in districts further east. The first City victim was a man from Bearbinder Lane in the parish of St Mary Woolnoth, just a fifteen-minute walk away from Cloth Fair.

Nevertheless, the parish of St Bartholomew the Great managed to evade the plague throughout the spring – during March, April and May, Henry Downing recorded between six and seven burials each month, which was average for the time of year. However, when June brought a heatwave, the epidemic began to escalate. Daniel Defoe wrote:

> The infection spread in a dreadful manner ... for all that could conceal their distempers did it to prevent their neighbours shunning and refusing to converse with them; and also to prevent authority shutting up their houses, which though it was not yet practised, yet was threatened, and people were extremely terrified at the thoughts of it.

By the end of June, plague was rife and anyone who could afford to flee London did so. The royal court moved to its old Civil War headquarters at Oxford and took with them many tradesmen who relied on the king's custom for their living. These exiles were compelled to obtain certificates of health from the Lord Mayor's office before they could use the roads leading out of the city or lodge at any inns. However, they were easily obtained, even by those already infected with plague, so long as they were not displaying obvious symptoms.

Those Londoners who had to stay put laid plans to protect themselves from infection. Some measures, such as staying away from plague hotspots, were effective up to a point. Others were useless, particularly the medications purveyed by street sellers, one of whom set up a stall outside St Bartholomew's Hospital. As the epidemic worsened, billboards in Cloth Fair became plastered with advertisements for 'Infallible Preventative Pills' and 'Plague Water', and the fearful populace took to carrying lucky charms, the cheapest of which was an intricately folded piece of paper on which the magic word 'abracadabra' was written to form an inverted pyramid.

The residents of Cloth Fair and their neighbours also employed the services of countless charlatans who claimed to possess curative powers. Among them was a supposed physician from Holland, who claimed to have cured numerous victims of the epidemic in his homeland, and an old woman who specialised in drawing the plague out of stricken women.

Of course, the soothsayers and snake oils did not stop the irrepressible spread of the plague and by July it had reached the parish of St Bartholomew the Great. From his home above the Eagle & Child, Henry Downing witnessed its horrific progress and was mortified when his sister Deborah and her husband, John Hobbs, began to display its awful symptoms.

There is no way of telling how the couple contracted the disease. It may have been from a flea bite, a scratch from an infected animal or through the contaminated body fluids of another sufferer. Whatever the method of contagion, Deborah and John Hobbs would have first felt unwell two to five days after coming into contact with the deadly bacterium and henceforth their illness took one of three courses that were succinctly described by Daniel Defoe:

> Some were immediately overwhelmed with it and came to violent fevers, vomitings, insufferable pains in the back ... others with swellings and tumours in the neck or groin, or armpits, which, till they broke, put them into insufferable agonies and torment; others, as I have observed, were silently infected, the fever preying upon their spirits insensibly, and they seeing little of it till they fell into swooning, and faintings and death without pain.

Although it hardly appeared to be the case while afflicted, people who contracted the bubonic strain of plague – characterised by the excruciatingly painful swellings – were most likely to recover. Those 'silently infected' with the pneumonic and septicaemic strains invariably succumbed to the disease, sometimes within hours of displaying the first symptoms. However, the nursery rhyme 'Ring a Ring of Roses' (thought to have originated during the plague year) hints that many victims of the 1665 epidemic contracted the bubonic and pneumonic strains simultaneously:

Ring A Ring of Roses [the buboes]
A pocket full of posies
A tissue, A tissue [a pneumonic symptom]
We all fall down

Could this simple song explain why this particular outbreak was so catastrophic?

With no cure available, the authorities' only option was to fight the plague by containing it. Emergency measures were discussed by the City's Common Council and it was just days after they were brought into force that Deborah Hobbs fell ill. In accordance with the new ordinance, her husband John was compelled to inform the City authorities at once and a 'chirurgeon' (doctor) was quickly dispatched to examine her.

Once satisfied that she had indeed contracted the plague, the chirurgeon sent word to the local constabulary, who were tasked with the awful duty of shutting up the Hobbs's home with all the other inhabitants, whether ill or not, locked inside. A foot-long red cross was then daubed on their front door, above which was inscribed the desperate plea, 'Lord have mercy upon us'. Two watchmen were then assigned to guard the property day and night to ensure no one (apart from chirurgeons or nurses) went in or out. Henceforth, the watchmen became the Hobbs' link to the outside world – they bought their food and drink, passed on messages from anxious relations and delivered medicines.

With no way of escaping the disease, Deborah's husband John soon began to display plague symptoms himself. Their home had become a death cell and all they could do was pray that they would somehow survive. It was not to be. On 20 July 1665, a distraught Henry Downing opened his parish register to record his sister's burial. Five days later, he added her husband's name and, on 25 September, that of their daughter, Elizabeth.

This unimaginable family tragedy was made harder to bear because those left behind were forbidden to properly grieve. Deborah, her husband and their baby girl died alone and their bodies were unceremoniously removed from their house on a rude wooden 'dead cart' that incessantly patrolled the streets, announcing its presence with the mournful cry, 'Bring out your dead!' Then, with no family or friends in attendance for fear of contagion, they were hurriedly laid to rest in a fenced-off section of St Bartholomew's Churchyard. Henry Downing and his mother were not even allowed to visit their graves.

After the Hobbs family died, their home remained in quarantine for twenty-eight days to make sure no other inhabitants had contracted the disease. Afterwards, all their possessions were burnt and the rooms in which they had met their end were covered in a thick layer of antiseptic lime wash. By the time a white cross was painted on the front door to show the house had been cleansed, all trace of its former occupants had been obliterated.

The brutal treatment of the Hobbs family and their fellow plague victims unsurprisingly provoked fear and outrage across London. Daniel Defoe branded it cruel and un-Christian, writing:

> The misery of those families is not to be expressed; and it was generally in such houses that we heard the most dismal shrieks and outcries of the poor people, terrified and even frightened to death by the sight of the condition of their dearest relations, and by the terror of being imprisoned as they were.

Panicked at the prospect of being left for dead in their own homes, many people attempted to escape by clambering over rooftops into back rooms of neighbouring houses, thus evading the eyes of the watchmen. One ingenious household even blew up a supply of gunpowder to create a distraction while they stole away. Clandestine escapes were particularly common if a servant rather than a family member fell sick. One so-called gentleman, whose maid had succumbed to plague, told the watchman in no uncertain terms that if a nurse was not immediately summoned, the poor woman would die of starvation as he would not let his wife and children go near her. By the time the nurse arrived, the man and his family had absconded by breaking through a wall into a cobbler's workshop next door. Their abandoned maidservant died soon afterwards and it fell to the nurse and watchman to organise collection of the body.

Of course, the fugitives ultimately made matters worse. Those already infected with the plague were known to drop dead in the street; others carried the disease to the countryside where, after being unable to produce a certificate of health, they were refused admittance to any inns and died a lonely death in rural barns. The nurses they left behind to tend the sick were often little better than the people who had absconded. Dr Hodges, who tended many London victims during the plague epidemic of 1665, was horrified to find that many of the nurses exploited the dire circumstances for personal gain. He wrote, 'These wretches, out of greediness to plunder the dead would strangle their patients and charge it to the distemper in their throats', and cited the case of a 'worthy Citizen' stripped naked by his nurse, who then made off with his clothes and personal belongings. The gentleman subsequently recovered and 'came a second time into the world naked'.

By the end of July 1665, the parish of St Bartholomew the Great and its surrounds had become eerily quiet. As the number of red crosses on doors rose, the inhabitants of the neighbouring houses fled and the annual August fair was cancelled. Other popular entertainments such as bear baiting and plays were also banned by the Lord Mayor and the Eagle & Child was ordered to close its doors at 9 p.m. each night to prevent drunken patrons from roaming the streets, potentially spreading plague in their wake.

In this strange, apocalyptic atmosphere, no one bothered to go into mourning as the sheer number of deaths rendered the tradition unmanageable. However, as science failed them, people turned to religion. Bereaved citizens driven out of their minds by grief and confusion took to the streets where they loudly declared that the 'Day of Judgement' was upon them. The most famous of these false prophets was Solomon Eagle, an eccentric Quaker who patrolled Cloth Fair and its surrounds with a pan of burning charcoal on his head, beseeching bemused passers-by to 'Repent! Repent!' Those who had not completely taken leave of their senses preferred to attend traditional church services, and the pews of St Bartholomew the Great overflowed with a desperate congregation praying for an end to their relentless suffering.

The horrors endured in the summer of 1665 were unlike any other, before or since. Dr Hodges described the appalling situation, writing:

In some houses carcasses lay waiting for burial, and in others persons in their last agonies; in one room might be heard dying groans, in another the ravings of a delirium … Some of the infected run about staggering like drunken men and fall and expire in the streets; while others lie half-dead and comatose, but never to be waked by the last trumpet; some lie vomiting as if they had drank poison; and others fall dead in the market, while they are buying the necessities for the support of life.

Over at Cloth Fair, Henry Downing's loss of his sister, brother-in-law and niece was made all the more miserable by the fact that his tailoring trade had virtually ground to a halt. As we have already seen, the populace was not buying mourning dress and in the midst of the epidemic new clothes of any type were seen as totally unnecessary. In addition, the import and export of cloth had stopped.

The Port of London had continued to operate during the first few weeks of the plague outbreak, but word quickly spread and by July all trade with Italy, Spain and Portugal was vetoed. Shortly afterwards, the port temporarily shut down, forcing hundreds of dock workers into penury and leaving tailors like Henry Downing with no access to any foreign-made cloth. Even English fabrics were difficult to obtain as they had to be unloaded outside the city and brought in by carts, prompting their prices to rocket.

Somehow the people of Cloth Fair became accustomed to living in the midst of death. The sight of corpses on the streets became so commonplace that passers-by merely gave them a wide berth, surmising that the death cart would carry them away in due course. Over at Smithfield Market, the meat sellers paid stretcher bearers to be at close hand so bodies could be removed before they affected business. Butchers who were based outside London wisely set up stalls at Islington and Southwark, a safe distance away from the epicentre of the outbreak. If a journey into the capital was essential, they walked in the middle of the road, keeping well away from the 'pestilential houses'. In turn, their customers tried to avoid infection by removing meat from its hook themselves and dropping their payment into a pot of vinegar.

By the beginning of August, many parish churchyards had literally run out of space in which to bury the dead. Room was found in St Bartholomew's graveyard for most of the local victims, but those from other parishes were not so fortunate. Over the following months thousands of people were laid to rest in large communal pits hastily dug on waste ground at the city's edge. With coffins no longer available to anyone except the wealthy, most were simply wrapped in a shroud and thrown onto a cart already laden with other bodies, from whence they rattled ignominiously to their final resting place. As no mourners were permitted to be present, the drivers of the dead carts simply tipped the bodies into the plague pits like refuse, sometimes even removing their shrouds beforehand so they could resell them.

Amid this chaos, there were at least some attempts to arrest the seemingly unstoppable spread of the plague. From the safety of his court at Oxford, the king commanded the College of Physicians to study the disease at close quarters in a bid to find a cure. A number of eminent doctors, including Dr Glisson, regius professor at Cambridge University, bravely volunteered to live alongside sufferers, and several gave their lives as a result. Although their valiant work failed to unearth a cure, they learned a great deal about the progress of the disease and an advisory pamphlet they published did much to impede the duplicitous careers of quack physicians.

While the doctors endeavoured to research the cause and effect of the epidemic, the Lord Mayor decided to try burning fires in the streets in a bid to clear the air of deadly miasmas. Enormous bonfires were subsequently assembled across London, including three at the stricken Port of London, two at the Royal Exchange and one outside the door of the Lord Mayor's house. They had little effect and, in fact, the noxious fumes probably killed even more people. Nevertheless, they remained alight for four days until the authorities were persuaded that they were wasting valuable fuel.

By the beginning of September, many people feared that the plague would not cease until it had claimed the lives of the entire population. However, as the month progressed, the number of new cases began to subside and on 27 September Samuel Pepys wrote in his diary, 'I saw this week's Bill of Mortality, wherein, blessed by God! There is above 1,800 decrease, being the first considerable decrease we have had.'

Reports of plague continued to decrease in October and slowly life returned to the abandoned city streets. Dr Hodges, who had remained in London throughout the epidemic, wrote, 'The houses which before were full of the dead, were now again inhabited by the living; and the shops which had been most part of the year shut up, were again opened.' Hodges was also surprised to note how those who, just weeks previously, had been scared to meet their own family now happily 'venture into the houses and rooms where infected persons had but a little before breathed their last'.

Nevertheless, the plague left an indelible mark on those it spared. On 16 October, Samuel Pepys walked to the Tower of London and noted:

> So many sad stories overheard as I walk, every body talking of this dead, and that man sick, and so many in this place, and so many in that. And they tell me that in Westminster, there is never a physician and but one apothecary left, all being dead.

By the end of November, the authorities were confident that the plague epidemic was finally subsiding. Nevertheless, it left utter devastation in its wake – inside the City wall, nearly 10,000 inhabitants died of the disease. Of the parishes 'without the wall', St Giles Cripplegate suffered the worst, with 4,838 plague deaths, while the significantly smaller parish of St Bartholomew the Great buried 344 victims.

One of the last people to be interred in the churchyard in 1665 was Henry Downing. The record of his burial on 12 December does not state that he was a victim of the epidemic (all plague burials were marked as such) but, as he was only 38 years old, his death was certainly untimely. Thus, by the end of plague year, the only surviving members of the Downing family were Henry's wife, Judith, and his mother, Elizabeth. This catastrophic loss was mirrored across London and, as Dr Hodges noted, 'The whole British nation wept for the miseries of her Metropolis'.

5

LONDON WAS, BUT IS NO MORE

Or How the Oldest House in London Very Nearly Wasn't

As the people of St Bartholomew the Great tried to rebuild their lives after the horrors of the plague epidemic, little did they know that fate had another test in store that would change the face of their city forever.

Back in 1661, Parliament had agreed that the newly reinstated king and his Privy Council needed an annual income of at least £1.2 million in order to carry out their administrative duties. The bulk of this sum was expected to come from customs and excise but, as the year progressed, it became clear there would be a deficit of around £300,000. Tasked with finding a way to make up the balance, Parliament came up with a scheme that would fill the royal purse without making too much of an impact on their own personal wealth – the hearth tax.

Colloquially known as 'chimney money', the hearth tax levied 2s annually for every fireplace and stove in the country. The money was paid in two instalments (in March and September) by the occupier of the property and if a house was empty, its owner had to foot the bill. In order to keep track of who should pay what, annual lists of householders were compiled. Some survive to this day and the 1666 ledger for St Bartholomew the Great reveals that, after the death of her husband, Judith Downing moved to her mother-in-law's house on Long Lane, while John Tocock continued to run the Eagle & Child. The alehouse was listed as having four hearths in total; these were probably found in the drinking room, the kitchen and the two reception rooms on the first floor.

Needless to say, the hearth tax was universally unpopular, especially with tradesmen who relied on fires and stoves for their living. One such man was Thomas Farriner, a baker who lived in Pudding Lane, just over 1 mile east of the Eagle & Child. On the evening of Saturday, 1 September 1666, Farriner shut up his bakery and retired to his living quarters upstairs for the night, leaving the fire in one of the ovens still glowing. Around three hours later, he awoke to find his bakery so fiercely aflame that he and his family were forced to escape through an upstairs window. Their maid, too frightened to follow them, collapsed and suffocated amid the acrid smoke that billowed through the building.

In a desperate bid to save his neighbours' property, Thomas Farriner battled to extinguish the fire by dowsing it with water. Although several people quickly rushed to his aid, their efforts met with no success and with a strong wind fanning the flames they concluded that the only way to stop them from spreading was to create a firebreak by pulling down adjacent buildings.

However, there was a problem. Many of Farriner's neighbours, who had fled London during the plague, had yet to return and so permission to destroy their property was impossible to obtain. Faced with a conflagration that was rapidly getting out of control, word was sent to the

Lord Mayor, Sir Thomas Bloodworth, in the hope that he would order the buildings' demolition. Roused from his slumber and reluctant to make rash decisions that might result in multiple lawsuits, Bloodworth arrived on the scene in an irritable mood. 'Pish! A woman could piss it out,' he declared, before returning to the comfort of his bed.

In fairness, Bloodworth's initial dismissal of the fire was not altogether irresponsible. Restoration London was filled with narrow streets lined with tightly packed wooden houses and fires were a common occurrence. In most cases the flames were extinguished without causing a great deal of damage, but that night the fates were against the city. An unusually strong wind swept down Pudding Lane, sending sparks scuttling across the road where they quickly ignited the dry timbers of an old inn, before spreading southwards to dock warehouses on Thames Street. As vats of tallow, oil and spirits burst into flame the inferno began to seriously threaten the city, but still the Lord Mayor refused to permit the demolition of buildings.

As the residents of Pudding Lane and Thames Street desperately tried to quench the fire, John Tocock, Judith Downing and their neighbours at St Bartholomew's were asleep in their beds, blissfully unaware of the disaster that was unfolding. However, the conflagration did attract the attention of people living closer, including Samuel Pepys, who lived on Seething Lane, a ten-minute walk away. Pepys was first told of the fire by his worried maid, Jane, in the early hours of Sunday morning. After deciding it was too far away to be a threat, he went back to bed but awoke a few hours later to learn that it was still alight. Anxious to get a better view, he hurried over to the Tower of London and, standing on 'one of the high places', was appalled at the sight that met his eyes. He recorded in his diary, 'There I did see the houses at the end of the bridge all on fire, and an infinite great fire on this and the other side [at] the end of the bridge.'

Pepys rushed down to the riverside where he paid a ferryman to row him along the Thames past the fire which, by this stage, was rapidly moving eastwards causing widespread panic. From the safety of the boat, he witnessed:

> everybody endeavouring to remove their goods, and flinging into the river or bringing them into lighters that lay off; poor people staying in their houses as long as till the very fire touched them, and then running into boats, or clambering from one pair of stairs by the water-side to another. And among other things, the poor pigeons, I perceive were loath to leave their houses, but hovered about the windows and balconies till ... some of them burned their wings, and fell down.

After watching in horror for an hour, Pepys continued up the Thames to Whitehall where, as a familiar figure at the royal court, he was quickly granted an audience with Charles II and his brother James, Duke of York. After describing the terrible scenes in the City, he implored the king to order the demolition of property in the fire's path to create the essential fire breaks. Charles agreed and dispatched Pepys to pass on this instruction to Thomas Bloodworth, the Lord Mayor. He eventually tracked him down at Cannon Street, where Bloodworth looked like 'a man spent'. When Pepys informed him of the king's command, he cried, 'Lord, what can I do? People will not obey me. I have been pulling down houses but the fire overtakes us faster than we can do it.'

As the wind hastened the spread of the blaze, thousands of Londoners risked life and limb to effect their escape. Those making their way down to the river dodged showers of 'fire drops' that rained down from burning buildings igniting everything in their path. Even on the Thames itself, weary oarsmen repeatedly beat out glowing embers that blew onto their boats, threatening to set their cargo alight. As every vessel on the Thames filled with goods rescued from the fire, the riverside evacuation ground to a halt, forcing throngs of terrified people to seek alternative methods of escape. On Sunday evening Samuel Pepys gave sanctuary to his colleague, Tom Hayter, who had been driven from his house on Fish Street Hill. However, just hours later, Pepys' home itself was under threat. He wrote:

> The newes coming every moment of the growth of the fire; so as we were forced to begin to pack up our owne goods; and prepare for their removal; and did by moonshine … carry much of my goods into the garden, and Mr Hater and I did remove my money and iron chests into my cellar, as thinking that the safest place. And got my bags of gold into my office, ready to carry away, and my chief papers of accounts also there, and my tallys into a box by themselves.

A major problem faced by Samuel Pepys and his neighbours was how to carry large goods out of the city. By Sunday night, demand for carts was such that no London carriers were available. The lucky few who could afford to paid for carts to come into the city from outlying villages, but the vast majority of Londoners were forced to haul what they could in barrows, sacks and on their backs.

As thousands of exhausted and traumatised families flooded out of the narrow city gates, hundreds made for the parish of St Bartholomew the Great, hoping that the high wall that surrounded it would protect them from the flames. By Sunday night, the church and its graveyard resembled a refugee camp. Chests, paintings and other valuables were piled up around Rahere's ancient tomb, while outside, rugs and canvas were thrown over the tombstones to create canopies under which exhausted groups of people huddled, waiting anxiously for news of the fire's progress while ash fell like snow from the night sky, covering the churchyard in a sombre grey blanket. The evacuees at St Bartholomew's were more fortunate than those who had abandoned their possessions in churches within the City walls. Over the course of the following day most of these ancient buildings were reduced to ruins, leaving the goods stored within to be plundered by looters.

In the meantime, the political implications of the fire were not lost on Charles II. Fearing that the destruction of London would render the country vulnerable to invasion, he organised a team of firefighters. His brother, the Duke of York, was placed in supreme command and the Privy Council acted as deputies. The councillors were subsequently dispatched to strategic points on the perimeter of the fire where they were given royal assent to stop the advance of the flames by any means necessary. They were assisted by a 'fire team' comprising three local justices of the peace, thirty foot soldiers, the parish constables and 100 militiamen armed with buckets, pumps and fire hooks to pull down buildings. Realising this still might not be sufficient to stop the inferno, Charles also ordered the Lord Lieutenant's neighbouring counties to send soldiers, labourers and provisions without delay.

Despite the valiant efforts of the Duke of York and his teams, Monday, 3 September proved to be the fire's most destructive day. John Evelyn watched the inferno's dreadful progress from Bankside in Southwark and looked on in shock as St Paul's Cathedral – the city's most iconic structure – caught alight, its stonework exploding like grenades and the lead from its roof coursing in a molten stream down Ludgate Hill, heating the pavements so they glowed a fiery, volcanic red. By the time the sun rose on Tuesday, 4 September, the great cathedral had been reduced to a charred ruin, along with every other building that had once stood in its shadow. Evelyn wrote movingly of the traumatised city, 'There was nothing heard, or seen, but crying out and lamentation, [people] running about like distracted creatures ... London was, but is no more!'

Amid these apocalyptic scenes, Samuel Pepys was mightily relieved when a carriage sent by his friend Lady Batten arrived at Seething Lane in the early hours of Tuesday morning. After helping to load the vehicle with his most precious belongings, he rode in his nightgown to Bethnal Green where he handed them over to the safekeeping of his friend, Sir William Rider. He then returned to London where he and his wife packed up their remaining goods and, after burying their wine and, famously, their parmesan cheese in the back garden, they sought shelter behind the impenetrable walls of the Tower of London.

By this stage, the conflagration had moved so far west that it was threatening the precincts of St Bartholomew the Great. As the boiling river of molten lead from St Paul's streamed down Ludgate Hill, the timber buildings that lay in its path combusted and the inferno quickly spread through the narrow courts and alleyways that connected the cathedral to Newgate Street – a five-minute walk away from Cloth Fair. One can only imagine the terror felt by Judith Downing, John Tocock and their neighbours as they waited, powerlessly, desperately hoping that the thick medieval wall that enclosed much of the parish would hold back the fire. The flames were now so close that they could feel their heat and the sky was dark with the thick, choking smoke of burning buildings in nearby streets.

Over at St Bartholomew's Hospital, terror turned to panic as patients too sick to be moved faced the unimaginable horror of being burned in their beds. The parish was staring ruin in the face and news that the king had ordered the use of gunpowder to create larger firebreaks spurred the parishioners into a monumental effort to save their homes and businesses.

Armed with explosives and fire hooks, a gang of local men – quite feasibly including John Tocock, who was an ex-soldier – ran out of Cloth Fair, past the stricken hospital and into Giltspur Street. The scene that confronted them was terrifying: St Sepulchre's Church was lit up against the smoke-filled sky with a fire so intense it melted the bells in its steeple. As the adjoining houses hissed and cracked in the heat, the men began tearing at the brickwork with their tools, sending smouldering timbers and plaster crashing down into the street.

At first their labours made little difference but, undeterred, they systematically made their way back up Giltspur Street towards Smithfield Market, demolishing buildings as they went. As they drew almost parallel with St Bartholomew's Hospital, the fierce wind that had been fanning the flames to such devastating effect suddenly began to drop. Now able to overtake the fire, the men triumphantly halted its progress at Pie Corner, a popular haunt of street food sellers, at the junction of Giltspur Street and Cock Lane.

The sudden easing of the wind allowed the conflagration to be stopped across the entire city. The *London Gazette* jubilantly reported:

> On Wednesday morning we began to hope well, and his Royal Highness never despairing or slackening his personal care wrought so well that day … that a stop was put to [the fire] at the Temple Church, near Holborn Bridge, Pie Corner, Aldersgate, Cripplegate, near the lower end of Coleman Street, at the end of Basinghall Street, and Leadenhall Street, at the Standard in Cornhill, at the church in Fenchurch Street, near Clothworkers Hall in Mincing Lane, at the middle of Mark Lane and at the Tower Dock.

The final vestiges of the fire were successfully extinguished on Thursday, 6 September, and the following day, the people of London tentatively began to take stock of what had been lost. The results were calamitous: 436 acres of the City, from the Tower in the east to the Temple in the west, had been reduced to ashes. The fire had breached the city wall at several points and, had the wind not dropped, it probably would have destroyed the entire metropolis. As it was, fifteen of the twenty-five wards – comprising 13,200 houses in 400 streets – had been razed to the ground. The ruined property was valued at between £5 and £7 million.

Thanks to the heroism of the firefighters in Giltspur Street, the parish of St Bartholomew the Great survived the fire completely intact, but the once familiar streets nearby were rendered unrecognisable to its inhabitants. Soon after the fire was extinguished, John Evelyn surveyed the area around St Bartholomew's and wrote, 'Splendid buildings, arches, entries, all in dust; the fountains dried up and ruined, whilst the very waters remained boiling.'

The destruction had a direct effect on John Tocock and Judith Downing. The Holborn Conduit, which had supplied the parish of St Bartholomew with fresh, clean water since 1498, had been rendered inoperable. A few yards away, Newgate Gaol had suffered severe damage and rumours abounded that the fire had enabled dangerous prisoners to escape. The fugitives were said to still be at large in the area, waiting for the opportunity to murder people in their beds. Close to the gaol, busy Newgate Market, which had supplied everything from vegetables to candles, had been utterly destroyed, while across the road the abattoirs serving Smithfield Market and the traders' livery halls – Butchers Hall and Poulterers Hall – were burnt-out shells.

The districts east of St Bartholomew the Great had fared no better. The fire had been stopped just south of modern Little Britain on the parish boundary, but not before it had destroyed several important buildings: Cooks Hall, the headquarters of the Worshipful Company of Cooks (or 'pastelers') was ruined. A short distance away at Oat Lane, the public notaries' Scriveners Hall was burnt to the ground and the adjacent Church of St Mary Stayning, which had stood on the site since the 1100s, was reduced to a blackened carcass.

Slightly further east, the fire devastated the livery hall of the Barber Chirurgeons who had so valiantly tried to understand the plague just one year before. The only part of the building to remain intact was their anatomy theatre, in which they performed public dissections. The final resting place of the dissected corpses – St Olave's – was also destroyed, but sometime in the 1700s a plaque bearing a skull and crossbones was put up as a memorial. It is still there today, bearing the inscription, 'This was the Parish Church of St Olave, Silver Street. Destroyed in the dreadful fire in the year 1666.'

Another notable building destroyed in the fire would have been very well known to Judith Downing. Haberdashers Hall stood minutes away from Cloth Fair on the corner of modern Wood Street and Gresham Street (in 1666 the area was known as Maiden Lane). As the headquarters of the Worshipful Company of Haberdashers, it would have been frequented by Judith's master tailor husband and interestingly it had also been sequestered as a parliamentary HQ during the Interregnum. Now, this historic and important building lay in ruins.

In addition to the shock of witnessing the destruction of their city and the challenges brought by disruption to water and food supplies, the residents of St Bartholomew's also had to contend with an enormous influx of displaced families. In the immediate aftermath of the fire, Charles II once again proved his worth by taking control of the refugees' welfare. On his command, St Bartholomew's Church became a temporary home for the orphan scholars of Christ's Hospital School. The children remained there for six years, despite the accommodation being 'very inconvenient', and became a familiar site in Cloth Fair, clad in their Bluecoat uniforms.

The king also assisted homeless families by supplying hundreds of tents that were hastily erected on any available open spaces. The largest encampment was at Moor Fields, a vast, tree-lined park outside

Moorgate, twenty minutes' walk away from St Bartholomew's. This site proved to be a great leveller as rich and poor set up camp alongside one another. John Evelyn described the scene in his diary, 'Some under tents, some under miserable huts and hovels, many without a rag, or any necessary utensils, bed or board, who delicateness, riches, and easy accommodations in stately and well-furnished houses, were now reduced to extremist misery and poverty.'

The paucity of food in London caused great hardship at the encampments, especially for the poorest inhabitants. Samuel Pepys visited Moor Fields and, after burning his feet on the overheated pavements, he was shocked to discover that plain loaves of bread were being sold there for double their usual price. He informed the king, who quickly realised that if this wretched state of affairs continued, famine would cause far more deaths than the fire itself – miraculously only a handful of people had perished in the flames. In an attempt to rectify the situation, he warned that severe punishment would be meted out to any trader found to be profiting from the crisis. The parishes bordering London were also commanded to send bread to the camps and a consignment of ship's biscuits from the navy's sea stores was dispatched to Moor Fields. Unfortunately, they proved so inedible that most of them were returned.

To prevent the spread of disease, it was universally agreed that the encampments should be cleared as soon as possible. With this in mind, the king ordered that householders in unaffected areas should open their doors to the fire refugees. Henceforth, the Eagle & Child and the neighbouring houses at St Bartholomew's filled with families, and although this inevitably caused tensions due to overcrowding, the original tenants were placated by the money they received from subletting rooms. The opening up of private houses had a truly amazing effect. Within a week of the fire, almost every displaced family had been accommodated and the Earl of Clarendon noted, 'In four days, in all the fields about town, which had seemed covered with those whose habitations were burned, and with the goods which they had saved, there was scarce a man to be seen.'

Over at the Eagle & Child, drinkers inevitably began to discuss how the disaster had occurred. Although the king had done his utmost to stress that the fire was purely accidental, many of his subjects were convinced it was the work of hostile foreign agents. The most likely suspects were thought to be the Dutch, with whom Britain were at war, or the French. Indeed, one Frenchman had already been killed by an angry mob when the tennis balls he was carrying were mistaken for fireballs. On 10 September, the *London Gazette* reported:

> Divers strangers, Dutch and French were, during the fire, apprehended, upon suspicion that they contributed mischievously to it, who are all imprisoned, and Informations prepared to make a severe inquisition here upon by Lord Chief Justice Keeling, assisted by some of the Lords of the Privy Council.

None of these suspects were remotely culpable, but that did not stop one being summarily executed: Robert Hubert, a young watchmaker from the French town of Rouen, sensationally confessed to Justice Keeling that he had started the fire by throwing a grenade through the ground-floor window of Farriner's bakery while unnamed accomplices had stopped up nearby water supplies to sabotage any efforts to put it out. From the outset, Hubert's story was dubious. He initially claimed to have started the fire in Westminster and seemed unaware of the fact that Farriner's bakery had no windows on the ground floor. Few who heard his story believed it and a jury member admitted that he was 'only accused upon his own confession ... he was a poor distracted wretch, weary of his life, and chose to part with it in this way'. If Hubert had indeed planned suicide by proxy, he succeeded. Under immense public pressure to find a scapegoat for the fire, the court found him guilty, the unfortunate Frenchman was hanged at Tyburn and his body was handed over to the Barber Chirurgeons for dissection.

With a scapegoat conveniently dispatched, Londoners' thoughts turned to the rebuilding of their city. In a bid to raise funds for this monumental task, the king declared 10 October 1666 a national fast day when 'all well disposed Christians in the respective churches and chapels of the Kingdom' were encouraged to donate money for the rebuilding programme.

In the meantime, John Tocock and his neighbours ignored the king's warning not to profit from the fire and started to charge exorbitant fees to their temporary tenants. This allowed many of them to recoup losses sustained during the plague but caused even more hardship for victims of the fire. The Earl of Castlemaine complained that the Mercers' Company had doubled the rent for a house he leased from them at Charing Cross and Samuel Pepys learned that one man was receiving £150 in rent for a property he had previously let for just £40. This inevitably priced poorer families out of the market and they were forced to return to the desolate streets of the burnt city. The Earl of Clarendon recalled in his memoirs, 'With more expedition than can be conceived, [they] set up little sheds of brick and timber upon the ruins of their own houses.' Fearing London could quickly become a shanty town, the Lord Mayor prohibited the 'hasty rebuilding of any Edifices, till such speedy care be taken for the re-edification of the City, as may best secure it from like accidents, and raise it to a greater beauty and comeliness than formerly it had'.

To accomplish the London's 're-edification', money was diverted from the royal purse, customs duties and the hearth tax for seven years.

Once these revenue streams were in place, surveyor John Leake was commissioned to produce a detailed plan of the fire-damaged streets over which a new cityscape could be laid. Design ideas were invited and many architects seized upon this unprecedented opportunity to completely remodel London. Christopher Wren submitted an ambitious plan that dispensed with the narrow medieval streets in favour of wide avenues and elegant circuses. He described his vision thus:

> From the remaining part of Fleet Street … a straight and wide street crosses the valley, passing by the south side of Ludgate, and thence in a direct line through the whole City [terminating] at Tower Hill; but before it descends into the valley where the Great Sewer runs, it opens into a Round Piazza, the centre of eight ways, where at one station we see straight forward quite through the City.

In the event, neither Wren's nor any other plans came to fruition. Altering the intricate network of streets that made up the city proved impossible as the land was owned by literally hundreds of different people, none of whom were willing to sacrifice their valuable property. Thus, London's layout remained largely unchanged, although vast improvements in fire safety were made. All new buildings, whether private or public, had to be built from brick or stone and many incorporated useful cellars into their design as these had been of 'notable benefit' in the fire. The main thoroughfares of Fleet Street, Cheapside and Cornhill were widened to prevent fire from crossing from one side of the road to the other and the Port of London was redesigned to incorporate a 'fair quay' with warehouses set well back from the river. The noisome trades of the brewers, dyers and sugar bakers, who had previously occupied much space along the riverfront, were moved to new sites further east, 'as may be convenient for them without prejudice of the Neighbourhood'. Henceforth, east London became the industrial heart of the city.

Dozens of exquisite new churches and public buildings were also created in the wake of the fire. Judith Downing and John Tocock must have watched with interest as the southern perimeter of their parish became a hive of building activity. A new school for the Bluecoat scholars was created opposite the resurrected market at Newgate, while, close by, the butchers' and poulterers' livery halls were rebuilt. Meanwhile, the charred remains of Newgate Gaol were redeveloped to incorporate a new frontage of 'great magnificence' embellished with statues of London worthies, including Dick Whittington and his cat.

Across the road, work began on a new church for the parish of St Sepulchre. Particular attention was given to its bells, which had an important history: after being acquired from St Bartholomew's Priory at the Dissolution, they had been used to announce imminent executions at Newgate for over a century. However, following their destruction in the fire, this grim practice ceased and instead the sexton informed condemned prisoners of their appointment with the executioner by ringing a hand bell outside their cell. This 'Execution Bell' still resides in the church today. Meanwhile, St Sepulchre's main bells were replaced and went on to feature in the nursery rhyme 'Oranges & Lemons' as the 'bells of Old Bailey'.

The building works near St Bartholomew's were mirrored across London and less than ten years after the fire the city had been almost entirely rebuilt, with the lion's share of the cost borne by ordinary people. Nevertheless, London did not forget the fire. Outside Thomas Farriner's bakery, a memorial plaque was erected and in 1677 the Monument was unveiled close by. This towering column, topped with a flaming copper urn, encased a cantilevered stone staircase leading to a platform from which the new city could be surveyed. Its total height was 202ft – the precise distance between it and the source of the fire in Pudding Lane.

While the Monument marked the area in which the fire started, the places where it was heroically stopped remained largely unrecognised. However, sometime afterwards, a new memorial appeared near St Bartholomew the Great. Known as the 'Golden Boy of Pye Corner' today, this little wooden cherub hovers over the place where, over 350 years ago, local people saved the ancient parish from almost certain destruction. An inscription attributes the curious coincidence that the fire began and ended at places related to food (Pudding Lane and Pie Corner) to the fact that it was 'Occasion'd by the Sin of Gluttony'. Whether this was a popular perception in the 1660s is not known and there is no record of when the Golden Boy first made his appearance. Some sources claim he was unveiled in the 1700s, while others believe him to be the creation of an enterprising landlord of the Fortune of War pub, which stood on the site in the early 1900s. Whatever the true story, today the Golden Boy provides a fascinating reminder of how 41–42 Cloth Fair was very nearly destroyed long before it became the oldest house in London.

6

KNAVERY
IN PERFECTION

*The Riotous Heyday
of Bartholomew Fair*

The mid-1600s were tumultuous times in London. Over a period of just thirty years, the inhabitants of St Bartholomew the Great endured the chaos of civil war, witnessed the execution of a king and lived through the uncertain, paranoid times of the Interregnum. The relief felt by many at the restoration of the monarchy quickly dissolved into fear and panic when their very existence was threatened, first by plague and then by fire.

Amazingly, the people of St Bartholomew's managed to survive and prosper throughout this mayhem but as life gradually returned to normal after the Great Fire, John Tocock, the keeper of the Eagle & Child, decided it was time to hang up his apron and retire. He and his wife Mary subsequently moved away and the alehouse was taken over by John and Ursula Craford.

Originally from the City district of St Stephen, Coleman Street, the Crafords had first moved to the parish of St Bartholomew the Great in around 1635 with their two young children, Nicholas and Martha. A third child, named John, was born in 1638 and during the three decades that followed, the Craford family led a normal, unremarkable life. However, in 1665 the clan was decimated when the plague claimed Nicholas, Martha and three of their offspring in quick succession. All five were buried in the parish churchyard and, now bound to St Bartholomew's by loss, John and Ursula chose to reside there for the rest of their lives. Interestingly, soon after they acquired the lease to the Eagle & Child, the annual event that had given Cloth Fair its name experienced a magnificent renaissance.

The fact that the Cloth Fair had survived the Interregnum was largely due to the heroic efforts of Henry Rich's widow, Isabella. When Oliver Cromwell restricted it to a dull, three-day trade event, Lady Rich risked imprisonment by allowing its exiled showmen to perform in the grounds of her home. Thus, throughout the 1650s, a merry band of actors, singers and acrobats assembled at Kensington every August, where they entertained the public with banned productions while Isabella kept the local authorities at bay by greasing their palms with hush money.

Isabella Rich died in 1655 and, when the monarchy was restored five years later, her son Robert resolved to honour her memory by returning the fair to its former, riotous glory. Unfortunately, he soon met with a major problem. Over the course of the Interregnum, the centre of the cloth trade had moved north to Leeds and consequently many traders who would once have paid good money to hire booths at fair time were no longer interested. In order to survive, the fair had to be reinvented and in this Robert Rich excelled. Over the following two decades, he and his associates transformed the ailing trade show into Bartholomew Fair – the biggest, longest and most notorious public festival in London.

Taking place over two (and sometimes three) weeks from 23 August, the event burst through the parish walls of St Bartholomew the Great and spread across the adjacent marketplace at West Smithfield as far as Duck Lane and Pye Corner in the south and Hosier Lane in the west. Even Bart's Hospital got involved in the action.

Bartholomew Fair resembled an anarchic fusion of today's Glastonbury and Edinburgh Festivals. The open ground at Smithfield Market was packed with temporary stalls and stages, and rooms in adjacent buildings – including some in Cloth Fair – were let as performance spaces. Keen to get in on the action, several local alehouse keepers became event organisers for the duration of Bartholomew Fair. For example, 'The Whelp & Bacon Musick Booth' was run by John Sleep, landlord of the Rose in Turnmill Street and 'The Old Kensington Court' stage was managed by the landlord of the Red Lion in Hosier Lane.

Although the letting of the Eagle & Child's ground floor was controlled by the Rich family, John and Ursula Craford were at liberty to profit from performances in the building's upper rooms during fair time. Even if they chose not to, Bartholomew Fair was impossible for them to ignore. By the 1680s the event was attracting thousands of people from every walk of life. Lords and ladies of the royal court paraded in their finery, merchants consorted with masked mistresses of dubious reputation and apprentices took advantage of the endless supply of beer by drinking themselves into oblivion.

The egalitarian atmosphere of Bartholomew Fair was exemplified by the curious custom of it being declared open for business twice – first by the people and then by the authorities. The root of this unique tradition dated back to the 1650s when the Lord Mayor's attempts to curtail premature trading was vigorously resisted by Isabella Rich and her tenants. To cock a snook at the authorities, a group of traders known as Lady Holland's Mob assembled at the Hand & Shears ale-house on the corner of Cloth Fair in the early hours of 23 August, while the dignitaries who were due to open the event were still sleeping in their beds. After imbibing some Dutch courage, they set off on a wild parade through the fairground, carrying an effigy of their benefactress, ringing bells and banging on doors to proclaim that, in the people's eyes at least, the fair had begun.

By the time the Lord Mayor and aldermen arrived for the event's official opening ceremony, their speeches were drowned out by a rowdy cacophony of drums, penny trumpets and shrieks of laughter. Excited visitors streamed into the fairground, heading for the densely packed assemblage of colourful booths on Smithfield Marketplace. Although the interiors of these little temples of wonderment were obscured behind heavy curtains, brightly painted boards outside advertised the delights in store for anyone who cared to pay the entrance fee.

There was a huge variety of entertainment on offer. The fair's Great Booth in the centre of the marketplace housed the 'greatest performers of men, women and children', who accomplished daring feats on tightropes. Ned Ward, author and publisher of *The London Spy*, visited Bartholomew Fair in 1699 and described the rope acrobats he saw there:

> A couple of plump-buttock lasses, who, to show their affection to the breeches, wore 'em under their petticoats; which, for decency's sake, they first danced in: But to show the spectators how forward a woman, once warmed, is to lay aside her modesty, they doft their petticoats after a gentle breathing, and fell to capering and firking [dancing] as if Old Nick had been in 'em.

The tightrope display was followed by a turn on the 'slack rope', which dangled from the booth's rafters. Ascending it was a lithe young woman who, after reaching the top, 'began to play at swing-swang ... hanging sometimes by a hand, sometimes by a leg, and sometimes by her toes; so that I found, let her do what she would, destiny would by no means suffer the rope to be parted with her'.

Surrounding the Great Booth were a cluster of stages that specialised in the production of bawdy comedies. A perennial favourite was Ben Jonson's play *Bartholomew Fair*, which had first been performed back in 1614. Using the fairground as a backdrop, it lampooned stereotypes of the period such as inept authority figures and overzealous Puritans. Unsurprisingly, it was banned during the Interregnum but enjoyed a renaissance at the Restoration, not least because it ridiculed the very people who sought to suppress it. One of its biggest fans was Charles II, who attended command performances on several occasions.

Puppet plays were also a popular attraction at Bartholomew Fair, especially those featuring Pulcinella, the grotesque character from the Italian *commedia dell'arte* who eventually evolved into that seaside favourite, Mr Punch. Another successful puppet production was the story of 'Patient Griselda', from Chaucer's *Canterbury Tales*. Bartholomew Fair's version featured a poem by Thomas Dekker that read:

> Golden slumbers kiss your eyes,
> Smiles awake you when you rise.
> Sleep, pretty wantons; do not cry,
> And I will sing a lullaby.

Three hundred years later, in an unexpected turn of events, this ancient verse was adapted by Paul McCartney and today it can be heard on the Beatles' *Abbey Road* album.

In a bid to lure audiences, the producers of Bartholomew Fair's plays often added other attractions to the bill and in doing so they sowed the seeds for modern variety theatre. In charge of proceedings was Merry Andrew, a comic master of ceremonies whose task it was to provide a distraction while stage sets were being changed. Presenting himself as the voice of the people (servants were often referred to as 'Andrew') the great and the good were the main butt of his jokes, but frankly anyone was considered fair game – one Merry Andrew was notorious for blowing his nose on the sleeve of audience members. Unfortunately, Merry Andrew's riotous reign as King of Bartholomew Fair drew to an abrupt close in the 1680s when William Phillips, the event's most notorious clown, ridiculed a financial crisis in the City by singeing a pig with Exchequer notes. When word of Phillips' irreverent antics reached the ears of the Lord Mayor, he angrily banned all Merry Andrews from Bartholomew Fair for good.

Although the theatre stages were the most popular attractions at the fair, music booths in Hosier Lane also drew large crowds. Ned Ward visited one of these establishments and, after being shown to his seat by masked attendants, was regaled with a 'fine new Playhouse song' performed in seven-part acapella, a Hautboy (oboe) recital and a lively ballet called 'The Footpad's Robbery'. The titular character of the latter was so convincing that Ward feared, 'had he not committed the same thing in earnest, I am very apt to believe he could never have made such a jest on it'. Thankfully, the unnerving performance was brief and the show closed with a considerably less threatening 'young damsel' who performed a sword dance using weapons borrowed from gentlemen in the audience.

While the performances in the play and music booths changed with the times, one seventeenth-century attraction survived into modern times. During the mid-1600s, innovations in engineering heralded the invention of amazing automata that were displayed across Europe by travelling showmen. During the 1660s, Samuel Pepys was enthralled by these machines at Bartholomew Fair and wrote of seeing a tableau 'with Neptune, Venus, mermaids, and Ayrid on a dolphin, the sea rocking, so well done', and a mechanical face 'wherein the several states of man's age, to 100 years, is shewn'. Despite immense technological advances in the ensuing centuries, automata continue to fascinate. Today, the 300 automated dolls that form Walt Disney's 'It's A Small World' captivate children in theme parks from California to Tokyo, while older examples of the art form change hands for astronomical prices at auction houses across the globe.

Another innovation at Bartholomew Fair that stood the test of time was the concept of fast food. At the appropriately named Pye Corner halfway down Giltspur Street, myriad stalls and shops purveyed hot and satisfying dishes for hungry fairgoers. However, the menu was decidedly limited, comprising spit roast pork and fruit (especially peaches), and the unsanitary conditions in which the food was prepared caused a good deal of wariness. After sampling the fare at Pye Corner, Sir Robert Southwell warned that 'those who eat imprudently do but hasten to the physician or the churchyard', but this did not deter Ned Ward, who vividly described his experience in *The London Spy*: 'Cooks stood dripping at their doors, like their roasted swine's flesh at their fires; with painful industry, each setting forth with an audible voice the choice and excellency of his pig and pork.' However, after examining the delicacies on offer, Ward began to lose his appetite: 'Some pigs hanging upon renters [meat hooks] in the shop windows, as big as large spaniels, half-baked by the sunbeams, and looked as red as the thighs of a country milk-wench in a frosty morning.' Seeking out the most palatable looking fare, Ned and his companion ventured into a booth, 'where we had great expectancy of tolerable meat and cleanly usage', but, to their horror, they were met by a 'swinging fat Fellow, who was appointed over-seer of the Roast to keep the Pigs from blistering ... standing by the spit in his Shirt, rubbing his Ears, Breast, Neck, and Armpits with the same wet cloth which he applied to his pigs, which brought such a qualm over my stomach that I had much ado to keep the stuffing of my guts from tumbling into the dripping pan'.

After wisely opting not to eat at Pye Corner, Ned Ward made his way back into centre of the fairground, passing 'curiosity booths' that lay around the perimeter of Smithfield Marketplace. Precursors to Victorian freak shows, their melancholy exhibits – both animal and human – all suffered from real or fabricated medical conditions designed to horrify and fascinate in equal measure. For the price of a few pennies, fairgoers could wonder at the sight of a goose with four feet and a terribly maltreated horse whose untrimmed hooves resembled ram's horns. The human 'curiosities' were even more disturbing. A booth on the corner of Hosier Lane advertised 'a prodigious monster ... from the great Moguls' Country, being a man with one head and two distinct bodies', while the Black Raven alehouse's prime exhibit was a 9-year-old girl who stood just a foot and a half tall. Seizing on the public's love of the supernatural, her master billed her as 'a fairy child, supposed to be born of Hungarian parents, but changed in the nursing'.

Other curiosity booths unashamedly faked their 'exhibits'. The Victorian writer Henry Morley unearthed a seventeenth-century handbill from Bartholomew Fair advertising a child that had been artificially conjoined to a bear. 'Let anyone who loves children feel the abomination of the fraud that bound a child and a bear ... for the amusement of the public,' he wrote.

Henry Morley's opinion of the curiosity booths was shared by many who actually saw them. In September 1667, Samuel Pepys witnessed:

> a poor fellow, whose legs were tied behind his back, dance upon his hands with his arse above his head, and also dance upon his crutches, without any legs upon the ground to help him, which he did with that pain I was sorry to see it and did pity him.

Although the curiosity booths shamelessly exploited sick and vulnerable people, the authorities did little to suppress them. Neither did they much care about the prostitution that was rife at Bartholomew Fair.

The event's red-light district was found in the narrow confines of Duck Lane (now Little Britain), where impoverished women plied their trade among the tipplers who crowded into the street's shabby alehouses. Unfortunately, Samuel Pepys' sympathies did not extend to these sad and desperate women – after visiting a bawdy house with his friend, Peter Llewellyn, in 1661, he wrote in his diary, 'We had a dirty slut or two come up that were whores, but my heart went against them, so that I took no pleasure but a great deal of trouble in being there and getting from thence for fear of being seen.' Pepys' fear of discovery was shared by so many of Bartholomew Fair's patrons that, by the end of the 1600s, brothel keepers were advertising discreet escape routes. Handbills for Barnes & Finlay's strip-tease show noted that 'for the convenience of the Gentry, there is a back door in Smithfield Rounds'.

Secreted among Duck Lane's brothels were the surgeries of the mountebanks – itinerant charlatans who sold spurious remedies for all manner of ailments. Tom Jones, one of Bartholomew Fair's most successful practitioners, delivered his enthusiastic sales patter from a rickety platform outside his booth:

Gentlemen and Ladies, you that have a mind to preserve your own and your family's health, may here, at the expense of two pence apiece, furnish yourselves with a packet, which contains several things of great use, and wonderful operation in human bodies, against all distempers whatsoever.

His claims did not impress Sir Robert Southwell, who was so appalled at the brazen deceit that he warned his son, 'Tis from [the] more refined that the mountebank obtains audience and credit; and it were a good bargain if such customers had nothing for their money but words, but they are best content to pay for drugs and medicines, which commonly doe them hurt'.

Although the worst excesses of Bartholomew Fair lay just outside the ancient priory walls, temptation was a mere stone's throw away from John and Ursula Craford and their neighbours in Cloth Fair. Even St Bartholomew's cloister (which faced the Eagle & Child on the opposite side of the churchyard) was transformed into a den of iniquity during fair time. Its upper level housed a casino where, according to Ned Ward, 'money was tossed about as if a useless commodity'.

Beneath, the cloister's dark passages served as a knocking shop, known as 'Bedlam for lovers', while the open square at its centre was occupied by numerous lottery booths tempting punters with a dazzling array of goods that could be won for the price of a raffle ticket. The prizes were always high-value items that most fairgoers could not hope to afford under normal circumstances – in 1699, one Bartholomew Cloisters lottery advertised 'A quantity of curious filla-green [filigree] work, set with divers stones, the very best that ever was seen in England, formerly made in a nunnery and presented to a Lady of Quality lately deceased, which cost above £300'. When enough tickets had been sold to cover the purchase price (plus a healthy profit for the organiser), the lucky winner was selected by throwing dice. As is still the case today, there was little restriction on what could be offered as a lottery prize — the Adam Brothers disposed of most of the houses on their riverside Adelphi estate via a lottery — and the success of lotteries was not lost on the authorities. In 1694, the 'Million Adventure' became the first state lottery in England when 10,000 £10 tickets were issued to raise money for the Exchequer.

Although the majority of people who purchased a ticket from the rafflers in St Bartholomew's cloister went home disappointed, there was plenty of other merchandise to be had at the fair. Numerous retail stalls displayed a beguiling selection of overpriced mementoes known as 'fairings' that were snapped up by rich and poor alike. In August 1680, Lady Russel wrote to her husband, 'My sister and Lady Inchiquin are just come from Bartholomew Fair, and stored us all with fairings.'

There were a multitude of fairings on offer. At the fair's book stalls, vendors sold an early type of theatre programme that contained profiles of the event's biggest stars. A popular title was 'A New Fairing for the Merrily Disposed', which chronicled the career of William Phillips, the Merry Andrew who so angered the authorities. More controversial were the political fairing books, which contained comic strips of national events — in 1689, 'The Prince of Orange Landing; The Jesuits Scampering' was a particularly popular title. Other fairing books somewhat ironically railed against the fair's debauchery. In the 1660s, the cover of 'News from Bartholomew Fair, Or the World's Mad' carried an illustration of a rope dancer being tempted with an elaborately embroidered coat (perhaps a lottery prize?) by an eager salesman under which was written, 'What Christian can refrain from bewailing this present age, detesting and abhorring the pride and luxury the execrations, oaths and curses, profaneness and blasphemy, ebriety [drunkenness], fornication and adultery, that infatuated mankind is now immersed in?'

Alongside the book stalls were booths selling a colourful array of cheap pottery mementoes. Fairgoers snapped up gaudy figurines representing the celebrities of the day to take home and place on their mantelpiece. Over the centuries, these crude ornaments became collectable and today they change hands at auction for sums that would make the original vendor's eyes water. However, the most popular fairings during the fair's heyday were the Bartholomew Babies – elegantly dressed dolls (known at the time as 'poppets') which came in fancy packaging, thus making them excellent gifts for children and adults alike. The first mention of Bartholomew Babies appeared in a 1638 play and by the end of the century they had become so famous that the term was used to describe an elaborately dressed woman. For example, a 1695 handbill for a fortune teller promised to tell 'farmers what manner of wife they shall choose; not one tricked up with ribbons and knots like a Bartholomew Baby'.

Although the myriad delights of Bartholomew Fair excited its visitors, they drove the local residents to distraction. By the end of the 1600s, the frenzied atmosphere combined with a dramatic increase in crime at fair time prompted the parishioners of St Bartholomew the Great to petition the Lord Mayor, stating that, although the city had a right to hold the event:

That by length of time and depravity of manners, the lawful use and benefit thereof is of late wholly lost, and the same is become a mere riotous and tumultuous assembly of the worst of people of both sexes; by reason thereof, many great mischiefs and disorders have been committed … Your Petitioners are, by reason of the said disorders, very much prejudiced and hindered in their lawful callings and employments and in their passing to and from their habitations and are in continual fear of mischief to their persons and estates, and in great danger of fire, by the building of many great booths and sheds.

In response, the Corporation of London took drastic action and in 1708, the Common Council's Minute Book recorded:

> The Fair of St Bartholomew, according to the original grant thereof, ought to be holden annually Three Days, and no longer. And that by continuing the said Fair of Fourteen Days, as of late hath been practised, and the erecting and setting up of booths in Smithfield of extraordinary largeness, not occupied by Dealers in Goods, Merchandises, etc., proper for a fair; but chiefly used for Stage Plays, Music, and Tippling … Lewdness and debauchery have apparently increased, Tumults and Disorders frequently arisen and the Traffic of the said fair … greatly interrupted. And this Court being of opinion that no ways will be so effectual for the End aforesaid, as reducing the said Fair to its ancient time of continuance, doth unanimously resolve [that it] shall be kept Three Days only, and no longer, on the Eve of St Bartholomew, that Day, and the Morrow after, being the 23rd, 24th and 25th days of August.

Bartholomew Fair's showmen railed against the council's suppression and over the following decades, it was repeatedly limited to three days only to grow again the following year. However, the reckless abandon with which it had become synonymous in the late 1600s gradually faded, exposing a darker heart of petty crime and cynical exploitation.

As the character of the fair changed, so did the residents of Cloth Fair. John and Ursula Craford moved to smaller parish lodgings in the 1680s and henceforth, the Eagle & Child alehouse closed its doors after nearly seventy years of trading. 41–42 Cloth Fair subsequently took on a very different character when it became the home of a family who were destined to be closely linked to two of eighteenth-century London's most influential characters.

7

BY ORDINANCE
OF GOD

*The Wesley Brothers
at Cloth Fair*

In around 1680 the lease to 41–42 Cloth Fair was taken by a young man named Thomas Witham, who quickly set about transforming the Eagle & Child into a woollen draper's shop selling dress fabrics. By the time his business opened, the annual Cloth Fair had ceased to attract any serious fabric wholesalers and, instead, London's drapers purchased their stock at Blackwell Hall in Basinghall Street, near the Guildhall.

This ancient market had originally operated as an outlet for foreign dealers but in the early 1600s a group of enterprising English cloth merchants established a presence there, setting themselves up as weavers' agents. In this role, they took responsibility for all their employers' London orders, offering credit facilities to the retailers while also guaranteeing that the weavers would be paid for their work. The job was risky, but potentially lucrative as the agents demanded a generous percentage of the order value in return for their factoring services, and by the time that Thomas Witham visited Blackwell Hall to select stock for his newly opened woollen draper's shop, there were around fifty cloth agents vying for his business, offering a vast choice of fabrics. The market's Western Cloth booths sold medium quality, plain woollen stock designed for everyday use, which was the bread and butter of drapers such as Thomas Witham. The Suffolk Cloth agents specialised in woollen material dyed in myriad shades of blue, using a mixture of woad and indigo and the Kersey stalls purveyed a range of hardwearing cloth from Suffolk and Essex weavers, including firms in Witham, the village from whence Thomas's ancestors almost certainly originated.

While Kersey and Western cloth was practical, the most fashionable woollen goods on offer at Blackwell Hall were the 'Norwich Stuffs' – light but durable fabrics that were available in all manner of geometric and floral designs in colours ranging from bright yellow and brick red to pale blue and soft olive green. The best-selling Norwich Stuffs were the 'calimancoes' – thin, worsted cloths available in a variety of weaves. The striped version of this fabric became so fashionable in London that tabby felines were often referred to as 'calimanco cats'.

Norwich Stuffs were eye-catching by design and, consequently, they were popular choices for ladies' gowns and gentlemen's waistcoats. In 1709, *The Tatler* noted that the fashionable dress for a gentleman 'when he is at home, is light broadcloth, with calimanco or red waistcoat and breeches and it is remarkable that their wigs seldom hide the collar of their coats'.

Thomas Witham selected his fabrics wisely from the agents at Blackwell Hall, and his draper's shop at 41–42 Cloth Fair quickly prospered. By the end of 1685, he was sufficiently solvent to secure the hand in marriage of his sweetheart, Hanna Moore. The couple wed in Hanna's parish Church of St Martin Outwich on 31 December, and over the following decade they had six children: Sarah, Elizabeth, Mary, Thomas, Jane and Bethia.

The Withams' seventh child, Lidia, was born at 41–42 Cloth Fair on 23 November 1697 and was baptised in the Church of St Bartholomew the Great. However, when she was just 8 years old she became fatally ill. Her death in October 1709 was recorded in the parish register, but unlike most of the residents of Cloth Fair, Lidia was not laid to rest in the local churchyard. Instead, the family conveyed her coffin all the way to Dagenham for burial. This may have been because the Witham family had ancestral links to the Essex village, but none have been found. Another more intriguing explanation is that sometime between Lidia's birth and death, her parents had become involved with one of the dissenting religious groups that proliferated in London during the era.

As the debauched antics at Bartholomew Fair so keenly displayed, seventeenth-century Londoners were no strangers to drunkenness, prostitution or blasphemy. However, the established Church tended to turn a blind eye to the sins being committed in its midst, even allowing St Bartholomew's cloister to be used as a gambling den. This outraged many residents and resulted in the establishment of the 'Societies for Reformation of Manners', which were committed to reversing the tide of degeneracy that was sweeping through the streets of the capital. The societies welcomed anyone committed to reform and encouraged their members to report anyone caught swearing, drunk or 'profaning the Lord's day', to the authorities.

The Societies for Reformation of Manners were a high-profile example of the many Nonconformist groups in London. In 1699, Josiah Woodward wrote that there were around forty other religious groups in the capital that were not part of the established Church:

These persons meet often to pray, sing psalms and read the Holy Scriptures together, and to reprove, exhort and edify one another by their religious conferences. They moreover carry on at their meetings, designs of charity, of different kinds; such as relieving the wants of poor house-keepers, maintaining their children at school, setting of prisoners at liberty, supporting of lectures and daily prayers in our churches.

Some of these religious groups, notably the Quakers, grew so popular that they opened their own places of worship and purchased land in which their followers could be buried. Whether Thomas and Hanna Witham's membership of such a group might have prompted them to bury their daughter in Dagenham is a moot point. However, their only son, Thomas, and his wife, Elizabeth, were certainly enthusiastic dissenters and, through them, 41–42 Cloth Fair became a regular haunt of Charles and John Wesley, the founders of the most successful Nonconformist movement of all – Methodism.

The Wesley brothers' association with dissenting religious groups began at Christ Church College, Oxford, where both men studied during the late 1720s. During their undergraduate years, they inaugurated a 'Holy Club' where members were encouraged to test their faith by debating the Christian scriptures and exploring their personal religious convictions. John Wesley, the elder of the two brothers, was the driving force behind the club and presided over its weekly meetings in an inclusive and pragmatic fashion. Every member was held to account over their thoughts and activities and they were also encouraged to take their Christian message to the less fortunate inhabitants of Oxford, especially the town's criminal element, in the hope they would see the error of their ways. The club's efficient, practical approach to religion quickly earned them the nickname, the Methodists.

After graduating from Oxford, John and Charles Wesley were both ordained as Anglican ministers and, soon afterwards, they accepted an invitation to become Christian missionaries in the American state of Georgia. However, their adventure was not a happy one. Matters got off to an inauspicious start when the ship on which they were travelling was almost wrecked in a violent storm. As waves threatened to engulf the vessel, the Wesley brothers cowered below deck watching a group of Bohemian Nonconformists, known as Moravians, who were sitting nearby. Despite the perilous situation, the Moravians seemed to possess an inner calm and quietly sat and prayed together while those around them floundered in a state of panic. This left a great impression on John and Charles Wesley, who later concluded that complete faith in God was the key to a blessed life. However, their pursuit of that faith was to prove long and exhausting.

After arriving on the east coast of America, the Wesley brothers made their way to Savannah to begin their missionary work, but the experience did not play out well for either of them. Charles was repeatedly plagued with bouts of ill health and by July 1736 he had become so depressed that he decided to return to England. His brother stayed for another year, but by December 1737 his uncompromising stance on religious matters had caused so much consternation among Savannah's elite that he too decided to return to his homeland.

Once back in England, the Wesleys settled in London, where they became acquainted with Peter Böhler, a German pastor, who was in the throes of setting up a Moravian Society at Fetter Lane. Remembering the Moravians' impressive fortitude during the sea tempest, both brothers joined Böhler's new religious group hoping that, despite their discouraging experiences in America, they too might discover complete faith.

The Moravians' style of worship was intense and seemed rather alarming to many of their neighbours in Fetter Lane. John and Charles Wesley attended one of the group's regular 'love feasts' which, despite its modern connotations, restricted its fervour to the spirit rather than the flesh. John Wesley recorded in his journal:

> About three in the morning, as we were continuing instant in prayer, the power of God came mightily upon us insomuch that many cried out for exceeding joy and many fell to the ground. As soon as we were recovered a little from that awe and amazement at the presence of His Majesty, we broke out with one voice, 'We praise thee, O God, we acknowledge Thee to be the Lord'.

Despite the hysteria they experienced at the Moravian Church, the Wesley brothers remained doubtful of their faith until the spring of 1738. On 21 May, Charles found himself 'converted, I knew not how or when', and three days later, John also experienced a revelation. Charles later wrote, 'Towards ten, my brother was brought in triumph by a troop of our friends, and declared, "I believe". We sang the hymn with great joy and parted with prayer.'

Convinced that they had finally found the true path to salvation, John and Charles Wesley set about establishing their own religious group. Recalling their university nickname, they branded themselves 'Methodists' and began to disseminate a steadfast doctrine urging followers to resolutely place their faith in God above all else. The message resonated with many people who felt the established Church was failing society, but initially the brothers found it hard to establish a congregation. As ordained ministers they were perfectly at liberty to preach, but the severity of their sermons often meant that after one appearance at a church, they were not invited back. One of the few clergymen who fully supported their ideals was the Reverend Richard Bateman, rector of St Bartholomew the Great, who had known John Wesley at Oxford and may even have been a member of the Holy Club.

The Reverend Bateman first invited John Wesley to preach at St Bartholomew's on Christmas Eve 1738 and several more appearances followed. His sermons caused such outrage among some members of the congregation that the churchwardens were urged to write to the Bishop of London asking him to intervene, but the bishop replied, 'What would you have me do? I have no right to hinder him. Mr Wesley is a clergyman, regularly ordained, and under no ecclesiastical censure.'

One congregant who listened intently during John Wesley's controversial sermons was Elizabeth Witham, the wife of Thomas Witham junior. Originally from Waddesdon in Buckinghamshire, she had first arrived at 41–42 Cloth Fair after her marriage in 1715 and over the following years she and Thomas had taken over his father's woollen drapers shop and raised three children: Hannah, Thomas and Sarah.

By the time the Wesley brothers arrived in the parish, Elizabeth Witham's children were at school and the business was thriving. Thus, she had sufficient time and finances to indulge her interest in Methodism and she soon became one of Charles Wesley's closest friends, regularly holding prayer meetings in the upper rooms at 41–42 Cloth Fair. Her two daughters also became ardent followers of the Wesleys – Hannah Witham even travelled with Charles on his preaching tours and was a band-leader at the London meetings. However, her son and husband remained sceptical.

Thomas Witham senior and junior were not the Wesley's only detractors in the parish of St Bartholomew. In January 1742, John Wesley wrote in his journal:

> While I was explaining at Long Lane, 'He that committeth sin is of the devil', his servants were above measure enraged: they not only made all possible noise ... but violently thrust many persons to and fro, struck

others, and broke down part of the house. At length they began throwing large stones at the house, which, forcing their way wherever they came, fell down, together with the tiles, among the people, so that they were in danger of their lives.

The mob was eventually arrested and hauled off to the house of Justice Copeland, who bound them over to keep the peace.

Undeterred, the Wesley brothers continued to hold meetings in the parish of St Bartholomew and Elizabeth Witham and her daughters stoically dodged the brickbats to attend. Elizabeth also refused to give up on converting her husband and son. When Thomas Witham senior grew gravely ill in December 1743, she asked Charles Wesley to come and pray by his bedside. On arriving, Wesley was confronted by a man terrified at the prospect of his imminent demise. He wrote, 'I called upon Mr Witham, given over by his physicians; trembling at the approach of the king of terrors; and catching at every word that might flatter his hopes of life.'

Charles Wesley continued to visit 41–42 Cloth Fair over the following days and gradually Thomas Witham began to pay more attention to his unsolicited guest. Five days before Christmas, probably broken down by fear and exhaustion, he finally declared that he had accepted Jesus into his heart. Wesley triumphantly wrote in his diary:

I prayed in great faith for Mr Witham, the time of whose departure draws nigher and nigher … At half-hour past seven in the evening he broke out, 'Now I am delivered! I have found the thing I sought. I know what the blood of sprinkling means!' He called his family and friends to rejoice with him. Some of his last words were, 'why tarry the wheels of his chariot? I know that my Redeemer liveth. Just at twelve this night my spirit will return to him'.

Thomas Witham was eerily correct about his time of deliverance and he died as the church clock struck midnight.

In the months that followed her husband's death, Elizabeth Witham's relationship with Charles Wesley grew closer than ever before. Whenever time allowed, he would visit her at 41–42 Cloth Fair, occasionally even staying the night. However, his commitment to spreading the Methodist word sometimes tested Elizabeth's hospitality. On 12 June 1745, he agreed to stay with her, but as the night drew on, he became fixated on an idea to go and walk the dark streets. He later wrote, 'In Holborn I found the reason – a poor man, and countryman challenged me, who had been converted by occasional hearing us, but, through neglect of the means, had fallen from his first love, and into poverty. I exhorted him to return to God.' Nevertheless, Elizabeth Witham's kindness did not pass by unnoticed and Charles Wesley even temporarily succeeded in converting her son Thomas to the faith. On 16 January 1746, Charles wrote to her from Bristol, declaring, 'I rejoice in confidence that you and your children will walk in the truth and earnestly pray God whom I serve in the gospel of his Son, that ye may continue faithful unto death.' Enclosed with the note was a hymn he had composed, giving comfort to widows. Wesley urged Elizabeth to share the poem with several other Methodist 'sisters', telling her, 'Great fellowship I have with widows that are widows indeed. The Lord [shall] assure every one of your hearts that thy maker is thy husband. I commend you and yours to him who hath said I will never leave thee nor forsake thee.'

While Elizabeth Witham's friendship with Charles Wesley deepened, her elder daughter, Hannah, who was now in her early twenties, became engaged to Thomas Butts, a committed Methodist and member of the London congregation. The wedding took place at the Church of St Bartholomew the Great on 19 May 1746 with none other than John Wesley conducting the ceremony. Hannah and Thomas Butts subsequently moved to the parish of St Luke's, Finsbury, a short distance from Cloth Fair, where they raised three daughters and a son named Thomas who, in adulthood, became a close friend and patron of the visionary artist and writer, William Blake.

Back at the parish of St Bartholomew the Great, the Reverend Bateman was still being heavily criticised for his continued encouragement of the Wesley brothers' preaching. On 3 April 1747, Charles Wesley acknowledged his support in the face of adversity, writing, 'I met Mr Bateman at our sister Witham's. My heart rejoiced and ached for him. What has he to go through, before he has made full proof of his ministry?!'

On 31 May, John Wesley also witnessed the opposition faced by St Bartholomew's rector when he arrived to preach a charity sermon at the church:

> It was with much difficulty I got in; not only into the church itself, but all the entrance to it, being so thronged with people ready to tread on one another. The great noise made me afraid at first that my labour would be in vain; but that fear was soon over, for all was still as soon as the service began.

Charles Wesley agreed with his brother that St Bartholomew's congregation could be extremely unruly. On 8 July 1747, he assisted the Reverend Bateman with a service 'but was quite weighed down with the behaviour of the communicants, so contrary to the apostolic precept, "let all things be done decently and in order"'.

Throughout this opposition, Elizabeth Witham's devotion to Methodism remained undiminished and it was with great sadness that the Wesley brothers learned of her passing on 29 November 1747. John Wesley supplied a fitting epitaph when he wrote:

About six in the morning, Mrs Witham slept in the Lord. A mother in Israel hast thou also been, and thy works shall praise thee at the gates. Some years ago before Mr Witham died, she seemed to stand on the brink of eternity. But God renewed her strength till she had finished the work which he had given her to do. She was an eminent pattern of boldness for the truth, of simplicity and godly sincerity; of unwearied constancy in attending all the ordinances of God; of zeal for God and for all good works; and of self-denial of every kind. Blessed are the dead that thus lived and died in the Lord! For she rests from her labours, and her works follow her.

Days later, he composed a biographical verse entitled 'On The Death Of Mrs Elizabeth Witham', part of which described her efforts to convert her family at 41–42 Cloth Fair:

Resolved her house should serve the Lord
The parent unto him restored
The children he had given.
Her care and them on God she cast
The wife her husband saved at last
And followed him to heaven.

Elizabeth Witham was buried in the churchyard of St Bartholomew the Great on 1 December 1747. Her passing was considered a time for rejoicing by her great friend Charles Wesley, who wrote, 'Her dying prayers for me I found strengthening my hands, and comforting my hope of shortly following her.'

However, Charles' sentiment was not shared by Elizabeth's son, Thomas, who was now proprietor of the woollen draper's shop at 41–42 Cloth Fair. Although he embraced Methodism after his father's deathbed conversion he soon slipped back into the traditions of the established Church, but Charles Wesley never gave up trying to tempt him back into the fold. Three weeks after Elizabeth's funeral, he wrote to Thomas:

> Blessed be the name of the Lord! He calls you, my dear youth, by taking your mother. Follow her, as she followed Christ … Her words will now be brought to your remembrance and make a deeper impression than at the time she spoke them. You will not now, I am persuaded, think her too strict, too zealous, too much dead to the world, or slight her fears and jealousies over you, as needless and superfluous; but rather follow her example of self-denial, diligence, love of brethren, etc., till you also depart to God and her in paradise. Your parents are both waiting for you there. Her prayers in particular, God has often heard in your behalf and seen her tears: and the son of those tears shall never be lost … I know a little of what she suffered on your account, by the yearnings of my own heart towards you; and my frequent fears of you miscarrying in the great concern, especially when you left the society …[but] I am confident in this, that even your greatest loss (the loss of the best of mothers) shall be your greatest eternal gain.

Despite this plea, Thomas Witham did not return to the bosom of Methodism after his mother's death. However, Charles Wesley had no such problem with his younger sibling Sarah who, like her sister Hannah, was utterly devoted to the movement. By early 1748, Sarah, known to all as Sally, was courting fellow Methodist Thomas Hardwick and on 31 December that same year the couple were married by Charles Wesley at St Anne's Church in Soho. After the wedding, Thomas and Sally Hardwick went to live near the Thames Bridge at Brentford where they regularly socialised with Charles Wesley and his wife Sarah, whom he married in April 1749.

In the meantime, Sally's brother-in-law, Thomas Butts, was put in charge of the Methodist's publishing house, which printed the Wesley brothers' hymns and sacred poems. However, soon after he accepted the post, he found himself at odds with the brothers over the appointment and education of new preachers. In December 1752, he angrily wrote in his diary:

> The want of study ruins half our preachers …[it] makes their discourses so … trite and sapless; the same dull round notwithstanding the many different texts they speak from … I think Mr Wesley is highly to blame, in taking so many raw young fellows from their trades to a work they are utterly unqualified for.

Proposals for reforming the Methodists' recruitment methods along with ideas to increase dwindling funds were discussed, but very little change was effected. At St Bartholomew the Great, the church's open-door policy to the Wesley brothers abruptly ended when the Reverend Bateman suddenly died in 1760. An alternative Methodist place of worship was subsequently opened by James Relly in the old priory chapter house but it is doubtful that it was ever frequented by members of the Witham family. By the end of the 1750s, their names ceased to appear in any Methodist records, which suggests that Thomas Butts' frustrations were shared by his sister-in-law.

Over at 41–42 Cloth Fair, Thomas Witham continued to run the family business until the mid-1770s when he retired to New Cross. He died in 1809 at the ripe old age of 85, having never married. His last wish was to be buried in the churchyard of St Bartholomew the Great 'as near as possible' to his mother. The disappointment he had caused her in life was not great enough to separate them in death.

As for John and Charles Wesley, their Methodist ministry went from strength to strength, despite facing tough financial and organisational challenges. By 1769, John Wesley wrote that around 30,000 people in Great Britain and Ireland were members of Methodist societies. Over the following century this number grew dramatically as Methodism was embraced in North America. Today, the Methodist Church has millions of members across the globe – a fact that would have delighted John Wesley who noted on founding the first society, 'I look on all the world as my parish.'

8

THE NEWGATE SIX

Cloth Fair and the Gordon Riots

In 1779, the Witham family ended their long association with 41–42 Cloth Fair when Thomas Witham surrendered the lease to Charles Brunetti, a woollen draper of Roman Catholic descent. At the time Brunetti set up shop, the energetic persecution of Catholics that had blighted London since the 1500s had subsided into a grudging tolerance. Adherents to the faith were permitted to worship at chapels attached to foreign embassies and secret mass houses lay hidden inside buildings, especially in Moorfields, which had become the centre of London's Catholic community. To this day, St Mary Moorfields remains the only Catholic church in the City.

Nevertheless, London's Catholics were still subject to penal laws that set them apart from their Protestant friends and neighbours. They could not take military or public service roles without first swearing allegiance to the Anglican Church, there was a £100 bounty on the heads of practising priests and no Catholic could inherit or buy land or property. In addition to the restrictions on their civil rights, the lives of London's Catholic families were marred by prejudice and suspicion. In this testing atmosphere, it is unsurprising that when Charles Brunetti wed his sweetheart, Myrtilla Gregory, in the spring of 1779, he did so in the Anglican Church of St Andrew, Holborn.

At first, Charles Brunetti's draper's shop at 41–42 Cloth Fair thrived. Neat bolts of Kersey and Norwich stuffs lined the shelves alongside a seductive selection of luxurious satinettes, delicate floral cassimeres and sumptuous velvets. The shop's proximity to St Bartholomew the Great's churchyard also prompted him to diversify into the grim but lucrative business of supplying cloth for lining coffins. However, his Catholic heritage was a constant source of unease and after just one year of trading, Charles Brunetti's livelihood came under serious threat when simmering anti-Catholic sentiment boiled over into five days of unprecedented violence and terror, known today as the Gordon Riots.

The catalyst for this mayhem was Parliament's sanction of the Papists Act, which mitigated some of the official discrimination faced by British Catholics. Although this ruling was long overdue, it created widespread resentment and fear, especially when rumours began to circulate that it would pave the way to a return to an absolutist monarchy. Up in Scotland, the Papists Act was successfully blocked from passing into law by MP Lord George Gordon who, flushed with success, quickly turned his attention to south of the border.

Although a demonstrably effective and populist campaigner, Gordon was also a loose cannon who was prone to espousing outrageous and incendiary lies to further his cause. For example, while campaigning in London, he told his rapt audience that London's Catholics were planning to open a headquarters at West Smithfield, from whence they would launch a Spanish Inquisition-style crusade against the city's Protestants, burning heretics outside the entrance to Cloth Fair.

Although patently ridiculous, his supporters were only too willing to believe his hateful rhetoric and there is little doubt that Charles Brunetti's business suffered as a result. However, there was worse to come as in the early summer of 1780, Brunetti and his wife witnessed events that put them in mortal danger.

After failing to persuade King George III that the Papists Act should be scrapped, Lord Gordon decided to demonstrate the weight of his support by staging a public protest. A petition was signed by thousands of Londoners and on Friday, 2 June 1780, a 60,000-strong crowd, wearing blue cockades (rosettes) on their hats and brandishing banners declaring 'No Popery!', gathered at St George's Fields in Southwark to march on Parliament. Although the bulk of the protesters were young and excitable apprentices and disgruntled servants, there were also a surprising number of older, wealthier individuals in the crowd – a troubling thought for Charles Brunetti, who relied on the patronage of such people.

After delivering a firebrand speech, Lord Gordon led his supporters to the gates of Parliament, where they viciously attacked lords arriving in their coaches while their leader disappeared inside to deliver the petition. Politician Horace Walpole witnessed the scene and later wrote to his friend, Sir Horace Mann:

> Peers going to their own chamber, and as yet not concerned in the petition, were assaulted – many of their glasses were broken, and many of their persons torn out of carriages. Lord Boston was thrown down and almost trampled to death; and the two secretaries of state, the Master of the Ordnance and Lord Willoughby were stripped of their bags or wigs, and the three first came into the House with all their hair dishevelled. The chariots of Sir George Savile and Charles Turner, two leading advocates of the late toleration … were demolished.

Lord Gordon remained in the House for some time and when he eventually emerged, he did not bear glad tidings. In fear of their lives, the assembled peers had decided to postpone hearing the petition until the following Tuesday when they hoped the fervour might have subsided.

This proved to be the final straw for the crowd and the protest rapidly descended into a full-blown riot. Parliament's constables struggled to defend the gates while missiles torn from the vandalised carriages rained down on their heads. It took the arrival of armed soldiers to disperse the crowd who scattered into nearby streets and alleyways. However, this was not the end of the trouble.

As darkness fell, groups of protesters ran rampage through London, targeting Catholic-owned buildings. The genteel district of St James's was thrown into uproar when a mob raided the house and chapel of Bavarian Count Haslang, ruining his possessions before making off with his valuable supply of tea. Over at Lincolns Inn Fields, the chapel of Sardinian diplomat Monsieur Cordon was stormed by rioters who, according to Horace Walpole:

> stole two silver lamps, demolished everything else, threw benches into the street, set them on fire, carried the brands into the chapel and set fire to that, and when the engines came, would suffer them to play till the Guards arrived, and saved [Monsieur Cordon's] house and probably all that part of town.

Walpole's cousin Thomas lived near the property and it fell upon him to rescue Madame Cordon, who was confined to her bed by illness. 'She could scarce stand with terror and weakness,' Horace wrote.

The mob's modus operandi at Lincolns Inn Fields became the template for further violence. Over the following nights they raided over twenty more houses, taking the contents into the street before setting it alight. Thus, the owner was deprived of the opportunity to claim on his insurance policy because the fire had not occurred in his house.

As news of the raids spread through London, the little Catholic community at Moorfields braced itself. Fearing for their safety, local resident James Malo appealed to the Lord Mayor, Brackley Kennett, to provide them with armed guards, but his request was denied and the following night, Moorfields came under attack. With hatred pumping in their veins, rioters stormed the district, destroying the local mass house and sacking the homes of James Malo, George Beckett, Mary Crook and Father Richard Dillon, the local priest.

By the morning of Tuesday, 6 June, the streets of Moorfields were littered with the wreckage of the previous night. Ruined furniture and possessions lay smouldering in the streets amid the shattered glass and splintered timbers of broken windows and doors while the dazed community surveyed the devastation in horror and disbelief. As Catholics sorrowfully cleared away what remained of their homes, a crowd reconvened outside the gates of Parliament, eager to hear the outcome of Lord Gordon's petition hearing. However, the peers knew only too well what violence had occurred the previous night and opted to adjourn the sitting for two more days in the hope that order could be restored in the meantime.

The news of this second postponement was not well received by the mob, who refused to disperse, despite now being surrounded by armed militia. Eventually, Mr Justice Hyde emerged from the House and proceeded to read the Riot Act, warning the crowd that if they did not leave peacefully and immediately, the soldiers encircling them would open fire. No sooner had the judge uttered his valediction than a young watch-wheel cutter named James Jackson thrust a red and black flag into the air and cried, 'Hyde's house ahoy!' With that, the mob turned and ran towards Justice Hyde's home on nearby St Martin's Street and proceeded to set it on fire.

As Hyde's house burned, smaller groups of rioters broke away in pursuit of new quarry. Some targeted the Bloomsbury home of Stephen Maberly, a coach currier, who had bravely held agitators at Lincolns Inn Fields until they could be taken into custody. Others made for the home of the magistrate who subsequently committed them – Sir John Fielding – while a third party headed for Queen Street, Westminster, to destroy the home of Robert Kilby Cox, a wealthy and prominent Catholic.

These disparate gangs spread fear and panic through the city's streets. Ignatius Sancho, an African actor and composer who lived in Westminster, wrote that evening to his friend, John Spink, giving a minute-by-minute account of what was happening outside his front door:

> There is at this present moment at least a hundred thousand poor, miserable, ragged rabble, from twelve to sixty years of age, with blue cockades in their hats – besides half as many women and children – all parading the streets, the bridge, the park, ready for any and every mischief. Gracious God! What's the matter now? ... I was obliged to leave off – the shouts of the mob – horrid clashing of swords – and the clatter of a multitude in swiftest motion drew me to the door ... This is liberty! Genuine British liberty!

As Ignatius Sancho anxiously paced the floor of his Westminster house, Charles Brunetti and his neighbours at St Bartholomew's received the dreadful news that a huge mob led by standard bearer James Jackson were fast approaching, threatening to torch nearby Newgate Gaol and release all the prisoners. All along Cloth Fair, shopkeepers fastened their shutters and hustled their children into the upper rooms of the buildings, hoping that the parish's high walls would protect them. Nevertheless, curiosity got the better of many residents and, as the mob grew closer, a large company of spectators gathered at the end of Giltspur Street, where they had a direct view of Newgate.

As they waited for the onslaught, the onlookers wondered at how the rioters could hope to breech the seemingly impenetrable fortress. Rebuilt only two years previously, Newgate's cells were hidden away behind high stone walls and its entrance gate was protected by a sturdy iron portcullis. The only weak spots in its defences were the turnkeys' offices and the house of gaoler Richard Akerman, which had doors and windows fronting the street.

This concern was shared by Mr Akerman himself, not least because he had received an ominous warning earlier that day. At about five o'clock that afternoon, a well-dressed Quaker gentleman calling himself Richard Hyde had called at his house, demanding money from one of the gaol's inmates. When Akerman brusquely informed him that he was far too overworked to act as a debt collector, Hyde warned him, 'You say you have been busy; you shall be more busy presently.' Already anxious that the gaol could be targeted by the rioters, Richard Akerman mounted his horse and went in search of the Lord Mayor, hoping that he would order the deployment of the local militia. He was still absent when the onlookers in Giltspur Street caught sight of an enormous mob approaching. Its size of the mob was astonishing and was later described by Charles Dickens as comprising:

all the rioters who had been conspicuous in any of their former proceedings; all those whom they recommended as daring hands and fit for
work; all those whose companions had been taken in the riots; and a great
number of people who were relatives or friends of felons in the jail.

The heaving mass of people quickly filled the streets around Newgate until it was impossible to distinguish rioters from bystanders. John Steel, who was out running an errand for his father, recalled, 'Before I could get to Fleet Lane, I saw a parcel of people come with great sticks in their hands and great spokes of wheels.' Meanwhile, John Lucy, who had followed the mob from Westminster, noticed James Jackson's red and black flag waving above the crowd as it surged towards the gaol's gated entrance.

Inside the prison, turnkey Charles Burkitt was watching through a hatch in the portcullis when a man he knew as John Glover strode up to the gate, poked the barrel of a gun through the grille and screamed, 'Damn you! Open the gate and let the prisoners out or we will burn Newgate down!' When Burkitt refused, the mob set upon the gate with sledgehammers and pickaxes, but the strong ironwork refused to yield.

Inside a house opposite the gaol, a young woman named Rose Jennings watched in disbelief as the crowd gave up trying to break down the gate and instead turned their attention to Richard Akerman's house. Crow bars and chisels were thrust into the doorframe in a bid to prise it open while the spokes of coach wheels were thrown like javelins at the building. Errand boy John Steel watched as 'two men with a long [scaffolding] pole on their shoulders jammed it up against Mr Akerman's furthest window and broke the shutters and forced out the window frame'.

With the window now open, a man dressed in a sailor's jacket nimbly climbed through, quickly followed by a chimney sweep's lad. They lost no time in opening the other windows and, once the front door finally gave way, the mob streamed into the house, grabbing furniture, rugs, paintings and ornaments and tossing them out into the street. They then piled Richard Akerman's possessions up against the entrance gate and set them alight while the turnkeys and servants inside the gaol desperately tried to extinguish the flames by pouring water through the portcullis. When this had little effect, turnkey William Sheppard grabbed a broom and frantically tried to push the now raging bonfire away from the gate. The portcullis still refused to budge, so the rioters decided to gain entry to the gaol through Richard Akerman's house. Furniture outside the front door was torched and the fire quickly gained a hold on the property, burning the adjacent offices and prison chapel.

As the blaze spread, Rose Jennings realised she was in mortal danger. She and her servant, Ann Wood, raced out of their home beseeching the mob to help them stop the fire advancing across the street. To their utter amazement, the rioters obliged and moved the burning furniture a safe distance away. Nevertheless, Rose and Ann were relieved to witness the arrival of several fire engines, but the mob refused to let them near the flames until the prisoners had been released. Mr Wooldridge, a local alderman, offered to act as a mediator but by the time he began negotiating with the rioters, it was too late. The roof of Richard Akerman's house collapsed and, in the chaos that ensued, someone managed to get hold of the gaol keys.

John Pitt, one of Newgate's servants, was in a passageway when he suddenly came face to face with a rioter dressed in a red marine's jacket, who exclaimed, 'Damn my eyes, here is one of Akerman's bloody thieves. Let us do him first and we will do Akerman afterwards.' Terrified beyond belief, Pitt turned and fled, screaming for his colleagues to do the same as the mob stormed into the gaol. One by one, the cell doors were unlocked and felons ran jubilant into the street, dazed by their incredible luck. Meanwhile, the rioters celebrated their success by daubing the prison wall with a proclamation that the prisoners had been freed by 'His Majesty, King Mob'.

News of the prison break sent shockwaves through London. Horace Walpole opined, 'We have now, superabundantly, to fear robbery [as] 300 desperate villains were released from Newgate.' As word spread, rumours abounded that the escaped felons had immediately returned to their lives of crime, notably robbing Lady Albemarle on her friend's doorstep and shooting at Baron d'Aguilar's coach.

Although the Newgate prisoners were almost certainly innocent of these crimes, they still had to be rounded up without delay and the Lord Mayor hurriedly dispatched constables into the dark streets surrounding Newgate to rearrest them. This proved to be a fiendishly difficult task. Many of the felons had vanished into a labyrinthine network of rookeries that lay north of Smithfield Market and finding convicts in this den of thieves was like looking for a needle in a haystack.

As had been the case at Moorfields, the authorities' response to the riot at Newgate was woefully slow and dangerously chaotic. By the time armed soldiers arrived on the scene, the gaol was aflame and all its inmates had fled but that did not deter them from firing indiscriminately into the crowd, killing and seriously injuring rioters and innocent bystanders alike. The wounded were carried off to St Bartholomew's Hospital where the medical staff were quickly overwhelmed. The damage they saw was horrific. Surgeon Percival Pott treated a young woman named Hannah Stewart who had been hit by a musket ball at close range and described the injury in his journal:

The ball appeared to have entered externally a little above the head of the ulna and radius [the bones of the forearm] passing in an oblique direction through the joint, which it shattered and produced a very troublesome haemorrhage, which was soon stopped with a needle and ligature. From the appearance of the fracture … it was thought advisable to amputate, but the woman not giving her consent, the wound was put up in a common poultice, opiates were given to appease pain. She also received a shot through both breasts, possibly by the same ball.

Mr Pott saw Hannah again on 12 July and noted that, although the wound was less inflamed, her pulse was quick and she had a high fever. It is not known if she survived.

The military's brutal assault succeeded in dispersing most of the mob but some remained to continue with their mischief. Samuel Johnson ventured to Newgate at around midnight, where he found the gaol:

> in ruins, with the fire yet glowing. As I went by, the protestants were plundering the Sessions House at the Old Bailey. There were not I believe a hundred, but they did their work at leisure, in full security, without Sentinels, without trepidation, as Men lawfully employed, in full day. Such is the Cowardice of a commercial place.

Given the lack of resistance at Newgate, it is unsurprising that the rioters continued their destructive spree the following night. Already exhausted from the violence that had occurred in their midst, Charles Brunetti and his neighbours once again braced themselves when a baying mob assembled outside the premises of Thomas Langdale, a Catholic distiller, who owned a vast complex of buildings just west of Smithfield Market. Although the rioters claimed they wanted to destroy a mass house secreted inside, in truth they had their sights set on the gallons of gin that Mr Langdale stored in his cellars. Unfortunately, the mob failed to realise that alcohol is flammable. As they torched the upper floors of the distillery, the fire quickly spread underground, causing hundreds of vats to explode and a river of gin ran into the street where it was greedily scooped up by the assembled crowd in any receptacle that came to hand. Some even fell to their knees to lap the cobble stones and they got so drunk that Horace Walpole was moved to note, 'As yet there are more persons killed by drinking than by ball or bayonet.'

As Langdale's Distillery lit up the sky, the drunken mob made off for the nearby Fleet Prison, which was quickly sacked and all the prisoners released. From there they raged across the Thames to join forces with another group that had assembled at St George's Fields. The rampage that followed was stunning in its ferocity: Southwark became an inferno as rioters set fire to the King's Bench Prison, the New Gaol, the Surrey House of Correction and Marshalsea Debtors Prison. Close by, in Bermondsey, a Catholic chapel and several houses were pulled down and the southern end of Blackfriars Bridge was attacked, the raiders making off with the toll money.

Horace Walpole called the night of 7 June 'Black Wednesday' and wrote to his friend, Lady Anne Ossory, in the small hours of the morning:

It is impossible to go to bed ... I cannot be better employed than in proving how much I think of your Ladyship at the most horrible moment I ever saw ... I was at Gloucester House between nine and ten. The servants announced a great fire; the Duchess, her daughters and I went to the top of the house, and beheld, not only one but two vast fires, which we took for the King's Bench and Lambeth but the latter was the New Prison ... Colonel Heywood came in and acquainted his R[oyal] H[ighness] that nine houses in Great Queen Street had been gutted and the furniture burnt; and he had seen a great Catholic distillers at Holbourn Bridge broken open and all the casks staved – and since the house has been set on fire.

The devastation on Black Wednesday was not only restricted to prisons and large businesses. Ordinary working people were also targeted by the mob. After leaving Gloucester House, Horace Walpole visited Lady Hertford, where he witnessed the aftermath of a savage attack on one of her servants:

> Lady Hertford's cook came in, white as paper. He is a German Catholic; he said his house had been attacked, his furniture burnt, that he had saved one child and left another with his wife whom he could not get out; and that not above ten or twelve persons had assaulted his house.

It transpired that the cook's home had been targeted because he had refused to burn a torch in support of the rioters outside.

As dawn broke on 8 June, the authorities finally took control of the situation; 10,000 soldiers were mobilised and that night they managed to keep a lid on the violence, leaving London to take stock of the riots. The losses were sobering: over 200 militiamen had been killed while battling with the mob, another seventy-five had died in hospital and 173 others had sustained life-changing injuries; £65,000 worth of private property across the capital had been destroyed and the damage to public buildings (mainly the prisons) was assessed at just over £30,000 – an enormous sum of money at the time.

While London's loss adjusters burned the midnight oil, the authorities' attentions turned to the punishment of the mob's ringleaders. This was a daunting task, as over 450 arrests had been made. Of these, 160 people were sent for trial, the hearings being held at the Old Bailey, the Surrey Assizes and before a special commission in Southwark.

The rioters arrested at Newgate had been thrown into the Poultry Compter, a notorious prison near the Bank of England, where they languished awaiting trial while a succession of witnesses was brought in to identify them. As he had not been present during the siege of Newgate, Richard Akerman sent his turnkey Charles Burkitt and servants William Sheppard and John Pitt to the compter, where they were joined by Rose Jennings and Ann Wood, who had watched the riot from the house opposite. After touring the cells, they positively identified prisoners Benjamin Bowsey, Francis Monckford and John Glover as being ringleaders. Richard Akerman personally sought out Richard Hyde (the man who had threatened him shortly before the riot), and a fifth man named Thomas Haycock was indicted through his own admission of guilt. The sixth man to stand accused was flag bearer James Jackson, who had led the mob through the streets to Newgate, watched by numerous witnesses who clearly remembered him by his distinctive red and black flag.

The trials of the Newgate Six were held at the Old Bailey Sessions House on 28 June 1780. Much to Richard Akerman's disgust, Richard Hyde was quickly discharged through lack of evidence but the other five were not so fortunate. First in the dock was Benjamin Bowsey, a freed slave who had first arrived in London from America six years previously. Both Rose Jennings and Ann Wood swore that they had seen him knocking on Mr Akerman's door shortly before the house was attacked and Constable Percival Phillips proved Bowsey had been inside the property by producing a pocket book and monogrammed silk stockings belonging to the gaoler, which he had found when searching the prisoner's lodgings. Although his guilt seemed clear, Benjamin Bowsey put up a strong defence. Dr Sandiman, a friend of his employer, provided a glowing character reference and Robert Gates, a footman from Golden Square, told the court that in the six years he had known him, Bowsey had always been an honest, law-abiding man. The accused's paramour, Grace Roberts, even provided a dubious alibi by swearing he was at her home in Berners Street from

9 p.m. on the night of the riot. Unfortunately, the jury did not believe her story and Benjamin Bowsey was sentenced to death.

The trial of Thomas Haycock was trickier as he had only found himself in court through his own drunken confession. John Lambert, a tallow chandler of Jermyn Street, testified that at about 10 p.m. on 6 June he was drinking in the Bell at St James's Market when Haycock burst through the door and sat down beside him exclaiming, 'Damn my blood, I have done the business!' When Lambert asked him to explain himself, Haycock told him that after helping to sack Justice Hyde's house in Westminster, he had marched with the mob to Newgate, collecting weapons from coachmakers' and braziers' shops on the way. On arriving outside the gaol, he claimed that he demanded the keys and when they were refused, he had helped carry a bureau loaded with linen to the prison gate where he set it alight.

After John Lambert's testimony had been heard, Thomas Haycock's uncle was summoned to the witness box. He told the court, 'When I first heard the strange story Mr Lambert has told it alarmed me; but knowing that when [Haycock] is in liquor he would tell strange stories, I did not believe he was guilty of one little bit of it.' In a grave error of judgement, Haycock's uncle decided to hand him into the authorities in the hope that 'from his connections they might, through him, get at some persons more guilty than he was'. Unfortunately, this backfired when the court found his nephew guilty of rioting and the judge passed a sentence of death.

Next in the dock was Francis Monckford, whom Ann Wood and John Pitt had both apparently seen brandishing the keys to the gaol. He vociferously protested that they were mistaken as he had merely been an innocent bystander. 'Curiosity led me, as many others, to Newgate,' he told the jury. His friend Samuel Sheen corroborated his story, testifying that they had watched the riot together between the hours of 9 and 10 p.m., after which they had walked back to his lodgings in Covent Garden. Francis Monckford's most compelling defence came from Alderman Wooldridge, who had arrived at the gaol during the peak of the violence. He told the court, 'I recognise the prisoner, with others, taking hold of persons who had sticks in their hands, and making way for me to come up to the prison.' However, despite the alderman's praise, Monckford was found guilty and sentenced to death.

Following Francis Monckford into the court was John Glover. Like Benjamin Bowsey, Glover was black and his colour undoubtedly counted against him. Several witnesses had seen a black man in the mob attacking Richard Akerman's house and, as Bowsey and Glover were the only two black men in custody, they automatically assumed that one of them must be the culprit. John Glover's plea of innocence was not helped by the fact that Charles Burkitt swore he was the man who had pushed a gun in his face at the main gate to the gaol. However, not every witness was convinced of his guilt. Mr Savile, a watchmaker, had watched the riot from outside his shop on Snow Hill and while he agreed that a black man had attacked the gaol, he was certain that man was not John Glover.

Mr Savile's testimony offered a faint glimmer of hope that Glover's life might be spared, but this was soon dashed when his employer, Mr Phillips, took the witness stand. He explained that on the afternoon of 6 June, he had asked the accused to fetch a gun from his chambers at Lincolns Inn and he had not returned. This fitted perfectly with Charles Burkitt's testimony and, although Glover protested that he could not go back to his employer because he had been arrested, he too was found guilty and sentenced to hang.

The final prisoner to ascend the steps to the dock was James Jackson, the riot's flag-bearing ringleader. Understandably terrified for his life, he gave an impassioned defence, explaining that on the day of the riot he had been sick with a fever that rendered him 'totally unable to carry a flag, or even walk with the mob'. Rather, he had worked until six o'clock, 'when I went to my brother's lodging in Compton Street and ate a bit of bread and cheese', before returning to his place of employment. Later that night, he had ventured close to Newgate when he went to buy a file from a shop on Cloth Fair. He then met his brother for a drink in a nearby alehouse and, while there, they learned that Newgate was on fire and went to look. Several family members backed up James Jackson's story and witnesses Henry Jennings and James Clark both agreed that he was not the man they saw brandishing the infamous red and black flag. Nevertheless, he was found guilty and thrown into the cells to await his death.

The trials of the Newgate rioters were controversial even by eighteenth-century standards. Not one of the five convicted men had been proved guilty beyond reasonable doubt – for every witness who swore they had seen them outside the gaol, there was another who was equally certain they had not. This confusion, coupled with the fact that some so-called witnesses may have been attracted by a handsome reward, ultimately provided four of the five men with a lifeline. To their unimaginable relief, Benjamin Bowsey, Francis Monckford, Thomas Haycock and John Glover had their death sentences revoked. Their fate is unknown, but they may well have been on board one of the first transportation ships bound for Australia in 1788.

James Jackson was not so fortunate. On 20 July 1780, a scaffold was erected outside the ruins of Richard Akerman's house in preparation for his execution and at two o'clock, a cart carrying the bound and chained prisoner slowly made its way through an enormous throng of spectators and drew up beside the gallows. The crowd then watched in silence as a local minister climbed into the back of the cart to read James Jackson his last rites. After sitting silently in prayer for several minutes, the preacher climbed down and Jackson's distraught family bade him farewell as the rope was placed around his neck. Then, with a sharp crack of the horseman's whip, the cart lurched away and James Jackson was dispatched into the hereafter as the crowd openly wept.

Although James Jackson paid the ultimate price for his role in the riots, their architect, Lord George Gordon, managed to escape with his life. Although he was charged with high treason and thrown into the Tower, he was eventually acquitted on the grounds that he had no treasonable intent when he began his protest against the Papists Act. Nevertheless, his actions – and their effects – left London's Catholics in no doubt that they were despised by many.

Over at 41–42 Cloth Fair, the period following the Gordon Riots was not kind to Charles Brunetti. Soon after Newgate was destroyed, he moved out, and the property was subsequently converted into two separate dwellings for the first time in its history. The reason behind this major change is unknown but it is highly plausible that it was precipitated by damage caused during the violence.

After moving out of 41–42 Cloth Fair, Charles Brunetti and his wife took a shop overlooking Smithfield Market. Soon afterwards they had a son, but the child was sickly and he died in December 1783. Three years later, the business failed and the stock was sold off in a bid to repay the creditors. An advertisement for the auction placed in *The Times* on 20 November 1786 bears the last mention of Charles Brunetti. His eventual fate is unknown.

9

PROPERTY IS POWER

Cloth Fair at the Heart of Radical Politics

In the summer of 1789, news reached Cloth Fair that riots in Paris had forced the government to declare a state of emergency while King Louis XVI and the royal family barricaded themselves in the Palace of Versailles. At first, it seemed that the uprising would play out in a similar way to the London riots nine years before. However, it soon became apparent that the French partisans would stop at nothing short of revolution.

Like their London counterparts, the Parisian rioters targeted prisons but their operations were better organised and more murderous in intent. On 14 July, a mob assembled outside the gates of the Bastille fortress, their sights set on a large cache of arms and gunpowder that was stored inside. Alarmed by the size of the mob, Governor Bernard-René de Launay invited two of the ringleaders inside to negotiate but, when they failed to re-emerge, the mob took matters into their own hands and stormed the fortress. What happened next was shockingly brutal.

The governor and the commandant were captured and marched to the Place de Gréve, where they were executed. Their heads were then thrust onto tent poles and carried victoriously through the streets of the city.

The storming of the Bastille became the flashpoint of the bloody French Revolution and initially the savage event was celebrated across the Channel in Britain. William Wordsworth declared, 'Bliss was it in that dawn to be alive', and many of his contemporaries dared to hope that the French Revolution might become the catalyst for radical changes in Britain's government. In 1791 the writer Thomas Paine, who had witnessed the Paris riots first-hand, published *Rights of Man*, which argued that ordinary workers could justifiably overthrow a government that failed to protect their human rights. The following year, Mary Wollstonecraft's *A Vindication of the Rights of Woman* pressed for gender equality, particularly in education. In London, a shoemaker named Thomas Hardy founded the London Corresponding Society 'as a means of informing the people of the violence that has been committed on their rights, and of uniting them in an endeavour to recover those rights'. His movement was welcomed and embraced by the people of St Bartholomew the Great, not least because the district had been in steady decline since the troubles of 1780.

After Charles Brunetti left the property, 41–42 Cloth Fair stood empty for almost two years while it was converted it into two separate dwellings. The buildings were then taken on short leases by a succession of tenants. A gentleman named John Ball rented No. 41 between 1782 and 1784, while No. 42 was taken by James Conning and his wife, Betty. However, both households quickly moved on and by 1785, No. 41 had been let to George Redmile. Soon afterwards, No. 42 became the home of Richard Loving, a haberdasher and hosier, who filled the shop on the ground floor with a colourful array of ribbons, buttons, hats and stockings.

During Messrs Redmile and Loving's tenure at 41 and 42 Cloth Fair, the street gained notoriety as a dilapidated den of iniquity. Most of its properties had been standing for over 150 years and were showing signs of decay, but with limited funds at his disposal William Edwardes, Baron Kensington (the freeholder) simply could not keep up with the necessary maintenance. As the fine but ancient houses of Cloth Fair descended into ruinous slums, the street became a resort of London's criminal underworld.

In March 1786, City Marshal Mr Clark and his men arrested two men and a woman at one of the decaying properties after receiving intelligence that they had set up a coining operation in the basement. This highly illegal practice involved shaving the edges off legal tender, melting it down and stamping it into new coins, which were then illicitly put into general circulation. On entering the property, Clark caught the forgers red-handed, seated at a table strewn with coining tools and 'a great number of counterfeited halfpence'. They were hastily arrested and taken to Wood Street Compter to await trial.

The coiners were not the only criminals at Cloth Fair. In July 1787, *The Times* reported:

> Complaint having been made by many of the inhabitants of Cloth Fair and Long Lane, that they are afraid to stir out of their houses after the dusk of the evenings, on account of the number of thieves harboured in that neighbourhood; the City patrol have orders to apprehend all suspected persons, to find the houses where they are harboured and to see that the constables and watchmen do their duty.

This order clearly had little effect as, in April the following year, Mr Samuels' second-hand clothes shop at Cloth Fair was targeted by thieves. One Tuesday afternoon, a burly man named John Gilbertson entered the premises and began rummaging through the piles of old clothes, secreting any items that took his fancy beneath his coat. However, he caught the eagle eye of Mrs Samuels and, as he tried to make his getaway, she rushed out from behind her counter and, 'with the spirit of a David when he attacked Goliath', managed to keep hold of him until help arrived. At his subsequent trial, John Gilbertson was found guilty of theft and sentenced to death.

As the tradespeople of Cloth Fair contended with shoplifters, the state of the street's houses reached crisis point. When three properties suddenly collapsed on 20 April 1790, killing an elderly lady named Mrs Heathcock, the City's Court of Aldermen ordered that all other 'ruinous buildings in the neighbourhood of Cloth Fair' should be demolished without delay. However, the decision was too little, too late.

Well aware of what was happening in France and empowered by Hardy's Corresponding Society, many residents of the district became mutinous. Fearing that riots could break out at any moment, the Parish Vestry of St Bartholomew the Great called a meeting of the 'proprietors of lands and tenements, housekeepers and inhabitants' on 21 December 1792. Chaired by Rector Owen Perrot Edwardes (a cousin of the freeholder, Lord Kensington), the following resolution was carried:

Impressed as we are with a deep and sure sense of the many great and invaluable blessings which we enjoy under the present mild and happy form of government, and holding as we do with the utmost indignation and abhorrence the many daring attempts which have lately been made in several wicked and seditious publications to convert the fair scene of plenty, liberty and order into tumult, anarchy and confusion ... we avow that we bear true allegiance to his majesty King George III and will with

the becoming spirit of Englishmen support the constitution of King, Lords
and Commons as by Law established.

Similar declarations were made across the capital and thus London
became a divided city. On one side were successful merchants and
property owners whose best interests were served by preserving the
status quo. On the other were their poorly paid employees and impoverished residents, such as the family of the unfortunate Mrs Heathcock,
who were compelled to live in dangerous, squalid conditions but, with
no political voice, were powerless to do anything about it.

Perhaps concerned about the deteriorating conditions at Cloth Fair,
George Redmile left No. 41 in 1794 and the property was briefly taken
over by Margaret Nisbett before standing empty for around three
years. It was then let to Edward Sexton, a piece broker, who sold cheap
remnants of cloth. Sexton's profession reflected the falling fortunes of
Cloth Fair. By the end of the 1700s, the affluent merchants that once
populated its shops had been replaced by struggling tailors and impe-
cunious customers searching for bargains. This had already resulted in a
dramatic decrease in profits, but even greater problems lay ahead when
hostilities broke out between Britain and France.

In August 1792, the French revolutionaries stripped King Louis XVI
of all his political power, put him on trial for high treason and established the French First Republic. The monarch's subsequent execution
on 21 January 1793 effectively united the rest of Europe against
the Revolution and the First Coalition was formed to oppose the
Republic. By the end of the year, France was at war with Britain,
Prussia, the Netherlands, Spain, the Holy Roman Empire, Portugal,
Naples and Tuscany.

Despite mass opposition, the French revolutionary armies were for-
midably effective, mainly because mass conscription meant that they

had far more men at their disposal than their adversaries. After they successfully invaded Belgium, the Rhineland and the Spanish coastal district of San Sebastian in 1794, the allied coalition disintegrated, leaving Britain as the French Republic's primary antagonist. Hoping to end hostilities by destabilising the French government, British agents attempted to stage a coup at Paris but their plans were scuppered by the military garrison led by Napoleon Bonaparte.

The war with France had two major effects on the parishioners of St Bartholomew the Great. Firstly, their burgeoning campaign for social reform was viciously suppressed. Using national security as an excuse, the government bribed the press to portray the likes of Mary Wollstonecraft as dangerous revolutionaries and threw Thomas Hardy in gaol. Secondly, with their detractors silenced, they embarked on a rapid expansion of the military to meet the might of the French forces. As recruitment officers prowled the inns of Cloth Fair, William Blake (an old friend of the Witham family) wrote of their attempts to scare young men into signing up: 'Little blasts of fear, that the hireling blows into my ear.'

Nevertheless, the call to arms failed. At the time, the genesis of the Industrial Revolution was providing year-round (albeit badly paid) work across London and thus young men were loath to leave steady and relatively safe employment at a manufactory or dockyard for an uncertain fate as a soldier. Consequently, only the most desperate volunteered to fight, prompting the Duke of Wellington to callously describe them as 'the scum of the earth', although he did go on to add, 'it is really wonderful that we should have made them to the fine fellows they are'.

Army life proved the making of some rag-tag recruits, but nevertheless enlistment remained at a low ebb and by the end of 1794 the British military was in crisis. Over 18,000 men had been killed on active service against the French and another 40,000 had been discharged through injury or disease. As a result, Parliament hastily passed an Act that compelled the country's parishes to raise more men. Henceforth, the churchwardens of St Bartholomew the Great were twice called upon to find recruits. In 1795, a total of five men from the parishes of St Bartholomew's and St Martin Ludgate were ordered to present themselves at the naval recruitment office and, in January 1797, the Lord Mayor decreed that every London parish should supply fresh blood for the army. In response, the vestries of St Bartholomew the Great, St Bartholomew the Less and St Sepulchre held a meeting at which it was agreed that a total of thirteen men should be found. Three of these unlucky individuals had to come from the parish of St Bartholomew the Great, which undoubtedly caused a great deal of anxiety for Richard Loving at 42 Cloth Fair, whose sons William and Joseph were the optimum age for enlistment.

The names of St Bartholomew the Great's army recruits have long since been lost so it is impossible to know whether they included William or Joseph Loving. However, although the thought of sacrificing his own sons to the military was abhorrent, Richard almost certainly supported his country's forces. During the wars with France, patriotism was rampant and an enormous civilian network sprang up in London to help the British troops by supplying food, equipment and clothing. The drapers' and haberdashers' shops along Cloth Fair thronged with residents purchasing the fabric and thread to make soldiers' uniforms and young women congregated around billboards advertising military fundraising balls, excitedly imagining being whisked around the dancefloor by a dashing lieutenant.

The voluntary contributions made by Londoners during the French Wars was a positive result of the fierce nationalism that prevailed throughout the hostilities. However, this ethos also bred suspicion.

As French forces rampaged through Europe, thousands of refugees fled to London where they received a frosty welcome. In May 1797, city marshals were called to a house in Cloth Fair after locals reported that its eleven émigré inhabitants were 'suspicious characters'. Quite what the refugees had been doing to cause alarm was not revealed but, erring on the side of caution, a magistrate imprisoned them indefinitely in the New Compter.

Initially, the war had little effect on London's commerce but as the French navy made gains, Britain struggled to keep her lucrative European trading routes open and by the end of the 1700s the country was experiencing serious food shortages. As a result, the price of basic foodstuffs such as bread rocketed, driving cash-strapped families across the land into starvation. Even the relatively prosperous parishes of London were affected. In December 1799, Richard Loving and his neighbours were informed by the vestry committee that they were compelled to advance the parish's poor school in Enfield an extra 3s 6d every week to cover the vastly increased cost of provisions. To make up the deficit, the vestry ordered that the annual feast days of St Thomas and Ascension, along with the regular churchwarden's banquets, would be discontinued until further notice. Unfortunately, these measures proved insufficient and a year later the bread allowance for the parish's poorest families was reduced from 15oz a day to just 12oz.

As the people of St Bartholomew the Great struggled to cope with the escalating cost of living, repairs to the parish's already dilapidated properties ground to a halt. Although 41 and 42 Cloth Fair had benefited from refurbishment when they were divided into two dwellings, the environs were squalid. In 1802, antiquarian James Peller Malcolm visited the parish in search of its rich heritage and was shocked at what he found there. The historic priory cloisters were:

a scene of hateful degradation. Horses tied for the purpose of shoeing to the outside and horses standing in the inside of the beautiful eastern cloister. Why was not this precious remnant converted into a passage to the church; and thus, in some degree, preserved to its original sacred use?

Malcolm was horrified to discover that the rest of the ruined priory complex had degenerated into a chaotic and filthy labyrinth of tumbledown dwellings and shops, carelessly erected in spaces so tiny that opposing roofs almost touched one another, robbing the 'dark and dreary lanes' of even the tiniest sliver of daylight. This ramshackle rookery eventually opened out onto Cloth Fair, which although more expansive, was also in an advanced state of decay. From the windows of Nos 41 and 42, the churchyard that had been created from the remains of the original nave was barely visible through the crooked terrace of dwellings that now guarded its perimeter. 'Not one stone of the North side of the nave is left. A wretched door leads to the church in the North transept; and the first step within it shows a pile mutilated by no easy labour.'

By the time James Peller Malcolm surveyed Cloth Fair, Richard Loving had moved out of No. 42 and, in around 1802, the property was let to newlyweds Edmund and Sarah Wain. Soon after their arrival, a sign appeared outside the shop on the ground floor advertising the services of 'Edmund Wain, Woollen Draper & Man's Mercer', while inside the shelves took on a familiar appearance as they filled with woollen cloth.

At the time the Wains signed the lease to 42 Cloth Fair, the hostilities with France had officially ceased, causing a wave of optimism to sweep through London. However, the peace was not destined to last long. In May 1803, the Corsican General Napoleon Bonaparte (shortly to become Emperor of France) escaped from exile on the island of

Elba and amassed an enormous army at Calais in preparation for an invasion of England.

Although the British media made light of Napoleon's intentions, the public fully believed the invasion was imminent and finally answered the government's call to arms. Over the following months, thousands of young men, including parishioners of St Bartholomew the Great, signed up to defend their country not realising that in doing so, they were creating widespread destitution. As army policy restricted wages for married men to just six per company, any additional soldiers with families had to make do with single men's pay, leaving their wives and children at the mercy of the local parish overseers.

William Wordsworth publicised this terrible state of affairs in *The Excursion*, which described a woman driven to insanity after her husband enlisted. The Napoleonic Wars' effect on British women was also explored by Anna Laetitia Barbauld in her poem 'Eighteen Hundred & Eleven', which questioned the morality of the conflict, warning that Britain 'hast shared the guilt [so] must share the woe'.

It transpired that woe was in plentiful supply as Napoleon played a game of bluff with the British military. In preparation for the supposedly imminent French invasion, a fortune was invested in sea defences, notably the construction a line of Martello Towers along the east coast of England, many of which can still be seen today. However, the fortifications proved to be a monumental waste of money when (after the Battle of Trafalgar in 1805) Napoleon shelved his plan to invade Britain and instead concentrated on crippling her overseas trade by issuing the Berlin Decree, which forbade the import of British goods into European countries allied with (or dependent on) France.

As the British economy spiralled into recession, the government were faced with yet another huge cost. Thus far, Napoleon's military success was owed, at least in part, to the fact that he had access to a far greater number of soldiers – the population of France was double that of Britain. In order to make up the deficit, the government felt compelled to pay massive subsidies to its allies, Austria and Russia. Ultimately this cost was borne by ordinary members of the public as taxes were levied on an unprecedented number of everyday items, from candles and shoes to windows and ironwork.

Around this time, Edmund and Sarah Wain left 42 Cloth Fair for alternative premises in Smithfield and the house was let to another woollen draper named Thomas Hester. As he struggled to make a decent living, Hester would certainly have resented the high levels of taxation he had to contend with. However, he was a tenant of the property – not the owner – and as such was deemed unworthy of a voice in Parliament. His situation was shared by most of the population. Of the United Kingdom's 18 million inhabitants, only about 500,000 owned property, which gave them the right to vote. Consequently, the country's laws were designed to solely benefit its wealthiest citizens while penalising everyone beneath them. Hardworking traders like Thomas Hester had no choice but to make the best of this unjust state of affairs for the time being, unaware that an opportunity for change would soon manifest itself.

The catastrophically expensive war with France raged on until 1815 when the Battle of Waterloo finally put an end to the Napoleonic threat. In the aftermath, the full cost of the conflict was revealed. Of approximately 1 million British men and boys who fought for their country, a third were killed and thousands more were so diseased or horrifically maimed that they were unable to work. Nevertheless, the men that returned home unscathed were initially optimistic about the future, surmising that the lifting of wartime trade restrictions would provide plentiful work and reduce the price of food. However, they had forgotten how treacherously mercenary Parliament could be when protecting its own interests.

Shortly after the Battle of Waterloo the government passed the Corn Law Act, which prohibited imports of grain whenever the price in the British market fell below 80s a quarter. While this indisputably boosted the depleted bank balances of the country's landowners, it also ensured that food prices remained astronomically high, leaving their tenants close to starvation. As working families struggled to survive, their thoughts returned to the pre-war campaign for radical political reform and slowly a new movement emerged that was destined to directly involve Thomas Hester and his neighbours at Cloth Fair.

The leader of the new campaign was Henry Hunt, a Wiltshire farmer who, despite being a landowner himself, was a passionate advocate of workers' rights. Born in Upavon, Wiltshire in 1773, Hunt had become interested in radical politics during the Napoleonic Wars. During those testing times, it became painfully apparent that his tenants and workers were at the mercy of Parliament and could not make any meaningful protest as they had no voice. Realising that universal suffrage would result in a fairer, better country, he planned a public rally at Spa Fields, Clerkenwell on 15 November 1816.

The object of Henry Hunt's meeting was to drum up support for a petition calling for electoral reform that would close the enormous divide between the haves and the have nots. Advertisements were pasted up across London and, to his delight, they attracted a crowd so huge that Hunt was forced to abandon his original plan of speaking from the roof of a Hackney coach and instead repaired to the nearby Merlin's Cave pub, where he addressed his rapt audience from a large window in the front parlour. His speech resonated with the crowd and after collecting thousands more signatures on his petition, he declared that he would henceforth deliver it to none other than the prince regent.

Unfortunately, Henry Hunt's belief that he could place his petition under the nose of the prince was hopelessly naïve. Despite his best efforts to arrange a meeting, he was repeatedly obstructed by courtiers who abruptly informed him that 'neither any King of the House of Brunswick, nor the Prince Regent since he attained sovereign power, ever gave any answer to petitions except if they came from the Corporation of London or Oxford or Cambridge University'.

The palace's refusal to accept the petition strengthened the resolve of Henry Hunt and his supporters, but not everyone agreed with the object of their campaign. Soon after the Spa Fields rally, an anonymous gentleman calling himself 'Anti-Stasis' wrote to *The Times* claiming that Hunt 'loved his bottle' to such a degree that on Tuesday morning, while in a gin-induced stupor, he had fallen into a burst sewer and drowned in its filth. If that were not libellous enough, the mystery correspondent went on to claim that the corpse had prevented the sewage from destroying neighbouring houses, 'Thus by a felicity which will, in some degree, console the friends of Mr Hunt for his loss, his death was useful, if his life were otherwise'. The cruel author ended by noting:

A person who happens to bear a strong resemblance to the deceased orator has had the audacity to proclaim that he is the very man who now lies dead at the back of the tap-room in a house close to the Seven Dials. I can only say that I shall think it my duty to expose the unparalleled impudence of this novel sort of imposter; and I trust that the public will hiss him whenever he dares to show his face before them.

There is absolutely no doubt that the authorities (supported by the press) sought to silence Henry Hunt and his campaigners. On the morning of a second meeting at Spa Fields on 2 December, the

Middlesex Magistrates placed notices in the London papers recommending that:

> All Housekeepers and Masters of Families will prevent, as far as possible, their Servants, Apprentices, and Children, from resorting to Spa Fields from idle curiosity, or joining any disorderly proceeding which may result from such Meeting, as it is the determination of the Magistrates to put the Laws strictly in force in the event of any Riot, Tumult, or Disturbance of the Public Peace taking place.

Despite this, around 10,000 people attended the rally. According to a reporter from *The Times*, the Merlin's Cave pub (from which Henry Hunt was again to make his speech) 'was surrounded by 12 o'clock with a great assemblage that crowned the height of the door, and various detached parties spread over the fields, ready to fall into the general current directed to the quarter where Mr Hunt was expected to make his appearance'.

Henry Hunt eventually arrived at Spa Fields at one o'clock. He 'drove up to the Merlin's Cave in a handsome tandem, muffled in a great coat, apparently enjoying the applause that he excited, and disposed to show that he was both a man of substance and a skilful jockey'. He entered the front room of the alehouse, already almost filled with tobacco-smoking and gin-drinking patriots, and to 'tumultuous applause' took to his makeshift stage at the window.

Henry Hunt informed the crowd that 'disappointing though it was that the Prince Regent was unlikely to get involved', they should neither despair nor resort to violence as he intended to deliver the petition to Parliament when it sat on 28 January 1817. However, as these words left his mouth, news reached the Merlin's Cave that an angry mob had already broken away from the rally and was marauding through London, their sights set on storming the Royal Exchange, the Bank of England and the Tower.

By the time Henry Hunt learned of the mob's intent, they had reached Snow Hill, a bustling shopping street five minutes' walk away from Cloth Fair. After bursting into Mr Beckwith's gun shop and plundering firearms they rampaged along Cheapside, firing the weapons as they went, unaware that the authorities were about to stop them in their tracks. On arriving at the Royal Exchange, the excited mob found its gates were open and streamed into the courtyard, not realising that they had fallen into a trap. The gates were slammed shut, locking them inside.

Once the captive mob had been arrested, it quickly became apparent that the riot's ringleaders were a shoemaker named John Hooper and sailor, John Cashman. The latter admitted he had been driven to insurrection through despair. When asked by a city marshal why he had incited a riot, Cashman told him, 'I have no work, no home and no family. I do not care if I die.'

Hooper and Cashman were tried at the Old Bailey Assizes on 15 January 1817. In the chaos that had followed their entrapment at the Royal Exchange, it was impossible to prove they had led the riot and so John Hooper was acquitted. Nevertheless, the authorities were determined that someone should be brought to justice so they found John Cashman guilty of stealing guns from Mr Beckwith's shop. He was sentenced to death.

Saddened but undeterred by the violence that had blighted the second meeting at Spa Fields, Henry Hunt and his campaigners took their campaign across England. Hunt's talent for public speaking earned him the nickname 'the Orator', and over the following two years his impassioned speeches brought radical politics to the masses. As support for Hunt's campaign grew, more meetings were organised in London and in the summer of 1819, Thomas Hester and his neighbours noticed a series of placards had been erected in and around Cloth Fair, advertising a public rally led by Henry Hunt at Smithfield on 21 July. Soon afterwards, the Corporation of London responded to the placards by delivering a note to all householders in Cloth Fair. It read:

Sir:– Being directed by the Rt. Hon. Lord Mayor to return a sufficient number of proper persons to be sworn as special constables for this Ward, for the purpose of being in readiness, in case their services are required, to assist the Civil Power in the preservation of the peace, in consequence of the meeting advertised to be holden within this City on Wednesday 21 July; you are requested to signify your consent to the Ward Beadle, or to the Common Council, and afterwards to appear before me, at the Vestry Room, St Sepulchre's Church, on Friday next, at 11 o'clock in the forenoon precisely, for the purpose of being sworn. Signed, Robert Waithman, alderman.

It is not known if Thomas Hester answered the call to become a special constable. On one hand, he would have been eager to protect his business from theft and damage during the rally. However, as a man with no right to vote, it is likely that he would have been a supporter of Henry Hunt's reforms.

Whatever his personal views, a war of words soon broke out between the pro-government press and the campaign's supporters. On 16 July, the popular *Morning Post* newspaper reported that the owners of 'large manufactories, warehouses, etc.' in the areas surrounding Smithfield had 'particularly cautioned their workmen from attending the mischievous meeting'. In response, the rally's organisers erected more placards declaring:

While deprived of your just right to elect your own agents, and servants, for the purpose of protecting your lives, liberties and properties from lawless exaction and unmitigated oppression, are you not in fact reduced to the object conditions of Slaves? The right of self-defence is the first and most sacred law of Nature, and resistance to Oppression the constitutional privilege of every Briton!

As the date of the meeting drew closer, the public and the authorities alike became increasingly apprehensive. According to the *Globe* newspaper, no less than 6,000 Londoners were sworn in as special constables and the city's militia were poised in readiness for trouble.

The day before the rally, it was announced that armed soldiers would be posted in St Sepulchre's Church, the Compter, St Bartholomew's Hospital and Christ's Hospital with express orders to quell any riot, and the *Morning Post* published a satirical and downright offensive notice designed to belittle the protesters. Purportedly written by 'The Patriots of Smithfield Market', the piece likened Henry Hunt and his supporters to livestock, it declared that the meeting would 'commence as on cattle days, by the leaders taking the stalls nearest to the Hospital; with this difference, that they are not to be tied up as usual – This is a day of unrestrained freedom'. The repugnant prose continued:

As the show of Black Cattle is expected to be numerous, they will be under the care of Constables, to prevent them from goring each other. No horse market, but a plentiful supply of Asses instead. Mules in abundance ... Females not suffered to debate without proper credentials ... The Majesty of the People to be respected the whole day, but nothing else. The Orators to abuse freely and liberally all ranks above themselves, and to point out the propriety, and even the necessity of changing places.

In the event, no amount of media ridicule could stop widespread support for the meeting. By midday on 21 July, 'immense crowds' rumoured to number 50,000 had gathered in Smithfield Marketplace. The *Morning Advertiser* reported, 'The space from the houses to the pathway from St John Street presented one solid mass of people. Besides this, all the houses, the windows, the roofs, balconies, etc., were filled with persons of both sexes.'

The assembled audience watched intently as members of the campaign committee, 'holding in their hands white wands', were carried through the marketplace in an open wagon, which drew to a halt outside the entrance to Cloth Fair. Soon afterwards, Henry Hunt arrived on horseback and, accompanied by loud cheers, made his way through the crowd to the wagon, which served as makeshift hustings. As he climbed into the cart, his audience unfurled colourful banners bearing the slogans 'universal suffrage' and 'Peace & Goodwill' – a message of intent that was designed to allay the fears of the authorities. Two signs calling for 'Order! Order!' were then held up and Henry Hunt began his address, acknowledging that 'in the memory of man and in the records of history there never was assembled a meeting so numerous as the present'. He then introduced the men sitting beside him as 'Dr Watson, Messrs Thistlewood and Preston and the Reverend Joseph Harrison, a dissenting minister from Stockport, who stand here with simple wands in their hands, to shew their enemies that they are not afraid, on an occasion like this, to do their duty'. This drew huge cheers from the crowd, who were eager to show their detractors they were not the recalcitrant beasts portrayed by the media. Henry Hunt then proceeded to lay out the aims of the campaign:

1. Every Briton had a right to freedom and equality.
2. All rights being equal, no one should be taxed without being able to participate in universal rights.

3. That this universal right should be exercised in the choice of representatives.

4. That the present MPs in the House of Commons had not been fairly chosen by the votes of the largest proportion of the members of the state.

5. That a petition should be presented to the Prince Regent, requesting that the returning officers of every county in Britain be issued with writs causing the representatives to be chosen by the whole population, not the aristocracy alone.

Interestingly, his final resolution concerned Britain's old adversary Napoleon, who had been exiled on the island of St Helena since surrendering in July 1815: 'This meeting unequivocally disclaims any share in the acts of the Boroughmongers, in placing Napoleon a prisoner to perish upon a desert island, shut from human society, and from his only son'.

As the crowd shrieked and whooped with enthusiasm, Hunt took hold of a Union Jack, proclaiming, 'This is the Union Flag. The enemies of the people would call it the tri-coloured flag of the French Revolution, but it is nothing more nor less than what these words literally mean.'

Much to the authorities' disappointment, the Smithfield rally had thus far progressed peacefully, which was not part of their agenda. Consequently, they decided to up the ante. As Henry Hunt triumphantly waved his Union Flag, a band of constables were dispatched to the hustings where they dramatically arrested the Reverend Harrison for using seditious language during a speech in Stockport. However, their hope that the arrest would spark a riot was dashed when the clergyman calmly climbed down from the wagon and surrendered himself to the constables while Henry Hunt told the crowd:

There are those about who would be glad of anything like a breach of the peace. If I should be taken hold of, bail is ready and I will subpoena the whole assembly, which I believe to consist of 50,000, to my trial. If you were examined at a rate of 30 a day, the trial must last three years!

The rest of the rally passed off without further incident. This gladdened the heart of Henry Hunt, who was committed to peaceful protest despite the 'knaves of the London press wanting riot and bloodshed' to increase their circulation figures.

However, in the summer of 1819, the newspapers' wish was finally granted. Earlier that year, Henry Hunt received an invitation from Manchester's Patriotic Union Society to speak at a rally at St Peter's Field, a large open ground at the town. The society's secretary, Joseph Johnson, wrote, 'Nothing but ruin and starvation stare one in the face, the state of this district is truly dreadful, and I believe nothing but the greatest exertions can prevent an insurrection. Oh, that you in London were prepared for it.' Unfortunately, Johnson's letter was intercepted by government agents who interpreted his passionate prose to mean that riots were being planned on the day of the rally. In response, they instructed the local militia to be on high alert.

After two postponements, the Patriotic Union Society's rally finally took place on 16 August, attracting an immense crowd numbering around 60,000. Convinced that there would be trouble, Manchester's magistrates installed themselves in a house overlooking St Peter's Field and instructed the local constables to form a corridor through the spectators to give them a clear view of the wagons serving as makeshift hustings. The suspicious crowd assumed that the constables were preparing the stage for a theatrical arrest of Henry Hunt and decided to foil the plan by pushing the wagons further into the field where they could be protected by a human shield. In doing so, they unknowingly sealed their fate.

+ The Tomb Of Rahere
In The Priory Church Of St Bartholomew Smithfield

Monument to Rahere at St Bartholomew the Great. Illustration by J. W. Archer, 1851. (London Metropolitan Archives)

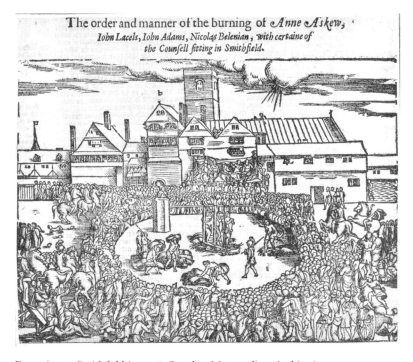

The order and manner of the burning of *Anne Askew,*
Iohn Lacels, Iohn Adams, Nicolas Belenian, with certaine of
the Counsell sitting in Smithfield.

Execution at Smithfield in 1546. (London Metropolitan Archives)

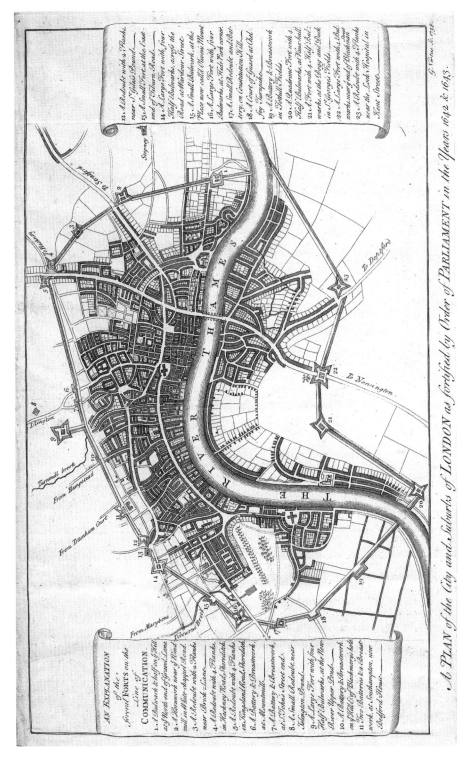

Plan of London showing fortifications erected during the Civil War, *c.* 1642. (London Metropolitan Archives)

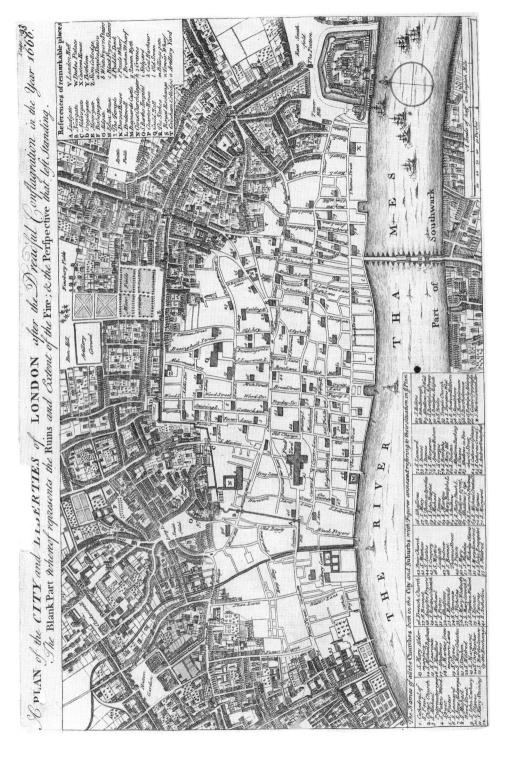

Plan of London after the Great Fire of 1666, by W. Hollar. (London Metropolitan Archives)

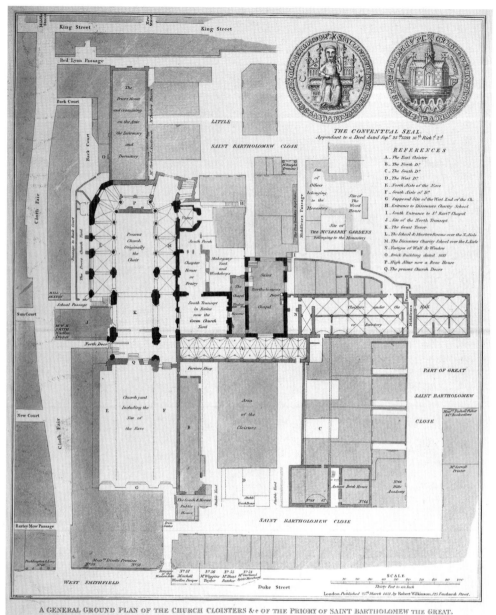

Plan showing the demolished sections of the priory, 1821. (London Metropolitan Archives)

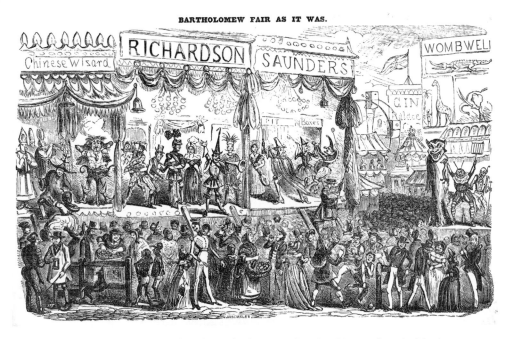

Bartholomew Fair As It Was, by John Walmsley, 1840. (London Metropolitan Archives)

Newgate Gaol during the Gordon Riots, 1780. (London Metropolitan Archives)

The church of St Bartholomew the Great in 1784. (London Metropolitan Archives)

Charles Wesley, by John Russell, *c.* 1775.

Old Smithfield Market, 1855. (London Metropolitan Archives)

Cloth Fair looking east, 1890. No. 41–42 is in the foreground. (London Metropolitan Archives)

Washing hanging in the churchyard of St Bartholomew the Great, 1877. (London Metropolitan Archives)

Cloth Fair looking west, showing Markham's workshop at 41–42, 1920. (London Metropolitan Archives)

Fine old houses opposite 41–42 Cloth Fair in 1908, shortly before they were demolished. (London Metropolitan Archives)

Bomb damage at Smithfield Market, 1940. (London Metropolitan Archives)

Cloth Fair in 2013.

Henry Hunt arrived at the rally at 1 p.m., accompanied by Joseph Johnson and several other speakers. As the crowd drew closer to the hustings, the crush of bodies became so dense that the spectators' hats touched together. Observing the scene from their distant house, the magistrates doubted that the constables could control such a massive crowd and, in a state of panic, they sent word to the local militia to present themselves at St Peter's Field without delay.

The Manchester & Salford Yeomanry were the first to receive the call and lost no time in mounting their horses and racing to the meeting, swords drawn. On their arrival at the magistrates' house, they were ordered to disperse the crowd around the hustings so the speakers could be removed. The cavalrymen galloped down the corridor formed by the constables, not realising that it was a dead end. As they plunged into the dense crowd, the horses reared in terror, their hooves pounding down on anyone standing near them while their riders desperately tried to reach the hustings by hacking at the crowd with sabres. Amid this mayhem, the constables managed to reach the hustings. They arrested Henry Hunt and his fellow speakers, while all around them people fell to the ground, battered and cut by the cavalry's onslaught.

The magistrates watched as the devastating events unfolded and, when reinforcements from the 15th Hussars and Cheshire Yeomanry arrived, they ordered them to disperse the meeting without delay. The soldiers quickly formed lines along the eastern and southern ends of St Peter's Field and, with a deafening roar, they charged into the crowd. The terrified spectators tried to flee but the main exit was blocked by a foot regiment armed with bayonets. As the scene turned into carnage, one of the Hussars screamed to his colleagues, 'For shame Gentlemen, forbear! The people cannot get away!'

Eventually the bayonet-wielding foot regiment stood down and the crowd surged out of St Peter's Field leaving a scene of absolute devastation. At least eleven people lay dead and hundreds more were so badly injured that veterans of the Napoleonic Wars who witnessed the carnage likened it to the Battle of Waterloo. Thus, the tragic blood-bath became known as the Peterloo Massacre, although many of those present felt the name was woefully inappropriate. Shortly before he died from wounds inflicted at St Peter's Field, army pensioner John Lees told a friend, 'At Waterloo there was man to man but there it was downright murder.'

The shock of the Peterloo Massacre reverberated through Britain and the government responded by suppressing all talk of political reform. Journalists sympathetic to the cause were silenced and Henry Hunt was charged with sedition and sentenced to thirty months' imprisonment at Ilchester Gaol. In contrast, the soldiers who had indiscriminately hacked away at unarmed civilians were acquitted of all blame when the courts inexplicably ruled that their actions had been justified in dispersing the crowd.

Although their leader was now languishing in gaol, Henry Hunt's supporters refused to give in. Immediately after the slaughter at St Peter's Field, Thomas Hester and his neighbours were invited to attend another meeting in Smithfield on 25 August. As soon as word reached the Lord Mayor that another meeting had been arranged, he ordered that on no account should it turn into a second Peterloo. On the morning of the meeting, at least 700 constables were dispatched to Smithfield. Once there, they were organised into groups and sent to six 'stations' around the perimeter of the marketplace, namely the Church of St Bartholomew the Great, the Hope Fire Station, the Bear & Ragged Staff alehouse and the yards of the Rose, Green Dragon and George inns. In addition, the East India Company supplied 500 men as security guards and men from the fire insurance companies were also on hand. They 'manifested the utmost zeal' by confiscating the coats and badges of colleagues who had refused to attend the previous meeting at Smithfield. As the time of the rally drew nearer, the gates of Cloth Fair and the surrounding streets were locked shut while the marketplace filled with people carrying banners, the most prominent of which bore the words 'Liberty or Death'.

Although the rally took a very similar form to the previous event in July, the events in Manchester and the absence of Henry Hunt conspired to make it a tense and anxious affair. Hunt's compatriot Dr Watson delivered the main address in which he implored the crowd to keep their temper, but as he was speaking, a horseflesh vendor's cart came clattering down Long Lane, causing those standing nearby to scatter in panic. The meeting pressed on but, without their great orator, the speakers struggled to galvanise the audience and gradually the crowd began to drift away. Puffed up with a mixture of relief and pride, the Lord Mayor made a point of walking to Newgate Gaol to observe the crowd's dispersal. He was greeted by a chorus of boos and hisses but most of the campaigners reluctantly accepted that, for the time being, the authorities had won.

Henry Hunt never achieved the parliamentary reforms he so passionately sought but the concept of universal suffrage was not forgotten. A quarter of a century after the Peterloo Massacre, two social reformers named Richard Cobden and John Bright finally achieved Hunt's goal by playing Parliament at its own game. Knowing that Britons were only eligible to vote if they owned property, they formed the National Freehold Land Society (later the Abbey National), membership of which was open to any working man willing to pay a subscription. The society's funds were used to buy estates across the country, which were then divided into small, affordable plots and sold to the subscribers. Now the owners of land, the subscribers were eligible to vote. The National Freehold Land Society quietly revolutionised

British politics and ultimately paved the way for the formation of the Labour Party and the Women's Suffrage Movement. It also gave rise to the saying that 'an Englishman's home is his castle' and kickstarted a national obsession with property ownership that has lasted into the twenty-first century.

Over in the parish of St Bartholomew the Great, Henry Hunt's campaign informed and inspired the shopkeepers of Cloth Fair, and when the Rich family began selling off the estate in the early 1800s the buildings were snapped up by their inhabitants, who now realised that owning property was power.

10

A PIECE OF TYRANNICAL IMPERTINENCE

Cloth Fair and the First Modern Census

While the acquisition of property gave Cloth Fair's more affluent inhabitants a voice in Parliament, their poorer neighbours remained silent and largely anonymous for the first four decades of the 1800s. However, this radically changed in 1841 when the government announced that, for the first time in the country's history, the names, ages and occupations of every man, woman and child in the British Isles would be recorded in a census.

Today, the population census is familiar to us all. We participate in one every ten years and the historical enumerators' books are an invaluable research tool for family historians the world over. However, back in the 1840s, the idea of the government having access to personal information on every citizen was regarded with a high degree of suspicion and scepticism by the media and public alike.

The roots of the ground-breaking 1841 census can be traced back to the beginning of the century when Charles Abbott, MP for Helston in Cornwall, resolved to improve the parlous state of Britain's historical archives. To achieve his aim, he formed a Parliamentary committee tasked with unearthing and cataloguing the records of every town hall, vestry and public institution in the land. The committee's findings were depressing in the extreme. Although the country had been recording births, marriages, deaths, manorial court proceedings and land exchanges for centuries, these precious documents were, in Abbott's words, 'in a condition so confused that no man could make use of them'.

In February 1800, Charles Abbott presented his damning report to the House of Commons, arguing that ignorance of the country's archive treasure trove was a wanton waste of resources that could, if properly organised, help resolve important arguments over property and common law. To remedy the situation, he proposed that every establishment that possessed historical records should make a list of their holdings so an accurate national directory could be compiled. The House agreed and appointed him the head of the Royal Record Commission, a body that paved the way for the founding of the Public Record Office later in the century.

Charles Abbott's success at establishing the Record Commission encouraged him to press for a full inquiry into the country's current population. In November 1800, he announced to Parliament that he intended to bring in a Bill for 'Ascertaining the Population of Great Britain, with the Increase and Diminution thereof'.

His idea was not new – population censuses had been conducted across the globe since biblical times. However, the exercise had never been attempted on a national scale in Britain, mainly because ministers were concerned that it would be seen as an attempt to levy more taxes or recruit more men into the military. In order to assuage these fears, Charles Abbott shrewdly used the chronic food shortage caused by the French Wars as a bargaining chip. He assured the House of Commons that an in-depth knowledge of the population would be indispensable as 'without such a criterion it must be extremely difficult to estimate the quantity of provisions necessary to support the inhabitants'.

Abbott's plan for a national census had its detractors in Parliament, but was well received by the press. After the first reading of the Bill, *The Times* declared:

> We have read with great satisfaction the motion of Mr Abbott for ascertaining the population of the country. The business could not be placed in abler hands, nor could anything more useful or necessary be devised at the present moment. Whatever tends to elucidate the causes of the present crisis is beneficial in the extreme. When the number of mouths in the Empire is acquired, and the amount of produce established by certain proof, it will not be difficult to provide an adequate remedy for whatever may be the disproportion between produce and consumption.

Realising that the census might indeed solve the food crisis, Parliament somewhat reluctantly supported the Bill. An Act for taking account of the population was hurriedly passed and Charles Abbott's secretary, John Rickman, was charged with overseeing the monumental task.

Rickman and his team settled on a modus operandi designed to produce the required results quickly and efficiently, whereby the overseers of the poor, churchwardens and constables would take a written account of the following particulars within their respective parishes:

1. The number of uninhabited houses.
2. The number of inhabited houses.
3. The number of families occupying these houses.

4. The number of males, including children.

5. The number of females, including children.

6. The number of people chiefly employed in agriculture.

7. The number of people chiefly employed in trade, manufacture or handicraft.

8. The number of people not employed as above, including children.

The only people not to be counted in each parish were army and navy personnel as they were to be enumerated separately.

In addition to compiling information on everyone currently residing in their parishes, the churchwardens were also ordered to count the number of baptisms and burials registered in every tenth year between 1700 and 1780 and then annually, in order to establish whether the local population was increasing or decreasing. Annual marriage totals were also required, beginning in 1734. All the results were then to be painstakingly entered by hand on to paper schedules supplied by John Rickman's office, affirmed in front of a local Justice of the Peace and endorsed by the district's High Constable, before being returned to the Principal Secretary of State for the Home Department.

The first ever national census of Great Britain took place on Sunday, 10 March 1801. John Rickman's method of grouping the project into parishes worked exceptionally well and, by late summer, the first statistics had been extrapolated from the dauntingly high stacks of returned schedules. The figures revealed that the total population of England and Wales was 9.4 million, split almost equally between males and females. The least populated English county was Rutland, which had 16,300 inhabitants, followed by Huntingdon, which was home to 37,449 people. In contrast, 588,711 people lived in the county of Lancaster, while Middlesex (including the City of London) was by far the most densely populated county, with 817,710 residents. Within the Middlesex parishes, St Bartholomew the Great was home to 2,645 people, comprising 1,258 males and 1,387 females.

The information that emerged from the 1801 census proved so enlightening that further censuses were conducted along similar lines in 1811, 1821 and 1831. Detailed statistics from the latter still survive and reveal that in the intervening three decades, the population of St Bartholomew the Great had increased by 278 to 2,923. Living conditions were cramped – an average of nine people lived in each house – and nine dwellings were unoccupied, possibly because they were being renovated. A total of 588 of the parish's adult male residents were employed in either retail or handicrafts (Cloth Fair's numerous drapers and tailors fell into this category), while 195 more worked as unskilled labourers, most likely as porters at Smithfield Market. Six manufacturers and seventy-one 'capitalists and professionals' also lived in the parish, but few were sufficiently affluent to employ servants – just eight 'below stairs' staff were recorded.

For the best part of four decades, the government was satisfied with the relatively basic information provided by Charles Abbott's census model. However, as the century progressed, migration precipitated by terrible hardship in Ireland and the collapse of labour-intensive farming in rural England and Wales resulted in a population explosion in industrial cities as former agricultural labourers and their families arrived in search of work. In an attempt to establish the extent of this seismic shift, the government decided to dramatically increase the amount of information on their decennial census. A general headcount of parish residents was no longer sufficient. Now the authorities demanded to know their names, ages, professions and places of birth. Some MPs even pressed for the inclusion of a question about religious persuasion but this did not come to fruition.

Initially, the parish administrators did not consider the new demands in the least problematic. In order to complete the previous census schedules, the churchwardens had habitually recorded the names of the members of each household and could usually find out their ages by consulting the parish registers. The difference was that this personal information was now to be shared with the government. However, although the local authorities were confident that the compilation of the new, detailed census was well within their capabilities, Parliament thought otherwise. In 1840, the passing of the Population Act took overall responsibility for collecting the information away from the parishes and placed it in the hands of a commission led by Thomas Henry Lister, the Registrar General of Births, Marriages and Deaths, who set about organising what is now known as Britain's first modern census.

Under his new scheme, each parish was divided into districts containing between fifty and eighty houses, to which an 'enumerator' would be assigned. Predicted by the *Evening Mail* to be 'intelligent tradesmen and others', these enumerators would be responsible for delivering census forms to all the houses in their district in the days leading up to census night, which was originally set for 30 June. In the days following, they were expected to collect all the completed forms, assist any illiterate households and enter the results on to a schedule. In return for their services, the enumerators were to be paid 10s for every fifty houses they visited, with one additional shilling being added for every ten properties above that number.

As recruitment of the enumerators began, some major issues came to light. Firstly, it became clear that the end of June was not a good time to conduct the census because the county courts' Quarterly Sessions were due to take place the day after. This meant that thousands of people involved in legal proceedings across the land would be away from home on the night of Sunday the 30th, thus giving a false impression of population distribution. Secondly, statisticians pointed out that recording the specific age of every inhabitant was impossible because many people did not know the exact year of their birth.

The citizens employed to do the census groundwork also had reservations. When enumerators living in sparsely populated districts realised how long it would take them to visit fifty houses, they decided not to take on the role and their counterparts in the cities were loath to venture alone into rougher streets for fear they would be at the mercy of the lawless inhabitants. In an attempt to address these problems, the government changed the census date to 6 June and permitted the ages of respondents to be rounded up or down to the nearest five years. Thus, someone who believed they were 52 would be recorded as being 50 while 54-year-olds would be rounded up to 55, etc. (In the event, many ages were recorded exactly.) In addition, the enumerators' pay was increased to 15s for fifty houses and those working in inner city districts were assured that they would be accompanied by a local constable.

Although the concept of a census had been welcomed by the newspapers at the beginning of the century, the detailed nature of the 1841 enquiry caused outrage. On 6 May, the *Morning Post* declared that 'a more complete system of espionage into the private affairs and domestic arrangements of every family, poor or rich, in the kingdom, was never devised by all the wily acts of Jesuitism'. Other papers picked apart the census questions. *Bell's Weekly Messenger* pointed out:

The Government want to know where every inhabitant in the kingdom was born – whether in Scotland, Ireland, or 'other parts' – the latter being an exceptional clause, which of course can only include England and

Berwick-upon-Tweed! Then they want to know whether we are all born 'in the country' or not – a nice verbal distinction, which will puzzle 99 out of 100 to tell whether 'the country' means *this* country or merely the rural parts of it.

The *Weekly Messenger* went on to pour scorn on the government's desire to know people's ages, noting that when Samuel Johnson asked the age of a certain Miss Sewell, his friend Boswell replied, 'She will tell you she is five and twenty, and was five and twenty 25 years ago!' The article continued:

We do not agree with Johnson in his estimate of the repugnance of our fair sex to allow their age to be known; but for a Government to send a set of inspectors into every family to insist upon the name and age of every female is a piece of tyrannical impertinence never attempted in this country since the time of the Norman Conquest.

Despite the media's initial cynicism, as the date of the monumental census drew closer, opinion began to change. When the enumerators sallied forth on 1 June to deliver the forms, the *Morning Chronicle* reported:

The unreasonable prejudices and the scarcely less reasonable apprehensions or suspicions that deteriorated the accuracy and consequent value of the first census have now generally subsided. The chief drawback to be feared is from neglect, or from a careless perusal of the directions rendering the return in some way or other erroneous. But all that is required is so little, and so easily done, that we trust the heads of families generally will cheerfully facilitate the labours of those employed in a work which, by the statistical information it affords, is capable of being the source of so much interesting information on the state of society, and of so many useful measures for its improvement.

The *Chronicle's* prediction proved largely correct, although some people inevitably made a stand. For instance, an elderly lady in Marylebone refused to divulge her age and instead drew a picture of her head on the form, alongside the word 'guess', while in a narrow alley by the side of the River Thames, an Irish woman named Catherine Harvey barraged the unfortunate enumerator with verbal abuse and tried to prevent her neighbours from accepting their census forms. Harvey was later fined for her trouble but the aged artist was let off on account of her advanced years.

Although most English enumerators encountered some resistance to the census, they were largely able to complete their duties without much ado. Unfortunately, this was not the case in some counties across the Irish Sea. Gossip regarding a divisive hidden agenda was so widely believed in the counties of Limerick and Clare that the enumerators were greeted by angry mobs bearing burning torches, while in Westmeath there was scarcely any poultry left alive after a rumour circulated that a tax was to be levied on them. The *Morning Post* noted, 'The total ignorance in which the people were kept by the Solomons of the Commission has been a frightful source of annoyance and will tend to their acquiring data that cannot be relied upon for any statistical purpose.'

Problems in Ireland notwithstanding, the collection of the 1841 census data was more successful than anyone had dared to hope. While a few inhabitants inevitably managed to evade the enumerators (and some were recorded twice), the vast majority of the population were satisfactorily accounted for and comparison with later censuses shows that the information they gave was largely accurate.

As the completed schedules flooded into the Registrar General's office at Somerset House, a small army of clerks and statisticians began the arduous task of extrapolating useful information from the enormous amount of data. While they worked, worrying details began to emerge concerning the population of London. For years, the authorities had been aware that parts of the city were dangerously overcrowded and the census confirmed this. One of the worst examples was Calmell Buildings, a rundown tenement block in Orchard Street, near Portman Square. On 20 June, the *John Bull* newspaper reported that its twenty-four dwellings were occupied by no less than 944 people on census night: 'Several rooms contained two families each, having children, besides men and single women as lodgers. Two houses had 50 people in each; one house 60, and one had 71 ... The enumerator was seven hours correcting and collecting the particulars.'

At the end of October, more detailed statistics began to emerge, creating a fascinating and sometimes worrying snapshot of every street in Britain in unprecedented detail. However, the statisticians were only able to scratch the surface of what could be discovered from the returns, simply because of the number of man-hours it took to extrapolate results. The full riches of the 1841 census were destined to lay hidden within the paperwork for over 150 years until privacy restrictions were lifted and the schedule information was entered into a massive electronic database searchable by keyword and available to the public. Suddenly, the entire project could be examined in ways that the Victorian commissioners at Somerset House could only dream of.

Although the original census findings were basic by modern standards, they nevertheless yielded some interesting information. Over at the parish of St Bartholomew the Great, the total population was calculated at 3,414, an increase of 491 since 1831. Although overcrowding in the district was not as severe as some other areas of London, its

339 houses each accommodated an average of ten people, rendering privacy an unachievable luxury for most residents. At Cloth Fair, the clothing trade still dominated, with four woollen drapers, seventeen tailors and seven needle workers residing there. Unsurprisingly, the meat market at Smithfield was also a major employer – eight butchers and eight porters lived in houses along the street.

Close examination of the return for Nos 41 and 42 Cloth Fair revealed that great changes had occurred at the property during the first three decades of the 1800s. The house was still split into two dwellings but its links to the cloth trade had been severed. No. 41 was now the home and workshop of William Emslie, a copperplate printer, who lived there with his wife, Susannah, their four children and three assistants. His print shop on the ground floor housed machinery that reproduced a wealth of intricate images from artistically engraved copper plates etched by local artists and designers. On being delivered to the print shop, these plates were slathered with ink by Emslie's assistants, who carefully ensured that it seeped into the engraved lines. After wiping the excess off, the ink-charged plate was fitted on a printing press that transferred the image onto a dampened sheet of paper, the fibres of which moulded into the plate's indentations to create a slightly raised image. This ancient process, which was first developed in the 1500s, is still used to make some bank notes and passports today.

The modest dimensions of William Emslie's print shop meant that his machinery took the form of jobbing presses that could only take small paper sizes. Consequently, his work mainly comprised short-run orders that might be produced on a photocopier or computer printer today, such as advertising flyers and letterheads. However, the benefits his presses had over their larger steam-powered counterparts were manifold. Their simple but sturdy construction meant that repairs were rare, they could be set up extremely quickly and, once working, they could produce 1,000 impressions an hour.

Emslie's wages bill was kept to a minimum by the provision of free board and lodging for his three assistants and although the cost of paper and the services of a skilled engraver meant that any print job had to be carefully considered before an order was placed, it was still the most cost-effective way of disseminating information to the public. As literacy improved in mid-nineteenth-century London, flyers produced by Emslie's print shop became a very powerful advertising tool and the satisfying clunk of the presses became a familiar sound to passers-by as they traversed Cloth Fair.

Unfortunately, the hive of industry at 41 Cloth Fair was not replicated next door at No. 42. The property was leased to James Richardson, a boot and shoe maker, who supplemented the meagre income from his trade by subletting the upper floors of the house to numerous lodgers, including his assistant, John Wimpress, a policeman named Thomas Isitt and his family, Smithfield porters George Wiggins and James Power, and Joseph Ethell, a printer who may well have worked next door. By this stage, a garret had been built on the roof to provide extra accommodation, but nevertheless there cannot have been more than five rooms fit for human habitation, unless some poor souls were confined to the damp, cold cellar.

The cramped conditions at 42 Cloth Fair were partially the result of mass migration into Britain's cities, which rapidly changed the social geography of Britain in the mid-1800s. Although James Richardson and his wife were Londoners born and bred, only three of their sub-tenants had been born in the city. This trend was reflected throughout the whole of Cloth Fair – the 1841 census revealed that thirty of the street's 'heads of household' had not been born in London. Of these, the largest proportion (twelve) had been born elsewhere in England

and Wales, but they were closely followed in number by migrants from Ireland.

Much has been written on the Irish exodus during the devastating Potato Famine of 1845–52. However, there had been Irish communities in England, Wales and Scotland long before that particular crisis struck. Extreme poverty caused by religious prejudice had historically been the driving force behind Irish migration. Back in the 1700s, Catholic families were not permitted to own property in Ireland and consequently, most farms, cottages and houses, particularly in rural areas, were leased from a handful of powerful Protestant gentry.

Although some of the penal laws were relaxed at the end of the century, few Catholics could afford to make property investments and their landlords ensured that the scales of wealth remained tipped in their favour by operating the conacre system. Under this arrangement, land was leased to Catholic smallholders – known as cottiers – on an eleven-month contract which cunningly allowed enough time to sow and harvest a crop without establishing any legal rights for the tenant. Robbed of the opportunity to gradually build up a successful business, thousands of cottiers were forced to make a precarious living from tiny plots of land producing barely enough to feed their own families. However, their situation was about to get worse.

By 1800, the mechanisation of agriculture meant that it was profitable to farm expansive, open terrain. Consequently, former smallholdings were combined to make large fields and the amount of conacre system enclosures reduced dramatically. In one Irish county, land that had been leased to a single cottier in 1770 had over 300 occupants by 1845. With their families facing death by starvation, thousands of Catholic smallholders were forced to seek seasonal work on farms in England, Wales and Scotland, where they became known as 'spalpeens', from the Gaelic '*spailpín*', meaning itinerant labourer.

The spalpeen migration began in earnest in 1818 when the *Rob Roy* steam packet began operating a cheap ferry service between Belfast and Glasgow. The service was so popular that other ship owners jumped on the bandwagon and as competition grew, fares dropped as low as 3*d*. By the mid-1820s, at least one spalpeen ferry was making regular voyages to London carrying workers from the western districts of Ireland where poor soil had caused the most terrible hardship.

At first, only a small percentage of Irish migrants came to the metropolis as it offered scant opportunity for farm work. However, in 1838 the government introduced a new method of acquiring funds for poor relief that brought the situation in Ireland to crisis point. Under this new system, each parish's poor relief was paid for out of the inhabitants' rates. However, anyone leasing property worth less than £4 per annum was exempt and their share had to be paid by the freeholder. As thousands of Ireland's cottiers fell into the exempted category, their landlords refused to pay and evicted them. Now with no home, no land and no means of subsistence, they were forced take any work they could find and London, with its burgeoning economy and thriving construction industry, was an obvious place to look.

By 1841, Cloth Fair had become home to several Irish economic migrants, including James Dwyer, Daniel O'Brien and Edward Hare, who all worked as tailors; Edward O'Neil, who had found work as a builder's labourer; and Mary Crawley, who scraped together a living as a char woman. At No. 42, one of James Richardson's tenants, Edward Newland, had also abandoned his homeland after being discharged from the army. His paltry pension dictated an austere existence but one that was preferable to starving to death back in Ireland.

By the mid-1800s, Cloth Fair had descended a long way from its halcyon days at the thriving centre of London's cloth trade. As its ancient houses filled with newcomers, the population of the parish of St Bartholomew the Great peaked at almost 3,500 in 1851 – nearly 1,000 more than in 1801. This rapid influx of people was replicated in all Britain's industrial cities and as the local authorities struggled to cope, Parliament was forced to make significant changes to the way local government operated. By the second half of the 1800s, the traditional way of life, which had existed in parishes like St Bartholomew the Great for centuries, was swept away along with material relics of the past.

II

THE DEATH OF OLD LONDON

Part One

By the middle of the 1800s, the parish of St Bartholomew the Great was struggling to accommodate both the living and the dead. As demand for cheap lodgings reached unprecedented levels, rents rose so high that the district's poorest residents were forced to sleep rough in the animal pens at Smithfield Market. Meanwhile, lessees at Cloth Fair, including James Richardson, crammed as many subtenants as possible into their houses in a bid to profit from the chronic housing shortage.

The conditions in some of these makeshift lodging houses were appalling. The internal walls of their upper floors were torn down to create dormitories in which long lines of 'beds', often no more than a piece of board on bricks, were installed. These communal bedrooms gave inhabitants absolutely no privacy and tempers often boiled over in the wretched and claustrophobic atmosphere, making violent, drink-fuelled altercations depressingly commonplace. In a bid to cope with these dreadful conditions, the inhabitants of lodging houses withdrew into themselves, studiously ignoring their unfortunate roommates, which created an unhappy and sometimes deadly environment. At a miserable lodging house in Saffron Hill, a corpse lay unnoticed in a bed for several days and, when the landlady was questioned by the authorities, she seemed surprised at the notion that her lodgers should have realised they were sleeping next to a dead man.

The overcrowding in London's low lodging houses was only exceeded by that in its churchyards. By the mid-1800s, the unprecedented population boom had led to hundreds of burial grounds in the city being partially covered over by housing, and St Bartholomew the Great's ancient churchyard was no exception. In the 1830s, workmen demolishing an old house on Long Lane unearthed a 'considerable quantity' of human bones, but after disinterestedly concluding that the plot had originally formed part of the old priory burial ground, they simply threw them back into the soil where, perhaps to this day, they still lie.

More intriguing discoveries were made in January 1843, when labourers excavating a sewer in Cloth Fair not only uncovered more bones but also an ancient tombstone engraved on one side with a cross and the letters B.G. (standing for St Bartholomew the Great). Antiquarians called to view the relic tried to decipher the Latin inscription on the reverse but could only make out a few letters. Nevertheless, they agreed that the stone had been erected around the time of the priory's suppression, making it at least 300 years old. The excitement over the find caused the labourers to keep a keen eye out for other relics and, in early February, their vigilance was rewarded when they uncovered a wall buried around 10ft below ground that seemed to extend from the west side of the church. Near the base of the wall they discovered the fragmented remains of a tessellated pavement on which lay a Roman silver coin, a decayed cross and many more human bones, described by the *Morning Post* as 'of very large dimensions, and the teeth in some of the jaw bones were in a good state of preservation'. There is no doubt that the earth in that small site contained 1,000 years of history but, as was so often the case in Victorian London, the precious finds, with the exception of the coin, were considered valueless and reburied.

While St Bartholomew's subterranean depths held fascinating secrets from its ancient past, more recent artefacts could be seen above ground by anyone who cared to venture into the churchyard. In 1850, a journalist from the Ecclesiological Society took a walk around the site and was horrified by what he found there. Bone fragments, some of them possibly human, lay strewn across the consecrated earth, intermingled with dead rats and rotting food surreptitiously tipped from the windows of the surrounding houses when no one was looking.

The section occupying the north side of St Bartholomew's Church was in the worst state. This once peaceful place of rest had been reduced to a filthy alleyway running between the walls of the church and a soot-blackened line of dilapidated tenements on Cloth Fair. As the journalist picked his way through the household detritus that carpeted the route, dogs snarled at him from makeshift kennels abutting the tenements. He cautiously crept past them, only to find his exit at the other end blocked by a haphazard collection of chicken coops. Enquiries soon revealed that the coops were the property of the parochial schoolmaster, who proudly claimed that the alleyway had been even more disgusting before he took it over, with human excrement from the adjacent dwellings lying ankle-deep along its path. The schoolmaster also revealed that St Bartholomew's incumbent rector, John Abbiss, enthusiastically encouraged householders to use the graveyard and even allowed them to extend their properties over the sacred ground in return for a generous donation to the church.

On concluding his conversation with the schoolmaster, the Ecclesiological Society journalist ventured into the main burial ground at the church's western entrance. Here he found the most shocking sight of all. Those unfortunate enough to have been recently interred amid its filth had been stacked on top of older burials and lay so close to the surface that hoops had to be placed over the graves to stop them being dug up by dogs. Nevertheless, effluvia from the coffins still oozed up to the surface during heavy rains, creating a nauseating stench that caught in the throats of anyone standing nearby. The appalled journalist declared:

> I have not seen anything called a graveyard so thoroughly disgusting, and so revolting to every sentiment of common decency, not to mention religion, as this ground; nor did I ever leave a place where I knew that my fellow creatures had been laid, with feelings of such indignant regret.

The shameful state of St Bartholomew the Great's graveyard was the unhappy result of challenges wrought by an ever-growing population combined with years of mismanagement by the parish's governing body – the select vestry.

First established after the Reformation, parish vestries had taken their name from the room in which the clergy's vestments were kept. These rooms were traditionally used to discuss local affairs and the meetings took on the same name as the place in which they were held. When the vestries were first inaugurated, all parishioners had the right to attend their meetings but in more populous districts, such as the City of London, it was thought sensible to elect a committee of representatives from the body of local ratepayers. This system worked perfectly well until some vestry committees, including St Bartholomew's, stopped holding public elections and instead began to choose members themselves, thus becoming known as 'select vestries'.

As early as 1720, residents of St Bartholomew the Great launched a protest against the parish's select vestry after its members announced that they were levying a household tax to pay for the repairing and 'beautifying' of the church. However, after a good deal of argument, the select vestry prevailed and, in 1755, its powers were increased when Parliament passed a Private Act 'for the better enlightening and cleansing [of] the open Places, Squares, Streets, Lanes, Alleys, Passages and Courts within the parish of St Bartholomew the Great; and regulating the Nightly Watch and Beadles within the said Parish'.

The select vestry were appointed trustees of the Act and as such were permitted to claim the associated costs from parishioners by increasing their rates. An amendment to this Act in 1768 further empowered the vestry to 'pave the streets and other places within the Parish, and to remove annoyances and obstructions'. Interestingly, a codicil also ordered that all the district's streets should be officially named and numbered, but there is no evidence that this was done until around a century later.

Although St Bartholomew the Great's vestry endeavoured to conduct their business with honesty and integrity, many of their counterparts in other parishes did not. As reports of corruption within select vestries began to appear in the press during the early 1800s, the committee at St Bartholomew's inevitably got tarred with the same brush and rumours of unscrupulousness began to circulate, causing great consternation among the ratepayers.

In 1830, as the select vestry sat discussing the local poor rate, their meeting was stormed by a group of angry parishioners who 'forcibly rushed into the vestry and conducted themselves in a very improper and tumultuous and offensive way'. The leader of the protest, Samuel

Bagster, then presented himself before the shocked committee, demanding to know why the ratepayers were funding sumptuous vestry dinners and fripperies such as 'beautifying the Beadle's staff', when St Bartholomew's most impoverished tenants were living in virtual starvation. Bagster had a valid point, but when the incident was brought before the Consistory Court (which dealt with ecclesiastical matters) he was fined £20 for his insolence. Interestingly, the court's judgement was recorded in shorthand by Charles Dickens, whose experiences at the Consistory Court eventually prompted him to pen a scathing article entitled 'Our Vestry' for *Household Words* magazine in August 1852. He wrote:

> Our Vestry is a deliberate assembly of the utmost dignity and importance … In asserting its own pre-eminence, for instance, it is very strong. On the least provocation, or on none, it will be clamorous to know whether it is to be 'dictated to', or 'trampled on', or 'ridden over rough-shod'. Its great watch-word is Self-government. That is to say, supposing our Vestry to favour any little harmless disorder like Typhus Fever, and supposing the Government of the country to be, by any accident, in such ridiculous hands, as that any of its authorities should consider it a duty to object to Typhus Fever – obviously an unconstitutional objection – then, our Vestry cuts in with a terrible manifesto about Self-government, and claims its independent right to have as much Typhus Fever as pleases itself.

While vestries across the land ignored the privations of their neediest parishioners, the government was inundated with demands for radical social welfare reform. In response, a royal commission headed by the Bishop of London was tasked with reviewing the situation. Its report, which was made public in March 1834, controversially concluded that poverty was invariably the fault of the individual, not the state.

Moreover, the commission believed that most recipients of poor relief did so out of sheer indolence and many were milking the system by having large families in the knowledge that benefits increased with every child. Blame was also laid at the feet of employers whom the commission felt were keeping wages deliberately low so they could claim subsidies. The fact that these people had taken responsibility for thousands of men, women and children who would otherwise be destitute appeared to be irrelevant.

In order to end this so-called abuse of the poor rate, the royal commission recommended that 'all relief whatever to able-bodied persons or to their families, otherwise than in well-regulated workhouses, shall be declared unlawful, and shall cease'. In response, the government established a Poor Law Commission in the palatial halls of Somerset House, overlooking the Thames. Amid these luxurious surroundings, the commissioners split the country up into poor law unions, each run by a locally elected board of guardians rather than the old parish vestries. These unions were to be funded by a new poor rate and only the ratepayers could be elected onto the boards. Thus, those most affected by the new law, namely impoverished subtenants, had absolutely no say in the matter.

The retraction of parish poor relief was not well received by the public or the press. On 30 April 1834, *The Times* declared:

The more we consider the new system of poor laws, the more do our apprehensions increase respecting it ... To say the truth, in one word, it is AGAINST the spirit, and method, and practice of the British constitution – it is AGAINST the deep-rooted and long-formed habits of this nation, the principle of all which is that the people should be made to govern themselves as much as possible, at least in their domestic concerns and relations.

These sentiments were shared by communities, especially in Wales and the north of England where an anti-poor law movement sprang up to oppose the new boards of guardians. Nevertheless, the reforms continued and quickly gave rise to the Victorian workhouses – the vilest, most degrading institutions ever to blight Britain.

The concept of the workhouse was not new. Back in the 1730s, the vestry of St Bartholomew the Great had opened one at Pelican Court, a narrow alleyway on the parish boundary. However, the experiment was not a success and, in 1741, the inmates were removed and placed in the charge of private individuals. This proved more satisfactory and, by 1766, the vestry had entered into an agreement with parishioner John Powell 'for wholly maintaining and clothing the poor of the parish'.

By 1796, the contract had passed to Mrs Sarah Showell of Bear Lane, who was paid the weekly sum of 4s 3d for every adult and 3s 9d for every child in her care. The vestry's aim was to give every inmate of Mrs Showell's establishment the opportunity to gain financial independence, especially the youngsters, and once children reached the age of 9 they were sent out to work. Mills at Watford and Hounslow were the principal employers of the boys while the girls were often sent to toil in the City warehouses of silk merchants, Bell, Carr, Dodgson & Co. In return for long hours of labour, the children were provided with basic lodgings, a 'good working suit of clothes' and 2s 6d a week.

The system of 'farming out' the parish poor continued until 1837 when St Bartholomew's Vestry was forced to surrender control of poor relief to the board of guardians of the newly formed West London Union – one of three new City bodies created by the contentious Poor Law Commission (the other two covered the central and eastern parishes).

On its inception, the West London Union took over St Sepulchre's old parish workhouse in West Street, near Smithfield Market, and turned it into a house of horrors. The establishment could not have been further removed from the area's original hospital for the poor, founded by Rahere back in the twelfth century. In an effort to deter anyone but the most destitute from entering, the workhouse deputies operated a shockingly inhumane system. Families driven to seek shelter there were immediately split up and sent to communal dormitories segregated by sex and age. Henceforth, contact with loved ones was severely limited, especially for older children, who were sent away to the West London Union School in Edmonton, several miles away.

As if separation from their families was not punishment enough, workhouse inmates also suffered the indignity of performing excruciatingly tedious tasks such as breaking rocks or 'picking oakum', which entailed unravelling endless quantities of old rope. The strength required for this degrading work was drawn from basic provisions such as gruel (a watery porridge) or bread and stale cheese. Charles Dickens (who was no fan of the previous system) visited a London workhouse and wrote of its utter repugnance: 'Groves of babies in arms; groves of mothers and other sick women in bed; groves of lunatics; jungles of men in stone-paved down-stairs day-rooms, waiting for their dinners; longer and longer groves of old people in up-stairs infirmary wards, wearing out life, God knows how.' Dickens tried to engage some of the inmates in conversation but was met with 'a sullen or lethargic indifference to what was being asked, a blunted sensibility to everything but warmth and food, a moody absence of complaint as being of no use, a dogged silence and resentful desire to be left alone again'.

Despite the dreadful conditions, workhouses were inundated, especially by young people. In April 1841, a table of weekly admissions to the West London Union Workhouse revealed that virtually all those taken in were below the age of 30 and most were aged 20 or under. These figures suggest that the bulk of the inmates were young families who simply could not afford to live in the overcrowded, overpriced city – a suspicion that is vindicated in the tragic story of Charles Swift, a 12-month-old baby, who starved to death in a dilapidated hovel in Black Bear Alley, Farringdon, in 1841.

Charles had been born in the West London Union Workhouse. His mother, Sarah, had been deserted by his father and, heavily pregnant, was unable to find work. No doubt she thought that the workhouse would give her unborn child the best chance of survival, but the conditions were so horrendous that, soon after Charles' birth, she took him and absconded to her sister's miserable lodgings in Black Bear Alley. Exhausted, destitute and almost certainly suffering from post-natal depression, Sarah sought solace in drink, leaving her baby in the care of neighbours while she trawled the local pubs with her sister. Charles Arrol, who lived next door, pleaded with her on several occasions to take the child back to the workhouse, but she refused, telling him that it was a fate worse than death. Over the following weeks, Sarah slipped further into an alcoholic abyss until, one night, when Charles cried relentlessly from hunger, she ended his short, pitiful life by beating his head on the wainscot of her miserable room.

The workhouse was just as demoralising for its older inhabitants. Three months after Charles Swift's awful death, Edward Wilkinson, a 64-year-old inmate of the West London Union's establishment, locked himself in a water closet, plunged a fork into his carotid artery and slumped onto the vermin-ridden floor, where he slowly bled to death. Dr Lynch, the workhouse surgeon, informed the subsequent inquest that Wilkinson had been feeling 'despondent' due to frequent bouts of ill health. However, the idea that the workhouse itself might have heavily contributed to the poor man's depressed state did not appear to cross his mind. Nevertheless, the wretched conditions inside the institution were soon to be exposed in the press.

On a cold December night in 1841, William Parker, a 52-year-old man whose shabby genteel clothes hinted at a more prosperous past, lay down on a flea-infested bed in the men's dormitory and breathed his last. As usual, a brief inquest was held, but this time Joseph Standen, the workhouse gatekeeper, decided to be brutally honest about the conditions the deceased man had endured. As local reporters leaned in to hear the shocking details, Standen told the coroner that William Parker had been admitted to 'the Refuge', a grim workhouse dormitory used by homeless men. Despite the freezing temperatures outside, inmates of this place were given no food on admittance and were provided with a blanket so thin that they were forced to 'lay two or three together to keep themselves warm'.

Joseph Standen's damning description of the Refuge was corroborated by one of the jurors, who told the court, 'The place is very cold, the windows are all broken and partially boarded up and the rain sometimes comes in.' It was in these conditions that William Parker had collapsed. When he could not be roused the next morning, he was quickly moved to the workhouse infirmary where house surgeon Mr Kinsey ordered some brandy and water, but before it could be administered the poor man had expired. The circumstances surrounding Parker's death were met with outrage in the press. The *Northern Star* newspaper wrote:

> It is hardly possible to conceive a place more wretched in appearance, and destitute of comfort and accommodation than 'The Refuge' within the precincts of the West London Union Workhouse. In this so-called place of 'refuge' the poor are treated as though they were hogs, so far, at least, as the sleeping part of the business is concerned; but as regards the eating and drinking, that is another matter. While the hogs are plentifully supplied with food, the miserable creatures who apply at the West London

Union for shelter receive, at this inclement season, but a scanty supply
of bread and a little water.

Despite this, the coroner concluded that the workhouse had not
been neglectful and, after a consultation of just fifteen minutes, the
jury returned a verdict of 'death from natural causes'.

The widely publicised circumstances surrounding William Parker's
death shone a very unflattering spotlight on the West London Union
Workhouse and brought the awful conditions therein to the attention of local residents. At Cloth Fair, James Richardson, William
Emslie and their respective tenants at Nos 41 and 42 would almost
certainly have discussed the appalling state of affairs, knowing full
well that the board of guardians, who were supposed to maintain
standards at the workhouse, never set foot in the place. If any change
was to be effected, it would have to be initiated by the people.

In 1842, the inhabitants of the West London Union district
raised a petition calling for a new board of guardians to be elected,
while at St Bartholomew the Great the parishioners also made
a stand against the select vestry by refusing to pay the church
rate that funded their operations. Their grievances reflected those
felt across London as thousands of families were becoming overwhelmed by demands for money from an ever-increasing number
of governing bodies. The *Morning Advertiser* summed up the situation by explaining:

> The refusal [to pay the church rate] was chiefly occasioned by poverty,
> the parties having met with accidents, or having aged parents dependant
> on them, or six or more children. One woman exhibited her tenth child
> in her arms, which she wished the rector to take in lieu of his claim.

The refusal to pay the church rate at St Bartholomew's eventually went to court. The residents inevitably lost the case, but the magistrate did make a point of recommending that they should petition Parliament to get rid of the parish's select vestry. Whether such a petition was ever raised is not known, but relations between the church and their parishioners certainly did not improve. In 1843, several residents indicted for not paying the church rate told the magistrate that the parish's declining fortunes had exempted most of their neighbours, placing the burden of the debt on the shoulders of just 150 householders.

The mood at St Bartholomew the Great was replicated across the country. Local newsvendor George Pollard summed up the national feeling when he declared, 'The Church absorbs £900,000 annually, and does nothing for it!' Seizing the opportunity to roll out the poor law model across other sectors of public service, Parliament began to introduce a raft of new civil committees that would eventually make the previously all-powerful local vestries redundant, save for their ecclesiastical duties.

The effect of this separation of Church and State was immense and directly led to the death of London's old methods of governance. As individual parishes combined into regional and sometimes national bodies, much of their unique character and tradition was lost. However, despite their manifold shortcomings, they at least began to improve the state of the nation's health by cleaning up the city.

A wave of sanitary improvements began in 1842 when Edwin Chadwick, secretary to the Poor Law Commission, became convinced that if public health was improved, far fewer people would be forced into the dreaded workhouses. At his own expense, he conducted a survey of sanitary conditions in communities up and down the country and discovered that the biggest problems involved that most essential of all resources – water.

At the time Edwin Chadwick began his survey, scientists were researching the possibility that disease was somehow transmitted through water supplies and, with this in mind, he investigated numerous sources of drinking water in London, discovering that many of the city's wells lay dangerously close to graveyards. Mr Barnett, the medical officer for Stepney, told him that a 'great number' of local people had been 'attacked with sudden sickness and fainting' after a build-up of gases in a coffin had caused it to burst and spew its malodorous contents into the earth, where it had seeped into the waters of local wells.

Another contaminant of drinking water seemed to be the sewer network. When Edwin Chadwick interviewed Mr Mills, the surveyor of the Holborn and Finsbury sewers, he admitted that the pipes not only 'came into contact' with several churchyards, but also 'must mix with drinking water as the wells of the houses adjacent to the sewers get dry whenever the sewers are lowered'. Mr Mills' colleague, Mr Roe, then recounted the story of Jacob Post, who lived in Church Street, Islington:

> When we were building a sewer close to Mr Post's house, he told our clerk that he had a pump that he formerly used for drinking water but since a burying ground was formed above his house, the water had become of so disagreeable a flavour as to prevent it being used.

Realising he was on to something, Edwin Chadwick took his findings to Dr Southwood Smith, physician to the London Fever Hospital, who confirmed that 'the introduction of dead animal matter under certain conditions into the living body is capable of producing disease and even death'. This crucial theory was quickly reinforced by independent investigations during a cholera epidemic in 1848–49 when John Snow in London and William Budd in Bristol diagnosed that the disease was caused by a living organism in contaminated water. Now convinced that sanitary improvements would ease the ever-increasing burden on the workhouses, ministers rushed a Public Health Bill through Parliament.

The imminent passing of the Public Health Act threatened to take away even more power from London's vestries by placing responsibility for the nation's health in the hands of metropolitan commissions. Some members of St Bartholomew the Great's select vestry quickly saw the writing on the wall and, in a desperate bid to save themselves from redundancy, moved to resolve that henceforth, every ratepayer in the parish would automatically be added to their committee, admitting that 'the system of self-election under which the parish has been so long governed is contrary to the spirit of the English constitution and abhorrent to this age of progress'. However, most of their colleagues were determined to wring the last drops of power from the dying vestry and the motion was rejected.

In the event, St Bartholomew the Great's vestry committee was not affected by the first major result of the Public Health Act. Soon after the legislation was passed, Edwin Chadwick was invited to preside over the newly formed Metropolitan Commission of Sewers to tackle the myriad dangers of contaminated water. The commission took control of the whole of Westminster, Southwark and 'any other such place ... being not more than twelve miles distant in a straight line from St Paul's Cathedral'. However, it did not have jurisdiction over the City of London itself, which retained its existing Sewer Commission, formed back in the 1660s.

The Metropolitan and City Sewer commissions immediately went into competition with one another over efficiency, and within weeks rumours were circulating that the Metropolitan commissioners were collecting evidence that would reveal the 'abominable' condition of its rival's sanitation. In response, the City Commission hastily employed its first medical officer, John Simon, who was tasked with producing annual reports on the cleanliness of the various wards. His findings were damning and paint a vividly revolting picture of streets like Cloth Fair in the mid-1800s.

On examining the City's water and sewage systems, he wrote:

> Now here is a removable cause of death. [Dangerous gases] rise from so many cesspools, and taint the atmosphere of so many houses, they form a climate most congenial for the multiplication of epidemic disorders ... In inspecting the courts and alleys of the City, one constantly sees butts for the reception of water, either public, or in the open yards of the houses, or sometimes in the cellars; and these butts, dirty, mouldering, and cover-less, receiving soot and all other impurities from the air; absorbing stench from the adjacent cesspool; inviting filth from insects, vermin, sparrows, cats, and children; their contents often augmented through a rain water pipe by the washings of the roof, and every hour becoming fustier and more offensive.

The disgusting state of the City's streets and water supply led to the passing of an Act to remove 'nuisances', described as follows:

1. Any premises in such a state as to be a nuisance or injurious to health.
2. Any body of water or privy, cesspool, drain or ash pit so foul as to be injurious to health or a nuisance.
3. Any animal that could damage health or be a nuisance.
4. The accumulation or deposit of anything that could cause a nuisance or be injurious to health, unless it had been approved for business or manufacturing purposes.

In order to enforce the Act, the City Sewer Commission appointed sanitary inspectors, who had the power to enter properties and remove anything considered to be a health hazard. Thus, the filthy church-yard at St Bartholomew the Great was finally returned to something resembling a place of rest and contemplation, much to the disgust of the locals, who were robbed of their convenient rubbish tip.

Over at 42 Cloth Fair, James Richardson's lodging house was care-fully inspected and he was ordered to clean up its filthy rooms at his own expense, or risk having the premises shut down. Outside his front door, the cleanliness of the street was put under the control of council surveyors who were responsible for ensuring that all ditches, gutters and drains were clean. Any infrastructure found wanting was repaired by the Corporation of London at the expense of the inhabitants.

The effect of this sudden war on filth created a positive mood for improvement at St Bartholomew the Great. However, in creating a healthier environment, many ancient features of the parish were sacri-ficed. In 1856, the old Coach & Horses Inn was deemed a health hazard and torn down, destroying part of the north walk of St Bartholomew's cloister in the process. The pub's owner, Mr Robins, also started removing what remained of the original south nave wall until the much-maligned vestry sprang into action and stopped him.

In fact, during this period of change, the vestry found a new and valuable purpose as conservators of the parish's history. In addition to opposing some demolitions recommended by the sanitary inspec-tors, they ordered the repair of the gateway leading to Smithfield Market (which had been damaged by fire in 1855) and commissioned a Mr Blyth to make new gates.

Unfortunately, the vestry were not successful in all their attempts at preservation. Shortly after the demise of the Coach & Horses, the owners of the property next door (70 Bartholomew Close) were ordered to take down their wall abutting the churchyard and, in doing so, the remains of the nave wall became dangerously unstable. Once again, the vestry tried to save this precious part of the original priory complex, but even they could not resist the might of the Sewer Commission who ordered it to be torn down. The ancient stones were subsequently sold to a local builder.

While the most deleterious parts of St Bartholomew's parish were being removed, the Sewer Commission turned their attention to the chronic overcrowding in the churchyards. In 1852, a Burial Board took control of all parish graveyards in the City, most of which were in the same state as the one overlooking Cloth Fair. In order to clean them up permanently, the board took the monumental decision to close virtually every one of them and open a vast new cemetery, well away from the crowded thoroughfares of the metropolis, as a replacement. After considering several sites they settled on an old farm owned by the Duke of Wellington at Little Ilford (modern Manor Park), 6 miles away from the city centre.

The Little Ilford land was purchased by the Corporation of London in 1853 and William Haywood, the Sewer Commission's surveyor, was tasked with laying out an enormous cemetery on the rolling, rural fields, aided by landscape gardener, Robert Davidson. Their plan was drawn up along similar lines to a housing estate. Accessed via a grand stone gateway, the most expensive burial plots (costing 17s 6d) lay by the side of an impressive central avenue leading to the main chapel, while cheaper, 'second class' plots (8s 6d) were available along less significant side roads. There were also catacombs in which up to 800 coffins could be entombed.

The first interment at the City of London Cemetery occurred on 24 June 1856, and by 1858 around 2,500 burials were taking place there every year, leaving the City's parishes free to concentrate on cleaning up their ancient churches and graveyards. Over at St Bartholomew the Great, the vestry, in its new capacity as heritage guardian, also decided it was time to restore the church – which had been badly damaged by fire in 1830 – to its former glory.

Back in the mid-1850s, architect William Slater had prepared plans for a refurbishment but intensive construction work taking place next door at the time had stalled the project. Thus, when the vestry employed Thomas Hayter Lewis as chief architect of the restoration in 1863, they thought it only right and proper that Slater should also get involved. That April, the two men undertook a detailed survey of the church and found that, although the fabric of the building was generally in very good repair, some ill-advised alterations made after the priory's demise had caused a raft of problems.

Firstly, the level of the floor inside the church had inexplicably been raised some 2½ft, blocking the circulation of air and causing damp to rise. Numerous precious monuments surrounding the altar and nave had suffered as a consequence and, by the time Slater and Hayter Lewis saw them, they had been painted black, probably to disguise their wretched condition. Outside, the graveyard that covered the destroyed section of the original nave had been raised 6ft above its original level to accommodate more burials, and its northern corner had been redeveloped as part of 9 Cloth Fair. The former south transept, which had been removed in the sixteenth century, had subsequently served as another graveyard and, even if the burials were exhumed, the site could not be redeveloped without affecting the light and air of Pope's Cottages, a haphazard cluster of tenements which had been thrown up on the foundations of the old Chapterhouse in the mid-1840s. On the opposite side of the church, the remains of the north transept were occupied by a blacksmith whose fiery trade rendered his environs in grave danger of being consumed by a conflagration. Meanwhile, the east cloister at St Bartholomew the Great had been divided up and let to private tenants, who had succeeded in almost totally destroying its 'very fine' remains.

After completing their survey, William Slater and Thomas Hayter Lewis recommended that phase one of the renovation should concentrate on returning the internal floor and entrances of the church to their original levels so they could be properly drained and ventilated. In addition, they suggested that the pews should be redesigned to provide more seating and the monuments returned to their original state with some intensive cleaning. The total cost of these works was estimated at £4,000.

At a public meeting on 27 May 1863, it was agreed that the restoration should go ahead and a fund was set up by the rector, the Reverend Abbiss, who gave an opening donation of 200 guineas. Galvanised into action, the parishioners set about organising a programme of fundraising events. On 13 July, the Reverend Thomas Hugo publicised St Bartholomew the Great's unique heritage by giving a talk on the history of the priory and Mr J.H. Parker, the distinguished keeper of the Ashmolean Museum, spoke of the building's fine and interesting architecture. His lecture, subsequently published in the *Gentleman's Magazine*, was printed up and sold on behalf of the restoration fund.

Although the church coffers quickly began to fill, the restoration could not begin until the thorny issue of encroachment had been addressed. Some owners of the properties partially occupying the church's land agreed to relinquish the offending parts of their buildings in return for compensation, but when Benjamin Winstone, the freeholder of a trimmings factory abutting the Lady Chapel, was approached he refused to comply unless the church bought his entire property for £4,000. This sum threatened to wipe out the entire restoration fund in one fell swoop and, consequently, the ambitious project had to be dramatically scaled back, leaving Winstone's factory in situ and sacrificing the less essential works.

After eleven long months of negotiations with the freeholders of adjacent properties, the restoration project was finally ready to proceed and the experienced firm of Dove Bros, Islington, was contracted to lower the church floor, rearrange the pews, take away the paint-daubed monuments for expert cleaning and move any mortal remains impeding the works. The latter proved to be a very tedious task as the labourers discovered thousands of bones, all of which had to be carefully reinterred. As the cost of their removal to the City of London Cemetery was estimated at a massive £400, it was decided that they should instead be reburied in a cavernous, 15ft-deep pit in the churchyard. Thus, numerous wealthy and important former residents of Cloth Fair and its surrounds were subjected to an ignominious end in a mass grave.

In January 1865, Dove Bros embarked on the second phase of restoration, which included repairing and making good the church's brickwork. By July the parishioners were growing impatient with the works, which had now dragged on for a year, but, as is so often the case with projects of this magnitude, the restoration of St Bartholomew the Great took far longer than anyone had anticipated. The church eventually reopened for worship in March 1868, and soon afterwards its vestry's centuries-old role at the heart of the community ended for good when the government abolished compulsory payment of the church rate. A voluntary tax was subsequently introduced but in the first year it realised just £48. Sensing defeat, the vestry committee reluctantly sold the parish watch house to pay off their outstanding debts and became a toothless, ecclesiastical committee that was a pale shadow of its former, grandiose self.

By this stage, the hated West London Poor Law Union had also ceased to operate as an independent body. In 1869, it was dissolved and combined with its central and eastern counterparts to form the City of London Union, the offices of which were located at 61 Bartholomew Close. The workhouse, which had loomed over the district, striking fear and loathing into the hearts of anyone who knew the horrors that lurked within, was subsequently shut down and the unfortunate inmates were rehoused in institutions at Holloway and Homerton.

With management of the parish now entirely under the control of central government bodies, the streets of St Bartholomew the Great were transformed when Home Secretary Richard Cross pushed the Artisans' & Labourers' Dwelling Improvement Act through Parliament in 1875. Its legislation allowed compensation to be paid to any owner of slum property willing to demolish it. However, it did not provide any funds for redevelopment and, as thousands of dilapidated but historically interesting properties vanished from London's streets, their former inhabitants were forced into the few slums that remained, creating an even bigger housing issue. By 1880 it had become clear that the death of old London's parish-based government threatened to create as many problems as it solved.

12

THE DEATH OF OLD LONDON

Part Two

As the ancient, parochial way of life diminished across London, the population of its central districts went into sharp decline. The parish of St Bartholomew the Great typified this trend. By 1881, it had just 2,373 inhabitants – almost half the number counted in 1851. There were two main causes for this exodus. Firstly, the council's attempts at slum clearance had reduced the amount of available housing dramatically – at St Bartholomew's it had decreased by around 25 per cent. Secondly, the construction of the city's rail network meant that workers no longer needed to live within walking distance of their place of employment.

By the 1880s, Cloth Fair and Smithfield Market had two stations within easy reach. Farringdon Street Station (now shortened to Farringdon) had opened in January 1863 as the terminus of the Metropolitan Railway, the world's first subterranean line, which ran under the city from Paddington. Aldersgate Street Station (now Barbican) opened two years later as part of the railway's extension to Moorgate. The line's 'workmen's fare' of just 3*d* for a return ticket meant that even the low paid could afford to live some distance away from their workplace.

As the Metropolitan Railway's extension was being constructed, the section running under Smithfield was covered by an enormous new market building. Designed by Sir Horace Jones, the 'Central Markets' comprised two vast wings separated by a Grand Avenue covered with a curved, cast-iron arch. Each end of this busy through-way was guarded by decorative bronze dragons bearing the armorial shields of the great merchant cities of London, Edinburgh, Liverpool and Dublin, while the buildings either side were embellished with octagonal pavilion towers, each with a dome embellished with carved griffins. On the south side of the market, a network of underground railway sidings connected to the Metropolitan Railway meant that meat could be brought in by train and taken straight into the marketplace via lifts.

As Smithfield Market was transformed, the character of Cloth Fair also changed as many of its former houses were converted into commercial units. One such property was 41 and 42 Cloth Fair, which became a cutlery workshop owned by Edward Tuthill Markham, a man whose life drew uncanny similarities to those of the property's previous inhabitants.

Born in 1847 in the East Anglian village of Terrington St Clement, Edward Markham spent his early years living above his father's drapers shop where he became well acquainted with the Norfolk fabrics that had once been the staple of the old priory's Cloth Fair. However, as an economic depression took hold in the second half of the nineteenth century, business at Markham's drapers declined and Edward's father was forced to seek alternative employment. After a stint working as a salesman for Langdale's Manures, he set himself up as an auctioneer and estate agent, which kept the wolf from the door but was far from lucrative.

Realising that his home town offered scant opportunity, Edward Markham resolved to seek his fortune in London. After leaving school, he used his considerable knowledge of the cloth trade to secure a job as a draper's assistant at Robert Waind's premises in Upper Street, Islington, where he became acquainted with a young Cornish shop assistant named Sarah Jane Hawkey. The pair married at Sarah's home town of Bodmin in 1877 and afterwards returned to London, taking a humble but well-appointed house on Fassett Square, Hackney. By 1879 they had a baby daughter named Florence, and Edward had taken the lease on James Richardson's old premises at 42 Cloth Fair, which he transformed into a workshop for finishing cutlery crafted from one of the Industrial Revolution's most successful innovations – mass-produced steel.

Steel, an alloy of iron, had existed in Britain since Roman times, when its hard but malleable properties were harnessed for weaponry. However, the amount of coke required to feed the blast furnaces in which it was produced made it an expensive commodity until the 1850s, when a 'converter' invented by engineer Henry Bessemer revolutionised the process. Bessemer's Converter took the form of a capacious, pear-shaped receptacle mounted on a pivot, into which molten pig iron was poured. Compressed air was then blown through, causing the impurities to oxidise and create steel. Depending on the size of the converter, between 5 and 30 tons of metal could be treated in one 'blow' and the entire process took just twenty minutes, greatly reducing the amount of fuel required.

Bessemer's Converter regenerated Britain's steel industry and the alloy was subsequently used to create all manner of items, from railway lines to cooking implements. At Edward Markham's workshop at 42 Cloth Fair, the business end of his cutlery was supplied by a manufacturer in the steelmaking heartland of Sheffield. His workers then fitted it with bone handles, sharpened the knife blades on revolving belts and, after giving the sets a thorough polish, packed them into presentation boxes ready for sale.

Markham's sturdy, reasonably priced cutlery proved popular with retailers and, as his workshop prospered, his thoughts turned to expansion. Taking advantage of newly available building society loans, he bought the freehold interest to 42 Cloth Fair and soon afterwards acquired Emslie's old print shop next door, thus reuniting the two properties. The increased amount of floor space was subsequently used to produce new cutlery lines featuring elaborate, electroplated silver handles that were snapped up by middle-class households who were keen to emulate the grand dinner tables of the gentry without spending a year's wages on solid silver services.

The success of Edward Markham's electroplated cutlery allowed him to move from his small home at Fassett Square to a considerably larger house in the prosperous north London suburb of Crouch End, which he shared with his wife, daughter and son, William, who had been born in 1883. While living there, he followed in the footsteps of the Witham family (his eighteenth-century predecessors at Cloth Fair) by joining the local Methodist congregation, where he became an enthusiastic lay preacher. Whether he was aware of 41–42 Cloth Fair's historical links to Methodism is a moot point, but for the remaining years of his life, Edward Markham became an avid collector of artefacts connected to the religious movement. In around 1900, the Wesley Historical Society noted in their magazine:

Mr E T Markham, of Crouch End, has an interesting book of sermons, which he picked up off a second-hand bookstall. It is an octavo volume bound in leather with a clasp and folding cover; a convenient packet for a saddlebag, so that an itinerant preacher's whole body of divinity could travel round the countryside with him. Opening the book we are immediately impressed by the bookplate ... In place of the text, in bold characters, we read 'James Rogers, 1781'. This is of course the husband of Hester Ann Rogers who was living in the preacher's house at City Road when John Wesley died there.

It would be pleasing to believe that Edward Markham was (or became) aware of the Wesley brothers' connection to his business premises. Indeed, at the time he acquired 41–42 Cloth Fair, the view from the windows had not altered much since the Witham family resided there.

However, the street's quaint character was about to change beyond recognition as much of London's architectural heritage was swept away in the wake of sanitary improvements and commercial redevelopment. As ancient parts of the city disappeared, many Londoners realised too late their significance as part of the city's cultural history. The great designer William Morris tried to stem the tide of redevelopment by founding the Society for the Protection of Ancient Buildings in 1877, but it had no power to oppose the might of the council. Thus, during this era of demolition, the scene was set for 41–42 Cloth Fair to become the oldest house in London.

Ironically, the destruction of medieval Cloth Fair began during a restoration project. In 1884, William Panckridge, the new rector of St Bartholomew the Great, formed a committee to oversee the purchase of 'certain buildings standing on the site of the ancient church'. There is no doubt that Panckridge's intentions were honourable. Although the filthy churchyard had been cleaned up, the church was still surrounded by a labyrinthine complex of dilapidated buildings which, as we have seen, stood directly on the remains of the

pre-Reformation edifice. In order to restore the church into something resembling the original, it was imperative that these structures
were removed.

The main offenders were the blacksmith's forge at 10 Cloth Fair,
which stood on the site of the former north transept, and the trimmings factory at 40–42 Bartholomew Close, which projected 20ft into
the east end of the church, covering the remains of the crypt and the
Lady Chapel. After the owners of these two buildings finally agreed
to vacate in return for a payment of £7,620, a fundraising appeal
was launched. Donations swiftly rolled in and by the end of the year
the restoration committee was ready to begin work. Dove Bros, the
firm that had carried out the previous restorations, were contracted to
demolish the forge and the factory, rebuild the north and south tran-
septs and restore the Lady Chapel. The remaining part of the factory
site was earmarked for a new school.

On 30 November 1886, a lavish lunch was held in the Great Hall
of St Bartholomew's Hospital to celebrate the start of the restoration.
Interestingly, this auspicious event was presided over by surgeon Sir
James Paget, whose grandson would become inextricably linked with
41–42 Cloth Fair in later years. In the meantime, the rejuvenation of
St Bartholomew the Great got under way, starting with the rebuilding
of the south transept and the demolition works at the east end of the
site. Once the trimmings factory had been erased from the landscape
the new school quickly rose on its footprint, allowing the local children to move out of their cramped and badly equipped classrooms in
St Bartholomew's north triforium (a gallery above the nave).

With the pupils now out of the church, Dove Brothers turned their
attention to the north transept, removing the ancient forge and erecting
a covered entrance porch embellished with a statue of St Bartholomew
in its place. As *The Times* noted, this new entrance provided 'easy access

to the church for the crowded population in and around Cloth Fair' and also gave a considerably better view from the windows of Edward Markham's workshop. The workmen then moved to the west entrance to the church where a statue of Rahere carrying a model of his beloved creation was mounted above a shield bearing the priory arms. Over this, a new vestry room was built, complete with a strong room to house the parish's precious registers.

The opening ceremony of the newly renovated church took place on 5 June 1893 and caused quite a commotion in Cloth Fair as people crowded at the railings to catch a glimpse of the special guests, the Prince of Wales and Princess Alexandra. The princess's attendance was particularly poignant as it was her first public appointment since the death of her eldest son and heir to the throne, the Duke of Clarence. The press noted, 'It was recalled that King Henry I, after the death of his son and heir in the wreck of the White Ship, had in like manner assisted in the founding of St Bartholomew's.' The Prince and Princess of Wales were joined at the ceremony by their daughters Princess Victoria and Princess Maud (later Queen of Norway) and their son, Prince George, the future George V.

Although much time and money was spent on the church's restoration, the population of St Bartholomew the Great and its neighbouring parishes continued to slowly and inexorably decline. The passing of the Houses of the Working Classes Act in 1890 expedited matters by allowing councils not only to demolish old properties but also build replacements. The development sites they purchased were often in the suburbs where land was cheaper and, thus, former inhabitants of inner London districts were rehoused many miles away. By the time the 1911 census was conducted, the population of St Bartholomew the Great had slumped to 913 and at night its streets acquired an eerie, abandoned atmosphere.

As the once thriving community at St Bartholomew the Great drifted away to new homes in the suburbs, the local authorities began to discuss how the area could be altered to meet the demands of the new century. The first outward sign of things to come appeared in the summer of 1913. On 4 August an article in *The Times*, headlined 'Cloth Fair in Danger', announced:

> It is said to be in contemplation, at a probable expense of £200,000, to effect an important street improvement in the neighbourhood of the London Central Markets by the demolition of the ancient and historic buildings known as Cloth Fair and the widening of Long Lane to a width of 60ft. The business of the markets is so rapidly increasing that outside additions in the way of cold storage facilities and other extensions are indispensable. It is expected that the large cost of improvement ... will be recouped by the increased assessments of the new buildings that will be erected on the site of the old-fashioned and picturesque dwellings which have played so interesting a part in the past history of the City.

It transpired that the council planned to demolish the entire eastern half of Cloth Fair, leaving only the church. This area comprised short terraces of fine and historically priceless sixteenth- and seventeenth-century houses, little altered since their construction. Directly in front of St Bartholomew's Church, backing on to the narrow strip of burial ground where the schoolmaster had formerly kept his chicken coops, a line of jettied properties dating back to 1597 were ordered to be removed so the narrow roadway could be widened. Opposite, a terrace of tall and thin Elizabethan townhouses and a picturesque old inn known as the Dick Whittington were also in the council's sights.

Before the introduction of the 1890 Housing Act, there is every chance that the twenty-two properties under threat on Cloth Fair would have escaped demolition due to their owners' refusal to sell. However, the Act gave the council the right to compulsorily purchase any dwellings they deemed unfit for human habitation and acquire buildings where it appeared 'that the closeness, narrowness and bad arrangement … is dangerous or prejudicial to the health of the inhabitants'. As the eastern part of the roadway through Cloth Fair was so narrow that the outstretched arms of passers-by could almost touch the houses on either side, the latter clause inevitably sealed its fate.

The news of Cloth Fair's imminent destruction caused a furore in London and beyond. In January 1914, the *Globe* newspaper warned, 'With the demolition of these houses the last of the city buildings (excepting churches) existing before the Great Fire will vanish.' The paper's view was shared by Guy Laking, first keeper of the newly opened London Museum, who wrote to the editor of *The Times* later that same month. His letter highlighted the prevailing threat to historic buildings in many other London districts but, he wrote, 'Of even greater importance, in my opinion, are the old houses in Cloth Fair, the circumstances connected with their approaching destruction being particularly scandalous'. The scandal to which Laking referred was the fact that the owners of the condemned buildings had offered to spend any amount necessary to improve their sanitation and structural repair. Nevertheless, the council persevered with their plans on the grounds that the road was too narrow.

By the end of January 1914, Cloth Fair had become the figurehead of a campaign to save old London. The *Daily Mirror* laid blame squarely on commerce, and asked its readers to consider:

Has beauty any rights? Any place in life? … We all talk much flap-doodle nowadays about 'thinking of the future'. What will be our future, possibly not enslaved to Business? Think of our treatment of things not our own, but only as it were left to us in usufruct; things that we, instead of handing on to others, wantonly waste and sacrifice to our immediate greedy notion that everything can be swept away, so long as Business profits in the sweeping.

The *Mirror*'s impassioned piece raised an interesting point regarding the council's role. Was it solely concerned with the health and financial welfare of the public, or should more esoteric factors be brought into consideration? To this day, this complex question has yet to be satisfactorily answered.

In the meantime, the council faced more opposition over its plans for Cloth Fair. In February 1914, its own Local Government Committee raised concern over the demolition scheme and letters poured into its offices pleading for the houses to be saved. The unprecedented interest in the capital's antiquities was exploited by Walker's Galleries in New Bond Street, which staged an exhibition of paintings by William Wiehe Collins, entitled 'Old & New London'. Among the exhibits were several renditions of the houses at Cloth Fair.

Elsewhere, new uses for the condemned properties were dreamed up in an attempt to preserve them. At a meeting of the Bishopsgate Ward Club, Edward Yates, a lecturer on London's antiquities, noted that people from all over the world came to see 'these relics of old London', and made the novel suggestion that they might be kitted out with period furnishings and opened to the public as museums.

This idea was later adopted to great effect at the eighteenth-century almshouses that now form the Geffrye Museum in Shoreditch. However, it failed to inspire the council in 1914 and, that March, the Society for the Preservation of Ancient Buildings reluctantly lent their support to the demolition project on the understanding that the Dick Whittington Inn, rumoured to be the oldest building on Cloth Fair, was saved. At a subsequent council meeting at the Guildhall, it was agreed that the building could remain standing as long as it was converted into an institute for Smithfield's market porters. However, weeks later, yet more of Cloth Fair's ancient heritage was placed under threat when the Corporation of London recommended that the freehold interest in the houses at Nos 6–9, which had loomed over the churchyard for three centuries, should be acquired.

With mass opposition to the destruction of Cloth Fair, there was hope that the unique street might still be saved. However, on 4 August, Britain declared war on Germany and the hostilities quickly diverted the public's attention. As the *Pall Mall Gazette* bluntly noted, 'People can hardly be expected to subscribe for such luxuries as the salvation of old houses. Cloth Fair is going, and public authorities and private owners will have little to stay them so long as the war and its effects last.'

Just days afterwards, the demolition crews arrived and began to dismantle Nos 6–9, thus opening up the burial ground and the north side of the church for the first time in over three centuries. As the ancient houses were reduced to dust, the *Sunderland Echo* likened the scene to the battlefields across the Channel. In a fictitious letter, 'Bertha', a woman living in war-torn Ypres, told her English friend 'Kathleen' that her town's 'wonderful Halle aux Drape [Cloth Hall] has gone, or is so mutilated as to have lost all its beauty … It is a coincidence that this same week sees the last of Cloth Fair in London: the old sixteenth century houses there are, I believe, all down now.'

Quite what Edward Markham thought of the destruction in his midst can only be guessed at. In any case, he had more pressing concerns as his son and business partner, William, was under increasing pressure to enlist in the British Army. William Markham's dilemma was shared by thousands of his peers. The destruction of the *Halle aux Drape* described so creatively by the *Daily Mirror* had occurred during the First Battle of Ypres, which raged from 19 October until 22 November 1914, maiming or killing thousands of British soldiers. Although servicemen were forbidden to talk about the horrors they had witnessed, the shattered bodies of the injured and the dreaded telegrams bearing news of the fallen spoke for themselves. By the end of the year, the military were desperate for new recruits but, unsurprisingly, the flood of volunteers that had marked the beginning of the war had levelled off considerably. Young men like William Markham, who had a good career and a close-knit family, were loath to give up the comforts of home for an uncertain fate on the battlefields of western Europe.

At this point, the possibility of introducing conscription was discussed in the corridors of power and, as a precursor, the government passed the National Registration Act in July 1915. Under the Act, forms were distributed to every civilian in Britain aged between 15 and 65 asking for the recipient's name, occupation, age and address. The forms had to be completed by midnight on Sunday, 15 August and during the following week they were collected by enumerators and sent to the Records Office at Somerset House. Over the following month, clerks waded their way through the returns, extrapolating data and by mid-September they had calculated that Britain had almost 5 million men of military age who were not yet in the forces. One of these men was William Markham who, although not yet a soldier, had already witnessed first-hand the violence of war when a Zeppelin airship wreaked havoc at St Bartholomew the Great on 8 September 1915.

From the onset of the war, it was common knowledge that Germany possessed airships capable of reaching Britain. The first ever air raid was launched on East Anglia on 19 and 20 January 1915 and that May, London got its first taste of aerial assault when bombs were dropped on its eastern and northern districts.

There is little doubt that Germany intended its air attacks to create mass panic. However, in the event, they simply strengthened the public's resolve. In his book, *The Defence of London 1915–1918*, Sir Alfred Rawlinson recalled that the May bombings produced:

a most effectual 'waking up' of London, who until that time had been inclined to be somewhat somnolent in their sense of fancied security … The result was that pressure from all sides was at once brought to bear on the Government, demanding that immediate steps should be taken to organise some form of defence, which, even if not capable of securing the safety of the town, should at least demonstrate to the enemy that no further attacks could be delivered with impunity.

Nevertheless, no immediate steps were taken and, during the summer of 1915, the defence of London – the most powerful city in the world – fell to a single branch of the Royal Naval Air Service under the command of Commodore Murray Sueter. His force primarily comprised special constables who each devoted four hours a day to manning a meagre armoury of heavy artillery and acetylene searchlights that possessed 'less power than many headlights on motor cars'. Sir Alfred Rawlinson noted:

The armament of this force was both inadequate and unsuitable for the purpose for which it was intended, as not only was it quite impossible for it to inflict any injury upon Zeppelin airships, but it was equally impossible that these guns could be fired over London without causing considerable injury to the unfortunate people they were intended to protect.

Over the summer of 1915 London endured more air raids, but none affected the parish of St Bartholomew the Great until 8 September.

That evening, a single Zeppelin, commanded by Kapitänleutnant Heinrich Mathy, loomed into view over the Norfolk coast just before 9 p.m. It silently made its way inland to Cambridge and then followed the line of a main road (the modern A10) towards London. Once it reached the outskirts of the city, the airship turned west, releasing two high explosives and ten incendiaries on the quiet suburb of Golders Green before continuing on its murderous course into central London, bombing Euston Station, Bloomsbury and Holborn as it ominously drifted through the night sky.

Over in the parish of St Bartholomew the Great, fireman Charles Henley was preparing for bed in his fire sentry box at Bartholomew Close when he received word that a Zeppelin was fast approaching. At first, he thought it was a false alarm as all was quiet save for the distant hum of traffic on Newgate Street. However, as he stood at the fire-box door, he gradually became aware of an unfamiliar whirring sound followed by a series of sinister thuds that seemed to be getting closer.

At that moment, William Fenge, the landlord of the Admiral Carter pub, stepped out of his premises with his friend Frederick Saunders. Charles Henley screamed at them to take cover, but it was too late. Seconds later, the Zeppelin dispatched a bomb that exploded directly on Bartholomew Close. A marble fountain that stood at its centre shattered, sending shrapnel flying in all directions – today the effects can still be seen on the pock-marked wall of St Bartholomew's Hospital. William Fenge and Frederick Saunders caught the full force of the blast and did not stand a chance. Charles Henley was knocked unconscious and came round to find his fire-box smashed to smithereens. If he had been in his bed, he too would almost certainly have been killed. Kapitänleutnant Mathy later revealed in his report that the 660lb bomb dropped on Bartholomew Close was the largest yet carried and the damage it wrought 'must be very great, since a whole row of lights vanished in one stroke'.

As the dawn broke, the full devastation caused by the bomb was revealed. The former site of the fountain had been reduced to an enormous crater 8ft deep, surrounded by a thick carpet of rubble. All around it, the wind howled through the glassless windows and wrecked roofs of the surrounding office buildings, scattering papers across their detritus-strewn floors.

It transpired that, after bombing Bartholomew Close, the Zeppelin crew had turned their attention to the heart of the City, dropping high explosives on the Guildhall and Liverpool Street Station before returning to base. In total, the raid killed twenty-two people, injured eighty-seven others and stimulated a complete reassessment of London's defences.

Nevertheless, the German airships continued to prove indestructible until September 1916, when Lieutenant William Leefe Robinson of the Royal Flying Corps finally managed to shoot down a Schütte-Lanz SL11 by repeatedly firing at a specific area of the craft. He later explained:

> I had hardly finished the drum before I saw the part fired at, glow. In a few seconds, the whole rear was blazing ... I quickly got out of the way of the falling, blazing Zeppelin and, being very excited, fired off a few red Very lights and dropped a parachute flare.

Lieutenant Robinson had every cause to feel elated. His valour earned him a Victoria Cross, he was hailed as a national hero and his fellow pilots began to copy his tactics.

After Germany lost five more airships to the Royal Flying Corps, the raids on London ceased. However, across the Channel, the British

Army was struggling against an enemy that was better equipped and more experienced at warfare. Realising that more manpower was essential to victory, Lord Derby, the director general of military recruitment, introduced a programme in mid-October 1915 that would alter (and in many cases end) the lives of millions of British men, including William Markham.

The Derby Scheme, as it became known, required all men between the ages of 18 and 40 who were not employed in essential work to either voluntarily enlist before 15 December or attest that they would join the army if and when they were called upon. William Markham chose the latter option, probably surmising that he was unlikely to be called up. Regular episodes of pneumonitis had rendered his lungs in such poor shape that the medical examiner noted on his form that he was 'fit for home service only'.

Nevertheless, as casualty figures rose, the War Office enlisted virtually every man who had signed the attestation form. Despite his poor health, William Markham was summoned to the Recruiting Medical Board's office at Mill Hill Barracks, where he was declared fit for general service. By July 1916, he was on board a ship bound for France where he joined the 12th Battalion, London Regiment, before transferring to the 7th Middlesex.

From this point on, his story heartbreakingly mirrored that of the Dick Wittington Inn on Cloth Fair. Albeit in very different ways, the man and the building had, against all odds, survived the threat to their existence since 1914, but 1916 brought a tragic reversal of fortune. On 2 September, a demolition crew suddenly appeared in Cloth Fair and, without warning, set about demolishing the historic inn, leaving nothing but a pair of carved figures that were subsequently donated to the Guildhall Museum. Fourteen days later, William Markham fell at the Battle of Flers–Courcelette aged just 32. His body was never recovered and the only tangible memory of his existence was a few paltry possessions he left behind at base.

By the time the bloody battles of the First World War drew to a close in 1918, Cloth Fair was unrecognisable. The 'divers fair inns and other comely buildings' that had gladdened the heart of historian John Stow in 1598 had been obliterated and all that remained from that period was St Bartholomew's Church. This shocking wave of destruction had been replicated across London where, between 1890 and 1918, a wealth of historic streets and iconic buildings were lost in the name of progress.

Within a few minutes' walk of Cloth Fair, two precious remnants of the area's past disappeared when Christ's Hospital School (the former home of the Bluecoat scholars) and Newgate Gaol were demolished between 1902 and 1904. Eight years later, the colossal Georgian edifice of the General Post Office at St Martin Le Grand fell prey to the wrecking ball, forcing the Central London Railway to change the name of their nearby station from Post Office to St Paul's. Further west, Clare Market, an ancient trading area founded in the 1650s by the Earl of Clare, was condemned despite having changed little since it was first developed. Its subsequent destruction erased several important seventeenth-century inns from the cityscape, including the Bulls Head Tavern, a favourite haunt of artist William Hogarth. Nearby, Wych Street's little terraces of Tudor houses and inns of chancery, including a former law school attended by Sir Thomas More, the home of music hall star Arthur Lloyd and a shop once run by America's first millionaire, John Jacob Astor, were also demolished.

A description of all the buildings and streets lost during this period would fill a book of its own and it should be noted that the demolition of some areas – the slums of Falcon Court in the Borough and the Old Nichol in Shoreditch, for example – was not mourned by anybody. Nevertheless, the fact that the authorities (or private individuals, for that matter) could demolish virtually any building they wished with impunity was a matter of grave concern for many people in the decades that followed. Indeed, during the interwar years, 41–42 Cloth Fair may well have fallen prey to the whims of developers had it not been for the passion and perseverance of two remarkable men who proved to be the saviours of not only the house but also many other iconic buildings in London.

13

SAVING LONDON

Seely, Paget and
the Second World War

Edward Markham's cutlery workshop finally closed its doors at 41–42 Cloth Fair in 1927 and the building subsequently stood empty and neglected for almost two years. It might well have suffered the same ignominious fate as the rest of old Cloth Fair had it not been purchased in December 1929 by two young and enterprising architects named John Seely and Paul Paget. Both men had a fascination for the hidden history of London and resolved to peel away the layers of the property's recent past to reveal its lost secrets.

Paul Paget was already well acquainted with Cloth Fair and its surrounds. His grandfather, James Paget, a surgeon at St Bartholomew's Hospital, had been involved in the restoration of St Bartholomew the Great back in the 1880s and his father, the Reverend Henry Luke Paget, had retained the family's links with both the hospital and the church. Indeed, soon after his son moved into 41–42 Cloth Fair, the reverend and his wife, Elma, took the house at No. 39, describing it as 'near St Paul's and St Bartholomew's – places of precious memories'.

Despite his familiarity with the area, Paul Paget did not persuade John Seely to move to Cloth Fair for purely personal reasons. At the time, the pair were planning to specialise in an architectural discipline that was decidedly unfashionable – the preservation and restoration of old buildings. The modern preoccupation with retaining Britain's architectural heritage is such a recent phenomenon that it is amazing that so many old buildings are still standing. Right up to the late 1940s, freeholders were permitted to do virtually whatever they liked with their property, unless it was of national importance or prehistoric. Consequently, every town in the land can today lay claim to an interesting, historic or simply beautiful property that was demolished at the whim of a previous owner.

The first seeds of change were sown in 1882 when responsibility for Britain's heritage passed to the government's Office of Works, which compiled a schedule of sixty-eight, mainly prehistoric, sites they deemed worthy of statutory protection. A decade later, a group of history enthusiasts, including the social reformer Octavia Hill and artist Sir Frederic Leighton, founded the 'National Trust for Places of Historic Interest or Natural Beauty'. The trust acted as guardians for large, rural sites (their initial acquisition comprised 5 acres of Welsh clifftop) and individual buildings, the first of which was a pre-Reformation clergy house at Alfriston in Sussex. However, the trust did not have sufficient funds to buy every threatened property.

The publicity generated by the destruction of Cloth Fair in 1913–14, coupled with the demise of numerous other historic houses in the capital, finally prompted the government to bestow new powers on its Office of Works, including the capacity to preserve lesser sites that, while not nationally important, contributed to the nation's history.

The legislation came just in time to save 75 Dean Street, a handsome townhouse linked to the celebrated artist James Thornhill. In a leader article about the property's preservation, *The Times* summed up the public's changing perception of old buildings by noting, '75 Dean Street has a charm greater than any due to mere personal associations. It represents an epoch.'

It was during this sea change in attitude that John Seely (born 1899) and Paul Paget (born 1901) were educated, and the revelation that ordinary buildings could unlock the secret history of Britain made a lasting impression on both of them. By the time their worlds collided at university at the end of the First World War, their respective obsessions with the past had been compounded by a shared loss of brothers on the battlefield. Paul Paget later described their meeting as a 'marriage of two minds'.

After graduating, Seely and Paget's first forays into restoration centred on their own property at Cloth Fair and at the sixteenth-century home of John Seely's father, Lord Mottistone, on the Isle of Wight. These two projects gave them invaluable experience of the unexpected challenges associated with preserving old buildings without the added pressure of having to deal with an anxious or impatient client. Their work at Cloth Fair was particularly rewarding, and by the autumn of 1930 all of the property's Victorian additions had been removed to reveal a building that would not have looked unfamiliar to the house's eighteenth-century residents. The only notable exception was the ground floor, which served as their architects' studio, rather than a draper's shop. That October, Seely and Paget announced in the press that they had moved into their newly refurbished premises and could be contacted by telephoning National 1191. However, business was initially slow and so they temporarily devoted their creative energies to a charitable project outside their front door.

Although the churchyard at St Bartholomew the Great had been cleaned up, it still presented a rather grim sight. The last burials had taken place back in 1863 and the graveyard had henceforth taken on a dejected air. Never short of money and generous with it, Seely and Paget offered to fund and oversee its clearance which would, of course, improve the view from the windows of their home. Work began quickly and soon most of the upright gravestones had been moved to the perimeter walls, with the exception of one memorial on which, according to local tradition, sixpences were placed for twenty parish widows on Good Friday each year. After the churchyard had been cleared, benches were installed and the site was planted with trees, which are still standing today.

The architects' sterling work resulted in John Seely being invited as guest of honour to the 1933 prizegiving at St Bartholomew's School, which stood in Red Lion Passage, behind the church. While delivering his speech, he cheekily employed some artistic licence to bring the history of the school alive, telling the children that the classrooms had to be moved from their original location on the church's upper floor because the pupils habitually dropped pencils onto the heads of the congregation below.

Soon after the prizegiving, Seely and Paget received their first major architectural commission. In the summer of 1933 Stephen Courtauld, a member of a wealthy textile dynasty, and his wife Virginia began hunting for a semi-rural home within striking distance of central London. Eltham Palace, a Crown property standing dejected in the south London suburbs, proved ideal and the Courtaulds snapped up a ninety-nine-year lease to the property on the understanding that they would be permitted to remodel its nineteenth-century parts. They subsequently commissioned Seely and Paget (whom they probably knew socially) to design a strikingly modern home while retaining as much of the fourteenth-century palace as possible. The result was an art deco masterpiece that showcased the very latest in technology. The living quarters, including the 'bedroom' of the Courtauld's beloved pet lemur, Math Jongg, were centrally heated; synchronous clocks installed throughout the building were regulated by the mains supply and an integrated speaker system allowed music to be broadcast in the ground-floor rooms during the couple's regular society parties.

Wisely, Seely and Paget employed the services of Sir Charles Peers, the Office of Works' chief inspector of ancient monuments, to assist them with the restoration of the older parts of the complex. This was a masterstroke as it not only silenced their critics, but also ensured that Eltham Palace was sympathetically brought back to life. The success of the project led to two more lucrative and challenging commissions: the restoration of the College of the Venerable Bede's Chapel in the University of Durham and the design of the Chapel of St Francis at Frodsham Hall in Devon.

However, just as the architectural practice was beginning to flourish, political crisis in mainland Europe intervened. On 2 August 1939, a notice appeared in *The Times' Court Circular* announcing that 'the Hon. John Seely and Mr Paul Paget will be absent from 41 Cloth Fair during the month of August, owing to their embodiment for a month's training in the Auxiliary Air Force. Correspondence will be dealt with as promptly as circumstances allow.' Just over four weeks later, Britain declared war on Germany.

By the time the Second World War began, London was already braced for an aerial onslaught. During the 1939 summer holiday, parents in the city had been informed that the government planned a mass evacuation of school-age children and a blackout was tested on 10 August. It was repeated when Germany invaded Poland on 1 September and remained in force for the next six years.

In the meantime, newspapers published instructions to civilians, warning that as soon as they heard the wail of the air-raid sirens, they should run for cover and not emerge until the 'raiders passed' signal was sounded. If poison gas had been dropped, they would hear the ominous noise of rattles followed by the chime of hand bells once the gas had cleared. Even if there was no imminent threat of an air raid, civilians were advised:

> Keep off the streets as much as possible. To expose yourself unnecessarily adds to the danger. Carry a gas mask with you always and make sure that you and every member of your household, especially children able to run about, have on them their names and addresses, clearly written.

Adding to the prevailing air of anxiety, all sports meetings were prohibited, theatres and cinemas closed until further notice and food rationing was introduced. At Smithfield, only the poultry and general provisions markets remained open for business and retail butchers were advised to apply at their local police station for the address of the nearest emergency depot. Across the way at St Bartholomew's Hospital, most of the wards were closed and the patients and staff were evacuated to St Albans in Hertfordshire.

For those who could not or would not leave London, the local authorities constructed public air-raid shelters and supplied citizens with corrugated steel with which to build Anderson Shelters (named after the head of air-raid precautions, Sir John Anderson). However, with little outside space at their disposal, the residents of Cloth Fair had to rely on basements and other subterranean spaces for shelter. At first, they were prohibited from using Tube stations on the grounds that they would impede the trains and, bizarrely, they might turn into a race of troglodytes, fearful of venturing aboveground, even when it was safe to do so. This peculiar ban was hastily lifted in the second year of the war.

At first, the manic preparations for enemy bombing raids appeared to be a waste of time and money. Almost as soon as the prime minister had finished his solemn announcement of war on 3 September 1939 air-raid sirens had wailed across London, but it quickly turned out to be a false alarm and for the following seven months the skies over the city remained quiet. Desperately missing their evacuated children, parents began to bring them back home, but on 25 August 1940 Germany delivered a blistering attack on the metropolis, devastating docks at Poplar, destroying vital railway lines and obliterating houses.

The raid was a taste of things to come. On 7 September, the Luftwaffe launched an eight-month blitzkrieg on London, designed to annihilate the RAF and bomb the inhabitants into submission. During this terrifying period, John Seely served as an Emergency Works Officer, tasked with surveying bomb damage as it occurred. The exhausting nature of this dangerous work was described in detail by one of his colleagues:

Little sleep was obtainable and the only rest was on the hard floor under the stairs, in the cellar, in the Anderson shelter in the garden or in the public shelters and Tubes ... The morning brought cold extremities and sore sleepless eyes and the excursion to work was subjected to cheerfully borne and constantly changing circuitous journeys and hold-ups ... The day was punctuated with all-clears, with the accompaniment of gunfire and bomb explosions, which never seemed quite so terrifying as during the long dark hours. The journey home was by ill-lit or completely unlit buses and trams and the walk from the station was through quiet, black streets with the ever-present menace overhead, turning up again for the night's performance.

Cloth Fair's proximity to the centre of the City meant that the inhabitants witnessed the ferocity of the Blitz at frighteningly close quarters.
On 11 September 1940, a device fell into the basement of the nurses'
block at St Bartholomew's Hospital, destroying part of the building and
fracturing the gas and water mains. The hospital was hit for a second
time on 23 September, when the Biological Laboratory was destroyed
along with the Anatomical Theatre, the Medical Theatre, the Lecture
Attendant's Room and the Photographic Department.

However, the district had worse in store. On 27 December 1940,
the streets immediately north of St Paul's Cathedral were subjected
to a massive aerial onslaught. District surveyor, Mr C.C. Knowles,
witnessed the aftermath and wrote:

> A considerable area north of St Paul's was devastated. The Cathedral escaped
> but practically the whole of the soft goods trade of the City including
> adjoining areas in Holborn, Finsbury and Shoreditch went up in flames.
> Other trades suffered also, the well-known lane of Paternoster Row, the
> home of books both sacred and secular, could not be saved and millions of
> books were lost. On the night of the great conflagration newspapers could,
> by the light of the fires, be easily read in the suburbs.

The Dean of St Paul's, Anthony Heap, surveyed the scene a few days
afterwards and described what he saw in his diary:

> Around St Paul's and Cheapside and for a good half mile north of that area
> there are few buildings left intact. Every street has its huge gaping wounds,
> gutted buildings and choked roadways. The odour of charred wood still
> lingers in the air. Never have I seen such widespread ruin and desolation.
> The damage in the West End is negligible by comparison with this – a
> harrowing sight.

The final major Blitz offensive occurred on 10 May 1941 when 500 Luftwaffe bombers appeared in the skies over London. The district situation report recorded:

> The alert sounded at 22.58 and continued until 05.50. Bombs began to fall within half an hour and there were two periods of great intensity, between 00.30 and 1.15 and 03.00 and 04.30. Large numbers of high explosives and incendiary bombs were dropped and eleven parachute mines, seven of which failed to explode. A sustained attack was made on the docks area and railway termini and several direct hits and fires were reported.

During the raid several hospitals were targeted, including St Bartholomew's which sustained severe damage to its student wing. A bomb also fell just outside the precincts of the hospital on Giltspur Street, blowing out nearby windows and damaging the roof of the pathology block. Luckily, no one in the area was killed but the inhabitants of buildings elsewhere were not so fortunate. The London Fire Brigade later reported that at least 1,436 Londoners lost their lives and thousands more required medical assistance in the aftermath of the raid.

Following the devastating onslaught on 10 May, the Luftwaffe turned their attention towards eastern Europe, but sporadic attacks on London continued, especially 'tip and run' raids where bombers would suddenly appear, drop their deadly cargo and then disappear as quickly as they had arrived. The worst of these occurred in January 1944 when Germany launched Operation Steinbock in retaliation for RAF attacks. Known as the 'Baby Blitz', the raids were typically brief strikes that occurred under cover of darkness. The last Operation Steinbock raid on London occurred on 22 April 1944, after which the enemy began targeting port towns on the south coast in an attempt to scupper preparations for an Allied invasion of the European mainland.

Although Germany had thus far succeeded in devastating large areas, London was by no means beaten. However, a new and more terrifying device was about to be unleashed on the city. On 13 June 1944, the first V-1 flying bomb fell on the capital at Grove Road, Mile End, killing six people and injuring several more. At first the authorities thought that one of the Luftwaffe's planes had crashed but it soon became apparent that the machine was in fact a 'pilotless aircraft'. Over the summer of 1944, many more of these devices dropped on London sites, including Bartholomew Close and the nearby crossroads at the junction of Long Lane and Aldersgate Street. To many of the inhabitants, the V-1 bombs were the most frightening element of the war. Harry Martin, who lived with his parents near the Royal Docks during the war recalled:

> We called them Doodlebugs because they made a whining sound like insects. You knew they were about to drop when the noise stopped and we'd all stand there, frozen, waiting for it to fall. It is awful to admit, but it was a relief when you heard the explosion because you knew it had missed you.

The Allies finally managed to capture the V-1 launch sites along the French and Dutch coastlines in September 1944 and, in triumph, government minister Duncan Sandys assured the press that the campaign on London was finally over.

The very next day, the first V-2 rocket hit the city. This final, formidable weapon was the world's first ballistic missile and could travel at three times the speed of sound, thus giving no warning of its presence until it was too late to run for cover. On 8 March 1945, a V-2 device fell on Smithfield Market in the middle of the morning, killing or injuring 448 traders inside. Germany may well have wreaked more havoc in London had its military might not faded. The last V-2 attack on London occurred at the end of March 1945 and, on 8 May, Hitler's forces unconditionally surrendered to the Allies.

As the threat of more air raids ended, London could finally take stock of the devastation they had caused. The reports made sobering reading: 19,415 citizens had lost their lives and another 38,716 had been seriously injured. In addition, 52,257 buildings had been destroyed (including 2,884 in the City of London) and another 17,171 had been damaged beyond repair.

Although Cloth Fair escaped any direct hits, the surrounding area had been damaged beyond recognition. Virtually all the buildings on the west side of Aldersgate Street, from Long Lane to Little Britain, had been reduced to rubble. The V-1 flying bomb that had fallen on Bartholomew Close had destroyed the houses and offices on its southern edge along with the whole of Montague Court, a little road that ran behind them. Parts of St Bartholomew's Hospital lay in ruins and the church school at which John Seely had awarded prizes in 1933 was so badly damaged that it was condemned. The V-2 rocket at Smithfield had not only demolished part of the market but also damaged the buildings on the opposite side of the road beyond repair. However, the worst of the district's devastation lay to the south of Cloth Fair, from Newgate Street to St Paul's Churchyard. This area, including the historic bookshops and publishers at Paternoster Row and the ancient warehouses of the Smithfield butchers, had been razed to the ground.

Throughout the war, London's economy had somehow managed to remain afloat. However, if the city was to retain its status as a financial capital in peacetime, it had to be reconstructed quickly. Mercifully, provision for the rebuilding of London had been put in place back in November 1940 when the government announced that all owners of damaged property were to receive compensation after the conflict ceased. In March 1941, a War Damage Commission was set up to handle claims, which were submitted by completing a form that was sent to regional assessors, who calculated how much compensation was due. Occupants of bombed property could also claim for furniture, clothing and other personal effects 'lost to enemy action', and were compensated on a scale of £200 for a single person, an extra £100 for a married couple and an additional £25 for each child under the age of 16.

In May 1941, War Damage Insurance was also made available for the loss of moveable goods, be they domestic or commercial. These items could be insured on the terms of £1 per cent up to the value of £2,000; £1 10s per cent for the next £1,000; and £2 per cent for the following £7,000. Generally, both insurance and compensation sums were deferred until after the war for obvious reasons, on the understanding that interest of 2.5 per cent a year would accrue, starting from the date the goods or property were damaged. However, immediate settlement was made in the case of some businesses if the Board of Trade deemed that the immediate replacement of their lost property, whether real or personal, was in the public interest.

The war damage insurance and compensation schemes understandably took time to process and consequently the rebuilding of war-torn London did not really get going until 1947. However, when finance eventually began to filter through, Paul Paget and John Seely (who had now succeeded his father as Lord Mottistone) were presented with an unprecedented opportunity to restore some of London's most historic and iconic buildings.

The architects' involvement in the restoration of London began in 1947 when the firm of Seely & Paget was commissioned to oversee the rebuilding of Lambeth Palace, the official London home of the Archbishop of Canterbury. This extraordinary complex of ancient buildings had stood overlooking the Thames for over 800 years but had suffered terribly at the hands of the Luftwaffe. During the Blitz, the property had suffered a direct hit from incendiaries, which gutted Lollard's Tower and destroyed almost half of the main chapel's handsome, hammer-beam roof, shattering all its windows. Today, scorch marks from the conflagration can still be seen on the marble floor. Lambeth Palace struggled on after the attack, moving services to the subterranean crypt, but in 1944 the archbishop's living quarters were also bombed, reducing the state dining room to rubble and causing severe damage to the adjacent rooms.

The intimidating amount of work involved in restoring Lambeth Palace was made more pressing by the fact that the incumbent archbishop, Geoffrey Fisher, was determined to hold the 1948 Lambeth Conference there. Consequently, Seely & Paget had to devise a restoration plan quickly, starting with the bomb-blasted chapel. Their greatest task at this revered place of worship was the repair of the hammer-beam roof, which was accomplished by skilfully matching homegrown oak to the surviving section and replacing all the cracked slates with tiles.

From the outset, the architects viewed the work as a chance to return the chapel to its seventeenth-century state. Consequently, a range of splintered, eighteenth-century bookcases were not replaced and the floor was lowered to its original level, allowing a blocked doorway in the south-west corner to be reopened for the first time in centuries. Even the shattered remains of the windows were preserved as much as possible, with the surviving fragments of glass set into a new oriel.

Once the public areas of Lambeth Palace were rebuilt, the architects moved on to the archbishop's private quarters, which had to accommodate his family of six sons, his sister-in-law and visiting clerics. With most of the budget spent on the chapel and Lollard's Tower, work on the rooms was necessarily functional rather than aesthetic and the installation of a lift caused particular problems. Paul Paget later recalled:

> The lift … was of somewhat massive design to accord with the nineteenth century architect Blore's neo-Gothic details and suffered some teething troubles in those early, post-war years. I recall that on our apologising for another of the all too frequent breakdowns, Archbishop Fisher, at once the most stimulating and most patient of clients, reassured us by saying that he really rather enjoyed a failure between the floors since remembering always to take his pipe and a book with him.

The publicity that accompanied the restoration of Lambeth Palace ensured that Seely & Paget received a raft of enquiries from the guardians of other wrecked historic buildings. In 1948, John Seely was appointed architect to the Dean & Chapter of Westminster Abbey and tasked with rebuilding their bomb-damaged canonical houses in the Little Cloister. Although this project was by no means as daunting as the Lambeth Palace restoration, later events would show that it was privately significant for the two architects.

Realising that the Little Cloister restorations would take up much of his time over the coming months, Seely decided to resign his position on the City's Common Council as representative of the ward of Farringdon Without. However, he was soon replaced by his partner, Paul Paget, who secured the post after a 'keen fight' with several eminent rivals including Mr F.A. Hoare, the managing director of Hoare's Bank, who counted two Lord Mayors among his ancestors.

Soon after Paget joined the Common Council, his office at Cloth Fair was contacted by the Reverend Philip 'Tubby' Clayton, the founder of the international Christian movement Toc H. The reverend's church, All Hallows by the Tower, had been ravaged by bombs, which had reduced the above ground parts to little more than an empty shell. However, its role as the guild church of Toc H and historic links to US President John Quincy Adams and Pennsylvania founding father, William Penn (who were both baptised there), resulted in a flood of donations from across the Atlantic.

With considerable funds at their disposal, Seely & Paget were able to rebuild All Hallows using steel donated by the residents of Boston, Texas, and timber provided by patrons in Canada. By midsummer 1949, the church's north aisle had been restored, revealing its precious collection of medieval brasses that had miraculously survived the Blitz, thanks to sheets of asbestos which had been placed over them as protection from fire.

With All Hallows now ready for worship, a special service was held on 16 July in the presence of Queen Mary. *The Times* reported, 'The area of Tower Hill was gaily decorated with flags and bunting in honour of this occasion and throughout the evening, the church's new carolling of 18 bells sounded gladly across the scene.'

In addition to restoration work on London's most precious buildings, Seely & Paget were also responsible for the creation of several war memorials. While work at All Hallows was still under way, they designed a table for St Martins in the Fields on which a Book of Remembrance, containing the names of nearly 2,500 members of the Reconnaissance Corps who lost their lives in the conflict, was to be displayed. Closer to their home at Cloth Fair, at St Bartholomew the Great they installed a new altar and a memorial to the Auxiliary Air Force Squadron in which they had both served.

Seely & Paget's burgeoning restoration skills were also employed at St Bartholomew the Less, which stood within the precincts of the hospital. This attractive little church had sustained severe damage when the nurses' quarters were bombed and looked a sorry sight immediately after the war. However, using their work at Lambeth Palace as a model, the two architects painstakingly returned the interior to its seventeenth-century state, lighting it with Dutch candelabra and redecorating the walls in a scheme of white, grey and gold. The windows, which had been completely destroyed, were replaced by stained-glass artist Hugh Easton, a regular collaborator, who lit the nave with handsome memorials to the medical staff who lost their lives in the service of their country. Above the altar, he designed a striking, three-light window containing figures of the Virgin and Child, St Luke (patron saint of physicians), St Bartholomew and the hospital's founder, Rahere.

As the work at St Bartholomew the Less got going, Seely & Paget received a commission from nearby Charterhouse, a fourteenth-century monastic building which lay a short distance north of Cloth Fair. This ancient edifice had been bombed in 1941 leaving its Great Hall open to the elements, a fine Elizabethan staircase smashed to pieces and the residents' accommodation uninhabitable. Work on this restoration project began in 1949 and proved to be one of their most interesting post-war commissions. As the rubble was moved away, the stone walls of the original Carthusian monastery were revealed alongside other long-lost treasures, including the coffin of its founder, Walter de Manny. The architects recommended that the monastery's outline should be preserved in a garden and, when the building was reopened by the Archbishop of Canterbury in December 1956, *The Times* noted, 'The most impressive view ... is in Master's Court, the centre of which now forms a small grass lawn on which are marked the lines of the original monastery walls.'

While Seely and Paget were busily engaged in restoration projects, their regular excursions around London and involvement with the Common Council caused them to worry that post-war rebuilding was spiralling out of control. Overwhelmed with the task in hand, the authorities were inclined to pass plans without giving them sufficient attention and there was a real danger that the historic character of some quarters of the city would be completely obliterated.

The development causing the most controversy during this period was the proposed Bucklersbury House, a fourteen-storey concrete and steel edifice that was about to be built on Queen Victoria Street. Seely and Paget were horrified by its brutal architecture and also realised that its erection would inevitably pave the way for more towering, concrete monstrosities. Unable to win support for rejecting the plan at the Corporation of London, John Seely appealed to the House of Lords to intervene. In his speech, he humorously explained that he was not making a mountain out of a molehill. In fact, Bucklersbury House was the very reverse of a molehill due to its immense size. More seriously, he explained that the London Building Acts prescribed that new developments should only reach 100ft above ground level but the height of the proposed skyscraper was 170ft – a full 60ft higher than the main roofs of St Paul's Cathedral. 'Is the dome of St Paul's no longer to dominate the scene and are the spires and towers of the City and Westminster no longer to grace the incomparable skyline?' he entreated.

In the event, John Seely's impassioned plea to the House of Lords did not stop the development of Bucklersbury House and in July 1953 he gave a speech at the London Society (of which he was chairman) warning, 'The London we know and love is threatened on all sides.' Admitting there was little use in fighting wealthy developers and adding that he had no desire to turn the city into a 'museum piece', he suggested that the London Society should henceforth do their best to ensure that new building projects did not irrevocably harm their environment's historic charm and character.

While John Seely led the charge to preserve the city's heritage, his partner endeavoured to highlight the longstanding problem of central London's decreasing residential population. As already discussed, the number of people living in the City had been in steady decline since the late 1800s. However, the Second World War had escalated the exodus. By the 1950s, some parishes, including St Bartholomew the Great, had tiny communities and this contributed to the problems associated with new developments as there were simply too few residents to raise a strong objection.

In April 1953, Paul Paget used his position on the Court of Common Council to suggest that the privilege of living in the City should be more widely shared in order to provide a 'healthy, mixed community', adding that there were surely numerous businesses who would find it convenient to have employees within easy reach. As a result, the council formed a special committee to investigate the prospect of building affordable homes in the Square Mile. Their findings were revealed at a meeting in October and, much to Paul Paget's disappointment, the response was not favourable. Sir Cullum Welch, the committee's chairman, concluded that, in view of the high rents chargeable on flats of the quality Paget suggested, he could not advise the council to enter into any such scheme. The committee's findings were backed up by Councilman Mr W.E. Sykes, who, referring to Paget's proposal to erect mixed-use buildings, painted a bleak picture of office workers contending with the noise of crying babies and blaring radios.

Exasperated but undeterred, Paul Paget took up his pen and fired off a letter to *The Times*, which read:

As a City resident of over 20 years' standing, may I once again enter the lists in support of the provision of some living accommodation in the Square Mile? Whenever this question has been raised – and it has often been the subject of vigorous discussion – the issue, so it seems to me, has been obscured by conflicting opinions which need to be segregated, and each considered quite separately, if any logical conclusion is to be reached. First, it has been suggested that there is in fact no demand for such accommodation. My own experience has proved the very opposite. The few habitations which I happen to control in the City have never for a single day been unoccupied, and any rumour that one is likely to become vacant evokes a host of enquiries. Secondly, the view has been expressed that the City is an unhealthy place for residents and that the more salubrious suburbs are to be preferred. Recently published statistics lend no support to this contention so far as London is concerned and members of my own staff to whom we have been able to offer accommodation nearby have frequently confirmed the improvement in their health and energy resulting from the avoidance of the racket of daily travel under rush-hour conditions. Thirdly, we are told that every square foot of the 'Golden Mile' will be required for commercial use and that the Corporation of London are reluctant to approve plans for residential purposes. The slow tempo of redevelopment under the restrictive conditions of the last ten years has, I submit, proved nothing conclusive in this regard, and there is no reason to suppose that commercial demand for sites just outside the perimeter will exclude some housing development hereabouts. The Corporation have shown no inclination whatsoever to turn down applications for residential use except in the riparian strip reserved for waterside commerce. Lastly, the financial argument is employed to demonstrate that it is quite impossible to develop residentially at economic rents. But has this aspect ever been as fully explored as it deserves by way of mixed development with a variety of uses, commercial, light industrial, and civic, incorporating some living accommodation adjacent to the open spaces which must in any case be provided, and on the upper floors of the higher blocks at rentals to suit a diversity of demand?

The post-war campaigns of John Seely and Paul Paget clearly demonstrate their passion for London, and in 1954 they met a kindred spirit in the form of John Betjeman, an ardent supporter of the struggle to preserve London's history. The architects were introduced to Betjeman by their mutual friend, George Barnes, and on discovering he was looking for a London pied-á-terre, they offered him a property they had purchased at 43 Cloth Fair for an eminently reasonable rent of £200 per annum.

The living accommodation was by no means grand, comprising a sitting room overlooking St Bartholomew's Churchyard and a tiny kitchen on the first floor, with a small bathroom and bedroom above. Nevertheless, the location was perfect for Betjeman's regular sorties around the city and he promptly moved in, papering the narrow stairway with William Morris willow pattern – a design he used at every house he lived in. His biographer, A. N. Wilson, noted:

> This was the first London base of his own which Betjeman ever had. A Londoner through and through, he had hitherto either lived with his parents, or as a lodger in other people's flats and houses … If Osbert Lancaster was right to say that Betjeman was married, had a mistress and was able to lead the life of a bachelor, then 43 Cloth Fair was what made this possible.

John Betjeman remained at 43 Cloth Fair until the onset of Parkinson's disease forced him to move away. During this time, he acquired a habit of visiting the sick at St Bartholomew's Hospital where Ward Sister Mary Bland recalled, 'John used to come and have coffee in my room every Thursday morning and then go round and visit the patients in my ward. He was able to make all the patients laugh – he was a wonderful mimic.'

Back at 41–42 Cloth Fair, Seely and Paget's longstanding battle to save London's old churches received a boost when the Inspection of Churches Measure obtained royal assent. This meant that historic places of worship throughout the country had to be inspected by an architect at least once every five years to ensure that any structural issues were dealt with quickly. Ivor Bulmer-Thomas, the chairman of the Historic Churches Preservation Trust, declared that 'if the measure is loyally accepted, it could be the biggest revolution that has taken place in the care of churches'. However, John Seely issued a word of warning that the atmosphere required to keep ancient buildings in good condition was not necessarily a comfortable one. 'Though we rather like it, the old, musty smell of country churches is a sure sign that they are damp because of stagnant air, and need ventilation,' he told *The Times*. 'Unfortunately, the things that people like least – cold and draughts – are the best preservatives of old churches.'

Probably the most important 'old church' in need of attention at the time was St Paul's Cathedral. During the war, this magnificent edifice had been badly damaged and, in 1956, the architect William Holford presented a plan to the Corporation of London that promised to transform it. Holford's overall intention was to improve the setting of the cathedral and ease the almost constant traffic congestion outside by diverting vehicles away from the road encircling the churchyard. This area would then be grassed and paved to form an impressive forecourt to St Paul's' principal entrance, with gardens featuring a large, marble fountain created along its southern wall. In addition, the forlorn, war-torn remains of Paternoster Row would be redeveloped into a new public square accessed via Sir Christopher Wren's Temple Bar, an old gateway into the City, which had been languishing in Theobalds Park, Hertfordshire, since 1880.

Holford's plan was seized upon by John Seely, who told the press:

As one who has lived and worked within 600 yards of the cathedral for 25 years, I think I can claim to know every brick and stone in the neighbourhood, although now it is perhaps more appropriate to refer to every willow herb and buddleia in the ruins. Day by day and year by year I have wondered and hoped that an acceptable plan would be produced and to my mind, it has now arrived.

However, not everyone shared this opinion and the project soon became mired in arguments, which Seely unavoidably got drawn into after he was appointed 'surveyor to the fabric of St Paul's' in January 1957.

While John Seely attempted to expedite William Holford's plan for the cathedral, Paul Paget got involved with a very different but equally important post-war restoration project. During the conflict, bombing raids had flattened much of the area now known as the Barbican, but as the derelict buildings were cleared, a large section of the Roman city wall was revealed running from Falcon Square to the churchyard of St Giles, Cripplegate. The ruins were eagerly surveyed by Paget, who declared:

Quite a small amount of clearance and repair work, together with the recovery of original levels to expose the ancient masonry to its full height, would effect a transformation to the great enjoyment of Londoners and their visitors who come in ever increasing numbers and eagerness to explore all that is extant of our historic past.

Unlike the St Paul's project, the plan to publicly display this section of the Roman wall received little opposition and the Corporation of London promised that work would be carried out without delay. However, by December 1957 so little had been accomplished that Paget asked his partner to produce a perspective drawing showing how the wall would look when restored to its full height. The illustration was reprinted in several newspapers and created such public interest that the works were expedited. Today, the part of the ancient wall accidentally uncovered by the Blitz forms a fascinating tourist attraction, visited by thousands of people every year.

Back at St Paul's Cathedral, the restoration plans remained contentious. The redevelopment of the churchyard and Paternoster Row eventually began in 1961 but only partially realised William Holford's vision. The revised open space at Paternoster Square was especially unsuccessful, with Lord Mayor Robert Finch describing it as being surrounded by 'ghastly, monolithic constructions without definition or character'.

The square was eventually completely remodelled by Sir William Whitfield and reopened in 2003. The following year, Temple Bar was finally rescued from exile in Theobalds Park and installed as its grand entrance. Debbie Morris, who was well acquainted with the structure in its former location, said:

> I was so pleased to see Temple Bar back in London. My school cross-country team used to run past it when it was in Theobalds Park and it was a sad sight, covered in graffiti and dirt. There was a legend that the statues at the top would move if you looked at them long enough. The gateway looks so different now it's been cleaned and rebuilt next to St Paul's.

In the meantime, John Seely continued his work at the cathedral, designing the Chapel of the Order of the British Empire in the crypt and a new carved oak and lime pulpit under the dome. He

and Paget's architectural practice continued to win important commissions and in 1960 they designed new buildings for Westminster
College, the teacher training foundation of the Methodist Church,
thus maintaining the astonishing link between 41–42 Cloth Fair and
the Wesley brothers.

Their restoration work also thrived, and in 1961 they rebuilt
St Andrew's Church in Holborn, which had been demolished in an
air raid some twenty years before. The new church remained true to
the previous Wren structure and incorporated the font, pulpit and
organ from the old Foundling Hospital, which was originally in the
same parish.

Although Seely & Paget made a huge contribution to saving
London's heritage from post-war destruction, not all their campaigns
were successful. A notable example of this was the ill-fated attempt to
keep the historic Coal Exchange on Lower Thames Street. This fine
example of early Victorian architecture had stood redundant since the
nationalisation of Britain's coal industry and by the late 1950s a pressing
need to widen the adjacent road brought forth the threat of demolition. At a meeting in March 1961 attended by John Seely, Paul Paget
and John Betjeman, a committee was set up (with Seely and Betjeman
at the helm) to devise a way to preserve the building. Campaigner Sir
Albert Richardson suggested, 'The City authorities in their blindness
and in their zeal for a new road have overlooked the French idea of a
dual road placing the Coal Exchange on an island site.' This gave John
Seely an idea and he quickly drew up a scheme whereby the road
could be enlarged to the required width by installing raised pavements.
However, although the British Theatre Association offered to give the
Coal Exchange a new purpose as a museum, all plans for its salvation
were rejected and this elegant and historically important building was
demolished in 1962.

Shortly after the wrecking ball ploughed into the stone façade of the Coal Exchange, John Seely grew gravely ill. He died at St Bartholomew's Hospital on 18 January 1963 and London lost one of its most dedicated and passionate champions. His obituary in *The Times* listed some of the numerous projects and campaigns he had been involved in since the end of the war, noting, 'Whether on the winning or losing side in any controversy, and whether in the company of those whose tastes accorded with his own or not, he was always tolerant and good humoured and delightful company.'

Seely's funeral took place at a church near his family home on the Isle of Wight on 24 January 1963. Three years later, Paul Paget erected a touching memorial to him in a niche of one of the clergy houses they had restored together at Westminster Abbey's Little Cloister back in 1948. It comprised a statue of St Catherine standing above a plaque flanked by two seahorses and bore the inscription, 'John Mottistone. This is a sign of love and sadness. P.E.P. 1966'.

14

PRESERVING THE PAST FOR THE FUTURE

John Seely was succeeded as surveyor of the fabric of St Paul's by Paul Paget, who resolved to carry out his partner's wish to restore the cathedral's exterior to its original, gleaming grandeur. The two architects had debated the pros and cons of cleaning the façade back in 1962 after reading a letter in *The Times* that complained of St Paul's' filthy appearance. After assessing the amount of work involved, they initially dismissed the project as prohibitively expensive, but shortly afterwards John Seely received an intriguing message inviting him to call at the Ionian Bank. He duly fixed an appointment while Paget wondered what the bank (with which they had had no previous dealings) wanted. He later recalled:

Imagine then the excitement which prevailed when my partner returned with a firm offer from the bank to finance the cleaning of the whole west front and towers [of St Paul's] on the single condition that until the work was finished, the names of the benefactors should not be disclosed.

With finance in place, 'the biggest spring-clean in history' began in May 1964 with the lower sections of the cathedral being cleaned first, using nothing but water and 'elbow grease'. The work removed centuries of dirt and soot which had turned the building black, revealing the intricate details of the carved stonework along with the graffiti of past visitors, some of which dated back to the early 1700s. Fascinated by these ancient etchings, Paul Paget admitted:

> The italic script of the bygone signatories is a good deal more decorative than the scribble with which, I regret to say, our present day visitors are wont to disfigure the walls. [In recent months] such inappropriate slogans as 'Up the Beatles!' have appeared.

The cleaning of St Paul's also dislodged a number of cloth-covered balls, thought to be around 100 years old, that had been nestling in the carved acanthus foliage atop one of the Corinthian capitals. Quite how the balls got there was a mystery, but Paget suspected that the culprits were choir boys who bet on 'who could throw the highest before hitting their high notes in the cathedral'.

After work on the lower part of St Paul's was complete, the contractors moved upwards to the dome, which desperately needed repair to damage caused by shrapnel and shocks from nearby explosions during the war. The resplendent cathedral was finally unveiled to the public in June 1968, when the scaffolding that had covered it for the best part of four years was finally dismantled.

While the cleaning of St Paul's was in progress, Paul Paget had grown even more apprehensive about the fate of London's architectural heritage. One of his most pressing concerns was the large number of war-damaged buildings that were still languishing in an unrepaired state. The foremost of these was Carlton House Terrace, a handsome, stucco-fronted range of buildings overlooking St James's Park, the fate of which had been debated since the early 1950s, mainly because no one knew what to do with it.

The matter had even been discussed in the House of Lords, where Lord Mancroft caused a furore by calling the terrace's creator, John Nash, 'an inspired jerry builder'. Lord Morrison, the parliamentary secretary for the Ministry of Works, added that the building's owners (the Crown Commissioners) had considered all possible uses for Carlton House Terrace but there were difficulties in converting it into a club, embassy, flats or a hotel. In fact, the only feasible proposal in recent years involved its complete demolition.

Eventually, the problems associated with leasing Carlton House Terrace to clubs and societies were overcome and it was preserved. However, other equally historic and important buildings remained under threat, especially disused churches. In a bid to stop these important reminders of bygone communities disappearing, Paul Paget helped to establish the Redundant Churches Fund in 1969. The charity was inundated with donations but still the Church Commissioners, who owned the buildings, refused to have many of them repaired. In response, the Friendless Churches Trust was formed so the properties could be purchased. Today, the trust owns fifty former places of worship in England and Wales, which are preserved for the local people.

Paul Paget's tireless campaigning, combined with his architectural practice and duties at St Paul's, left him precious little spare time. However, whenever his diary permitted, he left London for the bucolic surroundings of Northrepps Hall, a country house in Norfolk he had inherited from his uncle, Viscount Templewood, in 1959. It was here that, in 1965, he met Verily Anderson, a successful writer best known for her Brownie books and her memoir, *Beware of Children*, which was adapted into the film, *No Kidding*, starring Leslie Phillips and Geraldine McEwan, in 1960. Anderson lived in nearby Cromer and, although she and Paul Paget were distantly related, they first became acquainted while she was researching her book, *The Northrepps Grandchildren*, which told the story of the previous occupants of Northrepps Hall. The work was published in 1968 and, three years later, she and Paul Paget married in London with John Betjeman serving as best man.

After the wedding, Paul and Verily Paget spent an increasing amount of time in Norfolk and consequently they began to consider the possibility of selling 41–42 Cloth Fair. The prospect of giving up the house was almost certainly difficult for Paul. Over the previous four decades it had served not only as the centre of his personal and professional life, but also as a focus for his restoration passion. By letting go, he ran the risk that his and John Seely's painstaking work would ultimately count for nothing. Although 41–42 Cloth Fair had been statutorily protected since 1950, it could still be demolished if a developer could provide a good enough reason. In 1969, Paul Paget wrote to *The Times* about this very subject and his concerns still resonate today:

> Sir, For the past 40 years or so I have had the good fortune to be part owner of one of the very few seventeenth century houses to survive in the City of London. It is a listed building which has been factually recorded by the Royal Commission on Historical Monuments and generously described in Professor Pevsner's and Mr Ian Nairn's guides to London. As a result of these admirable works it has become something of a tourist attraction and gives evident pleasure to the increasingly large number of visitors who come in eager search of the ever diminishing evidences of London as it used to be. As compared with, for example, the Euston Arch

and the London Coal Exchange, No. 41 Cloth Fair is an insignificant work of architecture; the contribution of the little street in which it stands to the evolution of the great metropolis is less by far than was that of Woburn Square and as a bit of local colour it is perilously comparable with Carlton Mews. Sooner or later it is bound to get in the way of some developer's ambition as must inevitably happen where space at the centre of things is at a premium, and no one, as yet, has shown the initiative and courage to attempt a worthwhile counter-attraction on the perimeter of London. May I therefore seek the hospitality of your columns to bring this enjoyable corner of the City of London to notice before, as has now happened all too often, the bulldozers – not unlike the tanks in Prague – move in to show what a beneficent Authority has in store for us. And may I further suggest that all who are similarly interested in preserving historic buildings – whether they are immediately threatened or no – should write at once to their local planning officer or the Member of Parliament or the Minister of Housing and Local Government or to all three, so that we may never again be told that a scheme which involves the destruction of a national asset is so far advanced that, on financial grounds alone, there can be no reprieve.

Paul and Verily Paget finally took the decision to leave Cloth Fair in April 1975. They moved to Templewood, a property on the Northrepps Hall estate, where Paul passed away in the summer of 1985, aged 84. By this time, 41–42 Cloth Fair had become the premises of a surveyor and estate agent and, although the exterior of the building had altered little since Seely & Paget restored it, their elegant and comfortable living quarters on the upper floors had been reduced to functional offices. The house remained in this unloved state until the late 1990s when it was acquired by private individuals who sympathetically converted the entire property, including the original shop on the ground floor, into a residential house. The work resulted in a City Heritage Award in 2000 and the property remains in careful, private hands to this day.

During the last three decades of the twentieth century, national interest in preserving Britain's architectural heritage steadily grew. Time had proved that the wholesale destruction of historic properties after the Second World War had been a mistake, especially as many of them had been replaced by poorly conceived and cheaply constructed buildings that were at best ignored and at worst despised by the public. In response, the government reviewed their criteria for awarding buildings statutory protection in 1970 and grouped the properties on the list in terms of importance. This evolved into today's graded listings, which are divided as follows: Grade I properties, such as the Church of St Bartholomew the Great and St Paul's Cathedral, are considered to be of exceptional interest and are therefore given the most comprehensive protection. Grade II★ buildings are deemed to be 'of more than special interest' and include the Church of St Bartholomew the Less inside the hospital grounds, which cannot be developed or altered without reasons of the utmost magnitude. The vast majority of listed properties fall into the Grade II category, which demands that every effort should be made to preserve them. Most of the buildings that survived the early twentieth-century demolitions at Cloth Fair are now protected under the edicts of the latter listing. The only house on the street with Grade II★ status is No. 41–42 and it is fair to say that this is largely due to Seely & Paget's conscientious restoration work back in the early 1930s.

Nevertheless, a Grade II★ award does not necessarily mean that 41–42 Cloth Fair will be protected in perpetuity. While future owners of the house will require special consent to carry out any work that might affect its special architectural and historic interest, it does not mean that the building cannot be significantly altered or, in an extreme case, torn down. Indeed, a report compiled by the Policy Studies

Institute in the 1990s found that, in just one year, ninety of the country's listed buildings had been demolished and eight times as many had been partially destroyed.

A common way to overcome listing restrictions is to retain the façade of a property while removing everything behind it, thus rendering it meaningless. Examples of this can be found at building sites the length and breadth of the country, a notable example in London being a 350-room block of modern student accommodation behind the façade of a Victorian warehouse on the Caledonian Road. Oliver Wainwright wrote in the *Guardian*, 'With its grey flanks spilling out either side of the retained brick screen, it was like a whale trying to hide behind a seashell.'

A worse offender can be found at the junction of Gun Street and Artillery Lane in Spitalfields where developers made no attempt to incorporate the façade of the old Cock-A-Hoop pub into their housing scheme behind it. Instead, they merely attached it to the new building with a series of steel brackets. The stranded pub frontage looked so odd that most passers-by thought that it was surely destined for demolition, but there it stayed, strange and utterly redundant, presenting a surreal view of the twenty-first-century building through glassless Victorian windows.

Some developers, especially those in possession of listed buildings in less populated areas, overcome planning restrictions by ignoring them altogether. In 2007 the Grondra, a 250-year-old house in Shirenewton, Monmouthshire, was irreparably damaged when its owner decided to extend and modernise it without seeking planning permission. The *Telegraph* reported:

> Part of the property has been demolished and a sixteenth century cottage on the site has been gutted, while other buildings have been torn down …

Many fine examples of late eighteenth-century joinery and craftsmanship such as six-panel doors, moulded architraves, plaster cornices and marble fireplaces have all been ripped out. The tall Georgian sash windows have been replaced with modern units.

Paula Clarke, the local planning enforcement officer, damned it as 'the worst building work I have seen in my 25 years in the job'.

Nutter Cote Farm in Thornton-in-Craven, North Yorkshire, suffered a graver destiny in 2016 after it began to collapse during refurbishment work. Instead of informing the council of the problems, the owner simply bulldozed the entire building, leaving an adjoining property dangerously unstable. In both of the above cases the owners were fined, but the courts noted that if the penalty was too severe, there would be no money left to remedy the problem. Thus, the proprietor of Nutter Cote Farm was forced to pay just £17,500 with around £3,000 costs – a fraction of the sum that would have been required to properly restore the old farmhouse.

A greater threat than rogue builders is the absence of any statutory protection. A search for local landmarks in any area on the Listed Buildings Register will inevitably reveal that some much-loved and historically interesting buildings are notable by their absence. For example, opponents of the redevelopment of the Fruit & Wool Exchange, a handsome 1920s auction house overlooking Spitalfields Market, were shocked when they discovered that the building was not listed. An energetic campaign to save it succeeded only in preserving its façade, while its unique interior was reduced to a gaping hole ready to receive the foundations of a particularly uninspiring new office block.

A worse fate befell the Carlton Tavern, a charming pub that stood at the entrance to Paddington Recreation Ground in Maida Vale. The building was the only survivor of the street's intensive post-war redevelopment and was being considered for Grade II listing, but that did not stop its owner from sending in the bulldozers. The demolition works came completely out of the blue and stunned locals, some of whom had been drinking in the bar the evening before. Word of the destruction quickly reached council officers but, by the time they could stop the works, half the building had been destroyed. The owner (who had not bothered to apply for planning permission) was subsequently ordered to rebuild the Carlton Tavern, but he refused and today, two years later, the pub remains in a sad, semi-demolished state, its future uncertain.

Other culturally important buildings are at risk of destruction simply because they are too new. For example, Holborn Library on Theobalds Road was the first large, multi-function library to be built in post-war London. Opened in 1960, its bright and airy interior and wide range of facilities reflected a new era of optimism that placed London at the heart of the 'Swinging Sixties' later in the decade. Nevertheless, this reminder of a time long since passed is not on the Listed Buildings Register and may soon disappear beneath a new development.

The biggest danger for buildings, whether listed or not, is a decline in use. Supporters of the new development at the Fruit & Wool Exchange argued that the property had not performed a useful commercial role for decades; the Carlton Tavern was never that busy and it could be said that Holborn Library is an outdated relic now thousands of books can be accessed for free on the Internet.

Perhaps the most poignant examples of buildings with a lost purpose are the City churches. Despite having Grade I listings, St Mary Woolnoth, St Margaret Lothbury and St Bride's, Fleet Street, are all in a perilous state of decay. If the rot is not stopped quickly, these beautiful and historic places of worship will become ruins. However, the congregations they once served have long since drifted away, leaving the churches chronically underfunded.

The surest way to save London's heritage is to give it a valuable function. Across the city there are thousands of buildings, both public and private, which have been saved from demolition by evolving with the times. Would the stately Bankside Power Station still be standing today if it had not been converted into the Tate Modern art gallery? What would the future hold for the gracious churches of St Mark's, North Audley Street, or Holy Trinity, Marylebone, had they not found a new, albeit controversial, use as events venues?

The same can be asked of 41–42 Cloth Fair. Over the centuries, the house has survived, sometimes against all odds, because it adapted, however contentiously, to accommodate the needs of the era. Its ground floor, in particular, has seen many changes – it has been an alehouse, a shop, a workshop, an office and part of a private home – and it has succeeded in every incarnation. It is hoped that the remarkable story told in the pages of this book goes some way to show that every building in Britain has its own unique history – you just have to uncover it. As Paul Paget wrote in 1969, anyone who is interested in a property, whatever its size, purpose, age or grandeur, should bring it to the attention of those who have the power to preserve it 'so that we may never again be told that a scheme which involves the destruction of a national asset is so far advanced that, on financial grounds alone, there can be no reprieve'.

EPILOGUE

What Tomorrow Holds

With its historic buildings legally protected, Cloth Fair has acquired a status as one of the London's hidden gems and the dawning of the new millennium heralded some interesting projects that promise to transform its environs. In 2007, the government approved Crossrail – a new railway line connecting Berkshire to Essex via the centre of the city. Planned to be fully operational by December 2019, the Elizabeth Line, as it is now known, will run two separate branches from Reading and Heathrow that converge at Hayes & Harlington. From there, trains will run through the west London suburbs to the major rail network hub at Paddington before continuing east through the centre of the city before dividing once again with one line terminating at Abbey Wood and the other at Shenfield in Essex.

A key station on the Elizabeth Line – and one that will directly influence the fortunes of Cloth Fair – is Farringdon, from whence passengers will be able to access Canary Wharf in eight minutes, Bond Street in four minutes and Heathrow Airport in just over half an hour. In order to accommodate the new infrastructure a vast, partially subterranean building project got under way, stretching from Farringdon Road in the west to Charterhouse Square in the east, and as the construction crews dug into the soil, tantalising secrets of the area's past were revealed.

In 2013, Crossrail workers uncovered ancient skeletons arranged in rows 2.5m under the ground at Charterhouse Square. The uniformity of the burials suggested that the remains had been interred at roughly the same time and, intriguingly, the depth of the graves combined with fragments of pottery found at the site inferred that they dated back to the mid-1300s.

The discovery of the Charterhouse Square skeletons was quickly linked to an old mystery. Back in the 1500s, the historian John Stow had recorded that during the Black Death plague epidemic of 1348:

> Churchyards were not sufficient to receive the dead but men were forced to chuse out certain fields for burials, whereupon Raph Stratford, Bishop of London, in the yeare 1348 bought a peece of ground called no mans land, which he inclosed with a wall of Bricke and dedicated for burial of the deade, builded thereupon a proper Chappell, which is now enlarged and made a dwelling house, and this burying plot is become a fayre garden, retaining the old name of Pardon Churchyard.

This emergency burial ground was thought to have been near the Charterhouse, but despite intensive development of the area in the ensuing centuries, no evidence of it had ever been found.

In a bid to discover if the Charterhouse site was indeed Stow's 'Pardon Churchyard', twenty-three of the skeletons were carefully exhumed and sent to the Museum of London's archaeology laboratory for testing where DNA extracted from their teeth revealed traces of the *Yersinia pestis* bacterium – proof that they had been exposed to the plague. Interestingly, radiocarbon-14 dating also showed that the burial ground had been used in two distinct eras. The first burials had taken place during the Black Death of 1348 but then, around a century later, the graveyard had been reopened to receive more plague victims, revealing that London had been subjected to another major epidemic.

The bones from the Charterhouse burial ground also allowed scientists to discover fascinating details about London's medieval inhabitants, some of whom may have lived or worked at the nearby Priory of St Bartholomew the Great. Around 40 per cent of the people buried at the site had grown up outside London and had probably come to the city in search of work. However, the heavy wear and signs of malnutrition on their bones suggested that the only employment available was backbreaking, poorly paid manual labour. The most interesting and mysterious revelation of all was the fact that numerous skeletons from the second wave of burials had sustained injuries consistent with violence.

Soon after the secrets of the Charterhouse skeletons were divulged, the Museum of London announced that it intended to create a new museum at nearby Smithfield Market, bringing around 25,000 square metres of its redundant buildings back to life. The museum's plan promised to rejuvenate three parts of the old market complex. The long-deserted General Market overlooking Farringdon Road had originally been erected as a fruit and vegetable market in 1881 and, in typical late Victorian style, its design was confident and elaborate. A large iron pineapple topped the Charterhouse Street entrance and the roof was supported by rows of elegant and virtually indestructible columns made by the Phoenix Company of Pennsylvania; they were an expensive innovation in their day. However, from the outset, the market was something of a white elephant. With the renowned fruit and vegetable traders at Spitalfields only a short drive away, their rivals at Smithfield floundered and their stalls quickly gave way to dealers in general produce. Nevertheless, the building continued to form part of the Central Markets complex until it was shut down in the 1980s, after which it gradually degenerated into a dilapidated shell.

The second building earmarked for the new museum was the fish market and its additions on West Smithfield. Opened in 1888, its impressive entrance, embellished with cherubs astride dolphins, was connected to the General Market by a glazed, covered walkway, while below ground a maze of basements and tunnels led to the subterranean railway depot at the nearby meat market. The fish market's cavernous underground storage rooms were put out of use when trading ceased in 1983 and they henceforth became the depository for salt to grit roads rather than to preserve fish.

At the eastern end of the fish market an ugly warehouse, nick-named the 'Iron Mountain', was built in the 1960s alongside an older and altogether more attractive building known as the 'Red House'. Erected in 1898, this narrow brick structure was the first cold store to be built outside of the London docks and it revolutionised the stor-age of Smithfield's perishable commodities. Both the Iron Mountain and the Red House were vacated in the 1980s and they have since stood redundant, overlooking the cold stores' original engine house – a low building on a small, triangular piece of ground that in modern times was the location of some very insalubrious toilet facilities for the market traders.

The final site earmarked by the Museum of London was the base-ment of the poultry market. Like the General Market next door, this part of Smithfield had a chequered history. Originally opened in 1875, it was designed to complement and blend with the main meat market. However, the original building was almost completely destroyed by fire in January 1958 and a forbidding brick and concrete structure rose from the ashes. Nevertheless, the poultry market's fortunes fared better over the ensuing decades and its upper level is still in operation today.

While the three redundant parts of Smithfield Market were located in an accessible position for a potential new museum, the challenge of linking them together to form a coherent public space presented huge challenges, and in order to tackle them the Museum of London launched a competition. The brief, which was open to any architect, declared, 'This is a project rich with possibility; focussed on regenerating a nationally significant landmark and creating an atmospheric and sophisticated museum environment.' On a more practical level, the new museum had to be capable of receiving around 2.25 million visitors a year and also incorporate a 240-plus-seat theatre, offices for museum staff, a research centre with space for a laboratory and a considerable amount of warehousing for the museum's gigantic collection of artefacts.

In total, seventy-one architects responded to the brief. From these, a shortlist of six were selected and in July 2016 it was announced that the contract had been awarded to a partnership headed by Stanton Williams Architects and Asif Khan. On hearing of their success, Khan declared, 'To have a chance to create a new museum for London, in London, about London, at this moment in time is incredibly exciting for us … We want the Museum of London to be a museum where everyone belongs, and where the future of London is created.'

In preparation for the submission of a formal planning application in 2018, the architectural partnership worked with conservation architect Julian Harrap and landscape consultants, J. & L. Gibbons. The main features of the resulting concept include a centrepiece dome creating a light and bright entrance to the museum, spiral escalators leading down to the huge underground parts of the complex with a sunken garden and green spaces throughout. It is currently hoped that the new Museum of London will open in 2022. In the meantime, the meat and poultry markets at Smithfield continue to operate as they have done for centuries.

Today, the complicated and challenging projects at Farringdon Station and Smithfield Market are by no means the only schemes currently under way in Cloth Fair's midst. Over at St Bartholomew's Hospital, a campaign is afoot to save its majestic Great Hall from ruin. Created by architect James Gibbs in the 1730s, the hall was (and still is) a grand and opulent sight, designed to impress private benefactors on whom the hospital once relied for funding. Accessed via a staircase decorated with murals by William Hogarth, virtually all the wall space in the hall was filled with the names and portraits of staff and patrons, the most imposing being a portrait of Henry VIII, who famously saved the hospital when the priory was dissolved. This painting was surrounded by other important works, including Joshua Reynolds' rendition of Percival Pott, surgeon at the time of the Gordon Riots, and John Millais' portrait of Paul Paget's grandfather, James.

The Great Hall performed an essential function for St Bartholomew's Hospital for over 200 years. However, after the National Health Service was founded in 1948, funding became the government's responsibility and thus, the noble room lost its purpose. It was subsequently left to slowly decay while the whole north wing was blighted by the addition of an unsightly finance block and pathology laboratory in the 1960s. This state of affairs continued until 2012, when the NHS backed a proposal to replace one of the extensions with a Maggie's Centre for cancer care. Sensing that this was an unprecedented opportunity to restore the north wing to something resembling its former self, a group headed by royal gynaecologist Marcus Setchell formed 'The Friends of the Great Hall' and commissioned an alternative plan for the Maggie's Centre, detached from the north wing. The group also campaigned for the Great Hall's renovation so it could once again become a valuable part of the hospital. To their disappointment, the re-siting plan for the cancer centre was ultimately rejected but the proposed restoration of the Great Hall attracted a good deal of interest from press and public alike. It is currently hoped that the project will obtain sufficient funding to be completed in time for the 900th anniversary of St Bartholomew's Hospital in 2023.

Most of the current plans for the regeneration of Cloth Fair's surroundings are civic in nature. However, there is also a large private project under way at the historic enclave of Bartholomew Close. Uninspiringly renamed Bart's Square, the original site of the priory's outbuildings is being almost entirely redeveloped into a complex of luxury flats, designed to attract affluent City workers in search of a pied-á-terre close to their place of employment. The developers chose not to publicise the fascinating history of the close in their marketing materials, which is regrettable as Bart's Square stands on an area rich in heritage.

The Askew Building, which will occupy the northernmost part of the development, overlooking the Lady Chapel of St Bartholomew the Great, was originally the site of 50–53 Bartholomew Close, a small terrace of artisans' workshops with domestic quarters above. In the 1820s, No. 50 became the business premises of Joseph Smith, whose blacksmith's shop on the ground floor evolved into a hugely successful enterprise known as Smith & Turner, manufacturers of patented silent action door springs. Next door, Nos 51–53 were home to all manner of nineteenth-century craftsmen including watch engraver Charles

Holden and Messrs Brown and Sumersall, a firm of silversmiths. In 1913, the ancient buildings fell prey to the City's sanitary inspectors and, seven years later, a large commercial block rose in their place. This new building became the business premises for Bock & Engel's Ladies' Hat Manufactory, Moore & Mathes' print shop and a wholesale druggists, before being acquired by St Bartholomew's Hospital and converted into a centre for clinical research.

At the Askew Building's southern end, Abernethy House stands on the former site of the priory's farmery house and kitchen, overlooking an ancient pathway known today as Middlesex Passage. During monastic times, this narrow path ran past the mulberry garden to the priory's refectory and amazingly it survived throughout the following centuries, perhaps because it was a convenient shortcut through the close. At the height of Bartholomew Fair's notoriety, the passage became such an infamous resort of prostitutes that, in 1773, the vestry ordered a wooden gate to be erected at its entrance so it could be locked up at nightfall. This gate was still in situ in the early 1900s, but it was probably destroyed when Bartholomew Close was bombed in the Blitz. Today, Middlesex Passage connects Abernethy House to Hogarth House, another apartment block, which occupies the former site of the City Union's poor relief offices.

On the eastern side of the Askew Building, the surviving frontage of Dominion House, designed by Sir Aston Webb (the creator of Buckingham Palace's main façade), forms part of a new building of the same name. The original Dominion House was erected in 1879 for a pharmaceutical company and when its plans were exhibited at the Royal Academy they were heralded as 'worthy of the better time of Flanders'. However, the building was badly damaged when a bomb fell on Bartholomew Close in September 1915 and during the Blitz its southern section suffered a direct hit and was destroyed.

The Royal General Dispensary, which stood opposite Dominion House, was also badly damaged during the Second World War and in the 1990s the site was bisected by Albion Way, a new road connecting Bartholomew Close with Montague Street. Two new buildings known as Vicary House and the Underwood Building now occupy the old site of the dispensary.

Modern redevelopment has altered Bartholomew Close beyond all recognition and on the other side of St Bartholomew the Great, Cloth Fair has also seen its fair share of change during the post-war years. In 1982, the east end of the thoroughfare, which had existed in a dejected state after being deprived of its medieval houses just before the First World War, was finally purchased by a developer who planned to erect a range of townhouses on the site. However, progress was painfully slow and it was not until March 1986 that the properties were finally ready for sale, marketed by estate agents Chestertons as 'ideal for an entertaining lifestyle' at prices from £230,000.

Today, a walk along Cloth Fair is like travelling through time with each of its buildings representing an epoch in London's history. As we journey further into the twenty-first century, it is intriguing to wonder what new tales will be added to the unique and fascinating story of the house at 41–42 – the oldest home in the City of London.

AFTERWORD

41–42 Cloth Fair may be the oldest inhabited house in the City but it has been modernised – we have hot and cold running water as well as electricity! We no longer have to throw our human waste out on to the people below – though it can, at times, feel rather tempting when one listens to the same routines time after time from the many tour guides who come this way.

It is never just about any house. It is the area in which the house is built, it is the people in the house and the buildings surrounding it – looking over to John Betjeman's old flat, with its *trompe l'œil* window of the sailor's homecoming, difficult to see from the street because of the grime-encrusted plastic covering it, is the bell of the oldest church in the City, St Bart's (which does not keep us awake as it is 'turned off' from midnight) – and in old houses such as this one, it is the history. As this book teaches us, there is an extraordinary amount of important history in this area – so much so, that parts of it have been overlooked.

This was the case with the Great (Peasants') Revolt of 1381. Given that it was in West Smithfield where the dramatic climax of the revolt took place and where Wat Tyler was murdered, I was surprised to find nothing in the way of a memorial to this event. I spent over a year talking with the City, English Heritage and St Bart's Hospital trying to get agreement to instate one. When it was agreed, I commissioned the memorial, which is now on the corner of St Bart's Hospital, just by the entrance to St Bart's the Great.

I think when people come into the house, they are surprised, perhaps even disappointed, that it is not more palatial. The rooms, whilst a good size, are not as huge as the front of the house might suggest, though it is something of a maze and takes people a little time to get used to. These were merchants' houses and as such appear from the outside perhaps rather more baronial from our twenty-first-century perspective.

One only need look at pictures from the early 1900s to see other similar merchants' houses up and down Cloth Fair before the City of London Corporation tore them down due to early concerns about health and safety. Isn't it fascinating how our views regarding history change?

It is perhaps fitting that Betjeman was a neighbour, given his tireless protection of important historical buildings. I wonder how much his friendship with John Seely and Paul Paget and his frequent visiting of this house added to his conviction that such beautiful and historic buildings must be protected.

We were visited by the step-daughter of Paget, who told us that in what is now a wardrobe were two bath tubs side by side, where Seely and Paget would relax and talk about their various plans for the City. Following Seely's death, Betjeman apparently took over his bath for a time! She told me how much the place has changed. It has been sympathetically and beautifully modernised by Andrea and Penny

Cenci di Bello, whose work is recognised by the blue plaque next to the front door. It remains very much a home rather than a museum. This house was on the market for over two years before we found it. Perhaps it was thought that a twentieth-century house would be easier to live in than 41–42 Cloth Fair, but for my money, at least, there is none (from any century) better. There is not a right angle in the place; getting curtains made and hung was a nightmare for those who measured and cut them so carefully – some 'pool' nicely on the floor, others not so much!

Seely and Paget had about 400 of their guests throughout their time here sign some of the windows with a diamond-nibbed pen, and on a sunny morning those windows are white with signatures of the likes of Montgomery of Alamein, J.B. Priestley, Betjeman (several times) and Joyce Grenfell.

During a recent visit by two descendants of Seely they told me that they had been just too young to recall ever having visited the house, but were moved to find the signature signed by their brother, who had recently died, which he had made when he was a child. I suggested they add their early twenty-first-century signatures below that of their mid-twentieth-century brother's, which they were keen to do and it proved to be a moving moment.

I decided that this was a tradition that should be carried on, though perhaps rather more sparingly than it had been in the past; former Irish President Mary Robinson, Tony Benn, John Pilger and Ken Loach are some of the new-era signatories. The first Mayor of London, Ken Livingstone, accidentally locked himself in the loo when he visited a couple of years ago (I had a small blue plaque made up).

We are now at a significant crossroads in the history of this little pocket of London with the advent of Crossrail and part of St Bart's Hospital having been knocked down to make way for many new 'luxury flats'. There needs to remain the desirability for keeping quirky corners of a city in the face of the modern drive to make everything bland and functional. Where there is money, there will always be pressure to demolish and start again (Henry VIII wanted to knock down Hampton Court and rebuild it). There is a value to putting these little irritants in the path of the relentless drive for redevelopment. It leaves us a cityscape peppered with clues that illuminate the past, explain the present and inspire for the future.

Matthew Bell, Owner / Caretaker

August 2017

A WALK AROUND
CLOTH FAIR

Length: Around fifty minutes. Longer if you want to visit some of the landmarks en route.

Start/Finish: Farringdon Station (Circle, Hammersmith & City and Metropolitan Lines, or the Thameslink overground railway).

▷ **With the entrance to the Underground station behind you, turn right and walk down the passage to Farringdon Road**

▷ **Turn left and walk along Farringdon Road**

On your left, you will see the development of the new Elizabeth Line Station at Farringdon, which is due to open in December 2018.

▷ **Cross over Charterhouse Street**

On your left is the General Market building, erected in the

1880s as part of Smithfield's Central Markets complex. The corner of the market was rebuilt after sustaining bomb damage in the Second World War but the rest of the building is original. Straight ahead you will see Holborn Viaduct. This bridge, built in the 1860s to ease traffic in the area, was one of London's first flyovers.

▷ **Turn left into West Smithfield**

The buildings on both sides of this road are the planned site of the new Museum of London.

▷ **Turn immediately right into Snow Hill**

Smithfield's former fish market is on your left – note the carved fish above the entrances. At the end of the building, continue straight along Snow Hill, passing through a line of bollards marking the perimeter of the City of London. Looking up you will see the Old Bailey's 'Scales of Justice' alongside the tower of St Sepulchre's Church.

▷ **Continue along Snow Hill**

A short way along on your left you will find the City's most elaborate police station. Built on the site of the Saracen's Head Inn, it was erected in 1926 using an unusual combination of Moderne and Arts & Crafts architecture.

▷ **At St Sepulchre's Church, take a detour through its gate into Snow Hill Court**

This quaint enclave of ancient houses gives a unique impression of the area in times past.

▷ **Come out of Snow Hill Court into Snow Hill and turn left onto Holborn Viaduct, past the front of St Sepulchre's Church**

A place of worship has stood on this site since Saxon times. Named after Jerusalem's Church of the Holy Sepulchre in the twelfth century, it was rebuilt in the 1400s but suffered badly in the Great Fire of 1666, which left only the walls and tower standing. The church was subsequently rebuilt and today it is the largest parish church in the City.

▷ **At the next junction, turn left up Giltspur Street**

A short way along on your left, you will find a memorial to the great essayist, Charles Lamb, which was rescued from the ruins of Christ Church, Greyfriars, in the Second World War. Next to the bust is St Sepulchre's old Watch House. This building was erected in 1791 to guard St Sepulchre's Churchyard against bodysnatchers who sold corpses to St Bartholomew's Hospital for dissection. Unfortunately, the original Watch House was destroyed in the Blitz but was rebuilt in 1962.

▷ **Continue along Giltspur Street to Cock Lane**

The gilded wood statue of the 'Golden Boy of Pye Corner' marks the spot where the Great Fire of London was stopped and a plaque beneath blames the conflagration on 'the sin of gluttony'. The origins of the statue are shrouded in mystery. He may have been rescued from a gutted building after the fire or he may simply be the creation of an enterprising landlord of the Fortune of War pub, which stood on the site in the early 1900s.

▷ **Cross over Giltspur Street and turn right, then walk along the perimeter of St Bartholomew's Hospital to the cross-roads at Newgate Street**

The large building in front of you is the Central Criminal Court, where the country's most serious crimes are tried. The court stands on the site of the notorious Newgate Prison. The original gaol was inside a gate in the Roman fortification (or bailey) surrounding the city. It was rebuilt several times over the following centuries – a plaque on the wall facing Newgate Street records the demolition of the medieval incarnation in 1777. Its replacement was gutted by fire during the Gordon Riots three years later. From 1783, Newgate Prison was the site of London's public executions, the last of which was the hanging of Fenian Michael Barrett, in 1868. The prison was finally closed in 1902 and demolished two years later.

▷ **Cross over Newgate Street and walk down Old Bailey**

Warwick Passage on your left is the entrance to the court's public viewing gallery, where members of the public can watch trials in progress.

▷ **At the end of Old Bailey, turn left into Ludgate Hill**

The impressive sight of St Paul's Cathedral at the top of the hill causes most passers-by to ignore the little Church of St Martin Ludgate on the left. Nevertheless, this Wren church is well worth exploring, not least for the Grinling Gibbons wood carvings inside.

▷ **Continue up Ludgate Hill to St Paul's**

The pristine condition of Wren's monumental edifice is partly due to the efforts of 41–42 Cloth Fair residents, John Seely and Paul Paget, both of whom were 'surveyors to the fabric of St Paul's' after the Second World War. If you want to explore the cathedral there is a charge. However, if you wait until 5 p.m. (Monday to Saturday), you can usually take part in the Evensong service, during which you will hear some top-class choral music, free of charge. Check St Paul's website or ask the staff for more information on Evensong and other events at the cathedral.

▷ **Walk down the left-hand side of St Paul's and turn left through Temple Bar into Paternoster Square**

Designed by Sir Christopher Wren, Temple Bar originally marked the principal entrance to the City of London, where modern Fleet Street meets the Strand. However, as traffic into the City increased, its narrow archway began to cause serious congestion. Temple Bar was subsequently dismantled and in 1880 it was sold to Henry Meux, a wealthy brewer, who reassembled it in the grounds of his mansion at Theobalds Park, Hertfordshire. There it remained, in an increasingly dirty and graffiti-ridden state, until 2003 when it was returned to the City.

Paternoster Square was once the home of London's booksellers but the site suffered greatly in both the Great Fire of 1666 and the Second World War Blitz. The column topped with a flaming urn standing at the centre of the square serves a dual purpose as a ventilation shaft and a memorial to the two conflagrations that consumed the area.

▷ **Cross over Paternoster Square with the memorial on your right and continue straight on into the passage leading to Newgate Street**

▷ **Cross over Newgate Street**

Straight ahead of you is the parish Vestry House, built in 1768. The little park on the left is all that remains of Christ Church, Greyfriars' Churchyard. This ancient burial ground became a public open space in 1872 and now serves as an impressive entrance to the Bank of America and Merrill Lynch building.

▷ **Come out of the churchyard into Greyfriars Passage and follow it round to the ruins of Christ Church**

A religious house stood here from 1228, when a Franciscan monastery was built. After the Great Fire reduced the site to rubble, a new church was built by Sir Christopher Wren. However, this too was destroyed by fire during the Second World War and its ruins were subsequently transformed into the beautiful gardens you see today.

▷ **Walk through Christ Church Garden and turn left into King Edward Street**

Before the Great Fire of 1666, this thoroughfare was home to numerous warehouses and abattoirs connected to the trade at Smithfield Market.

▷ **Turn right into Postman's Park**

Named after employees of the General Post Office, which stood nearby, Postman's Park was originally the churchyard of St Botolph, Aldersgate. In 1900, it became the site of artist George Frederic Watts' 'Memorial to Heroic Self-Sacrifice', a wall of tablets commemorating those who died while saving others, which can be found at the centre of the park.

▷ **At the end of Postman's Park, turn left onto Aldersgate Street at its junction with St Martin's le Grand**

Fixed onto the park railings is a plaque commemorating the evangelical conversions of John and Charles Wesley – regular visitors to 41–42 Cloth Fair in the 1700s.

▷ **Continue a short distance down Aldersgate Street, then turn left into Little Britain**

About halfway along, a plaque over a rather uninspiring door marks the site of John Bray's house, the scene of Charles Wesley's evangelical conversion on 21 May 1738.

▷ **At the T-junction, cross over the road (a continuation of Little Britain) and follow it round to the left**

The land on the right-hand side of Little Britain was once Bartholomew Close, which originally housed the domestic quarters of St Bartholomew's Priory. The area was devastated by bombs in both world wars and today forms the site of Bart's Square, a residential development.

▷ **Continue to the end of Little Britain**

The road becomes pedestrianised about halfway down, before opening out onto the old Smithfield Marketplace, which was also the site of the notorious Bartholomew Fair.

▷ **Turn left and walk along the front of St Bartholomew's Hospital**

On the hospital's wall is a recently erected memorial to the Great Rising of 1381 (commonly known as the Peasants' Revolt). The leader of the insurrection, Wat Tyler, was killed by the Lord Mayor's guards near this spot after peace talks descended into violence. Close by is a plaque dedicated to William Wallace, the great leader of the Wars of Scottish Independence, who was executed here in 1305.

▷ **Turn left through the Henry VIII Gate of St Bartholomew's Hospital**

Straight ahead is the Great Hall, used to entertain the hospital's benefactors before the NHS was created. To the left is the Church of St Bartholomew the Less. If you go inside, you will see the results of Seely and Paget's restoration work after the Second World War.

▷ **Come back out of the hospital via the Henry VIII Gate and turn right**

The park in the centre of the old Smithfield Marketplace stands on top of former railway sidings that once brought livestock into the market. The site is now an underground car park.

▷ **On reaching the entrance to Little Britain (on your right), go through the archway straight ahead of you**

This is the entrance to St Bartholomew the Great. The church is well worth exploring (there is a charge) to see Rahere's impressive tomb and the elaborate monuments that line the nave. You can also find refreshment in the café in the ancient cloister.

▷ **Once you have finished looking round the church, walk back up the path and turn right up the steps into the churchyard**

You are now standing on the part of the nave that was destroyed when the priory was suppressed. According to local tradition, sixpences were placed on the flat gravestone in the centre of the burial ground every Easter for distribution among twenty parish widows. The trees were planted during Seely and Paget's restoration of the churchyard in the 1930s and if you look through the railings onto Cloth Fair you will get a timeless view of No. 41–42 – the oldest house in the City. This is still a private residence so please respect the privacy of its inhabitants. The little alleyway that runs around the house marks the perimeter of Launders Green, where the priory's washing was pegged out to dry. When it was developed in the early 1600s, the houses on Launders Green were built in a square with a courtyard in the centre. The only surviving building from this time is 41–42 Cloth Fair.

▷ **Turn right out of the churchyard and walk up Cloth Fair**

The street is built on the site of the medieval Cloth Fair, which took place annually in the priory grounds. The modern houses on your left stand on the site of Elizabethan dwellings that were torn down just before the First World War. At the end of Cloth Fair, the Hand & Shears pub has replaced an earlier structure that was the site of the Pie Powder Courts during the fair, which dealt with rogue traders and other petty criminals.

▷ **Turn around at the Hand & Shears and follow the road back to Smithfield**

The Rising Sun is another historic hostelry that has served market traders for centuries. At the back of the pub, some old stone tablets propped against the wall of an alley may well be ancient headstones from St Bartholomew's Churchyard. Further along, a blue plaque commemorates John Betjeman's home at No. 43.

▷ **On reaching the end of Cloth Fair, turn right, cross over Long Lane and walk through the grand arched avenue running through the centre of Smithfield's meat market**

This magnificent structure was built in 1868, replacing the animal pens that had stood on the site for centuries. Today, Smithfield is the City's last surviving large, wholesale market, operating from 4 a.m. to 12 p.m. every weekday.

▷ **Emerging from Smithfield Market, cross over Charterhouse Street into Cowcross Street**

This little thoroughfare is named after the cattle that were once driven up its path to the market. The Rookery Hotel on the corner of Peters Lane gives this part of the street a distinctly Dickensian atmosphere.

▷ **At the end of Cowcross Street, you will find Farringdon Station**

You have reached the end of the tour. I hope you enjoyed exploring Cloth Fair and its fascinating surroundings.

SELECT BIBLIOGRAPHY

A–Z Atlas & Guide To London, 1938 (2008) Geographers A-Z Map Co.

Ackroyd, P. *London: The Biography* (2001) Vintage

Barber, P. *London: A History in Maps* (2012) British Library Publishing

Booth, C. *Descriptive Maps of London Poverty* (2013) Old House Books

Centre for Metropolitan History *Hearth Tax: City of London 1666* (2011)

Clark, P. *The English Alehouse: A Social History* (1983) Longman

Dale, T.C. *Inhabitants of London in 1638* (1931) Society of Genealogists

Davies, P. *Lost London: 1870–1945* (2009) Transatlantic Press

Defoe, D. *A Journal of the Plague Year* (2003) Dover Thrift Editions

Evelyn, J. *The Diary of John Evelyn* (2006) Everyman

Hamilton, W.D. (ed.) *Calendar of State Papers Domestic: Charles I* (1877) HM Stationery Office

Harben, H.A. *A Dictionary of London* (1918) H. Jenkins Ltd.

Haywood, I. & Seed, J. *The Gordon Riots* (2012) Cambridge University Press

Hibbert, C. *King Mob: The Story of Lord George Gordon & the Riots of 1780* (1958) Longman

Hibbert, C. et al. *The London Encyclopaedia* (2010) Macmillan

HM Stationery Office *An Inventory of the Historical Monuments in London* (1929)

Hyde, R. (introduction) *The A–Z of Victorian London* (1987) Harry Margary

Hyde, R. (introduction) *The A–Z of Georgian London* (1985) Harry Margary

Jackson, L. *A Dictionary of Victorian London* (2006) Anthem

Jeaffreson, J.C. (ed.) *Middlesex County Records* (1892) Middlesex Record Society

Kelly, J. *The Great Mortality: An Intimate History of the Black Death* (2006) Harper Perennial

Kimbrough, S.T. *Charles Wesley: Poet & Theologian* (1991) Abingdon

Moorhouse, G. *The Last Divine Office* (2012) Blue Bridge

Morley, H. *Memoirs of Bartholomew Fair* (1892) Routledge

Noorthouck, J. *A New History of London* (1773) R. Baldwin

Pepys, S. *The Diaries of Samuel Pepys* (2003) Penguin Classics

Porter, S. *The Great Plague* (1999) Sutton

Purkiss, D. *The English Civil War: A People's History* (2007) Harper Perennial

Reddaway, T.F. *The Rebuilding of London After the Great Fire* (1940) Jonathan Cape

Rosewell, R. *The Medieval Monastery* (2012) Shire Publications

Stow, J. *A Survey of London in 1603* (1908) Clarendon

Thornbury, W. *Old & New London* (1878) Cassell, Petter & Galpin.

Tinniswood, A. *By Permission of Heaven: The Story of the Great Fire of London* (2004) Penguin

Ward, L. *The London County Council Bomb Damage Maps* (2015) Thames & Hudson

Webb, E.A. *The Records of St Bartholomew's Priory & St Bartholomew the Great* (1921) Oxford University Press

Weir, A. *Henry VIII: King & Court* (2008) Vintage

Worden, B. *The English Civil Wars: 1640–1660* (2009) Weidenfeld & Nicolson

Select Online Resources

Ancestry.co.uk

Bartholomew Fair – A Comedy by Ben Jonson (1614)

British Newspaper Archive

Charles Booth Online Archive (1890s)

Familysearch.org

John Strype's *A Survey of the Cities of London & Westminster* (1598)

Journal of John Wesley (1703–1791)

London Gazette Archive

Newgate Calendar Online

Oldmapsonline.org

Old Bailey Proceedings 1674–1913

Ordnance Survey Old Map Archive

The Times Online Archive

INDEX